CURRENCY USE AND PAYMENT PATTERNS

FINANCIAL AND MONETARY POLICY STUDIES

Volume 23

The titles published in this series are listed at the end of this volume.

CURRENCY USE AND PAYMENT PATTERNS

by

WILLEM C. BOESCHOTEN
De Nederlandsche Bank,
Econometric Research and Special Studies Department

SPRINGER-SCIENCE+BUSINESS MEDIA, B.V.

Library of Congress Cataloging-in-Publication Data

Boeschoten, W. C.
Currency use and payment patterns / by Willem C. Boeschoten.
p. cm. -- (Financial and monetary policy studies ; v. 23)
Includes bibliographical references and index.

1. Money. 2. Money--Netherlands. 3. Hoarding of money.
4. International finance. I. Title. II. Series: Financial and monetary policy studies ; 23.
HG222.5.B64 1992
332.4--dc20 92-2206

ISBN 978-94-010-5111-8 ISBN 978-94-011-2518-5 (eBook)
DOI 10.1007/978-94-011-2518-5

To Monique

CONTENTS

4 DEMAND FOR CURRENCY IN AN INTERNATIONAL PERSPECTIVE

5 EPILOGUE

ANNEX

"I have no doubt that in a few years' time such guesses will appear hopelessly amateurish and inaccurate, and will be replaced by scientific estimates. But by indicating what figures it would be interesting to know and by making doubtful attempts at their value, I may stimulate others, who are in a position to get better data, to correct me." (Keynes, 1930, pp 78)

PREFACE

Despite its everyday character, little is known about the use of currency (banknotes and coins) and the way we pay. The aim of this study is to throw light on this monetary field, starting from macro-economic data and theoretical and empirical knowledge available so far. Besides, we use, however, information that has become available from surveys, performed since 1983 for the Nederlandsche Bank. Two of them were specially designed by the author, one was designed and conducted by a market research firm in close consultation with Fase and the author, and one was a general budget survey in which the Bank participated from 1984 to 1986. The research for the Netherlands also profited from the detailed registration of the handling of banknotes by the Bank's Banknote sector. The multicountry analysis of the currency demand benefited materially from the information that became available through a questionnaire among central banks on currency use and payment systems in the context of the Bank Note Printers Conference Study Group on Trends in National Economies and in Payment Systems and their Effect on Note Circulation and Demand, of which the author was a member.

Considering the responsibility of the Nederlandsche Bank for the currency circulation and the payment system, which is embedded in the Dutch Banking Act of 1948, and thanks to the Bank's willingness to make available ways and means for the relevant research, we are now able to fill at least some of the gaps in our knowledge. Thus, this study is one of the fruits of the extensive research on this subject, started by Fase in the mid-seventies at the Bank's Econometric and Special Studies Department.

Acknowledgements

The work underlying this study was performed at the Econometric and Special Studies Department of the Nederlandsche Bank, where many contributed to it. I am indebted to all the statistical assistants of the department, especially to Anja Wouters and Rob Vet for their patient assistance in building up the data sets and analysing the survey data. Also Corina den Broeder rendered devoted and persistent research assistance with respect to the multicountry analysis during her stay at the Bank and I am grateful to Mike Clements of the Bank of England for his careful reading and commenting on that part. My collegues Peter van Els and Carlo Winder made some valuable suggestions. Liesbeth Klein and Coen Collee helped me avoid a number of errors in English, and thanks to the skilful efforts of Mariëtta Bakker, Gita Gajapersad and Carolien Verhoeven the text looks as it does.

Above all, I owe a debt of gratitude to Martin Fase, one of the pioneers in this field of research, for his efforts and contribution to the improvement of this study.

INTRODUCTION

We seem to be well on the way to a cashless society. Paradoxically, however, the majority of the transactions are still paid in cash even in the most advanced economies. A second paradoxical observation is that, despite the primary and common character of currency, the economic theory on the use of and demand for cash is only rarely supported by empirical evidence. In addition, some aspects of the theory have not been tested at all because of a lack of relevant data. Nevertheless, the interest in currency has flagged.

In view of these unsolved questions and the persistent importance of currency as a medium of payment and as an element of various economic key variables, such as base money, the money multiplier and seigniorage, this study aims to contribute to the knowledge on currency use and payment patterns. The analysis of the theory and the empirical evidence on currency demand and the replacement by alternative payments media afford an insight into future changes in the payment pattern and the demand for currency and plastic money. This insight is of basic interest to all financial intermediaries, and in particular to the banking system, which is primarily involved in the payments system by providing the means of payment and financial assets. The monetary and currency-issuing authorities are concerned with the subject both from the point of view of monetary policy and of their ability to meet efficiently the future need for currency. Obviously, these issues will remain as topical as they are now, even when we have made the transition to a single European currency after exchange rates have been irrevocably locked, by providing, for example, 'inter-operable' banknotes (*cf.* CEC, 1990). There is no fundamental reason why this transition would basically change public demand for currency. Moreover, an additional problem arises in the form of the question of how seigniorage should be distributed among the member countries.

The contribution of this study is twofold. First, it analyses the demand for and use of currency on a micro-econometric basis. There we provide a methodology for the measurement of cash management and payments behaviour and expected changes by means of surveys. These surveys are unique in that they have been specially designed for this purpose. Comparable, though less extended, approaches have, as far as we know, been applied only in the United Kingdom and the United States. For the practical implementation, the Netherlands serves as a case study, but the methodology has general applicability. Second, the study provides a macro-econometric approach, which consists primarily of a cross-section analysis for 1970-1989 of the currency circulation and composition of as many as 15 industrial countries, using unique information on their payments systems derived from a questionnaire sent to the central banks. Such a multinational approach seems especially useful for the analysis of the effect of new payments media on the demand for currency, because of the limited number of observations per country. Apart from this, we analyse the development of the currency circulation in the Netherlands in 1955-1990, giving explicit attention to the effects of financial innovation and technological change.

The study is rooted in a long-standing Dutch tradition in this field of research. The extensive studies of the demand for banknotes at the Nederlandsche Bank (*cf.* Fase and Van Nieuwkerk, 1976, 1977; COTOB, 1976; and Fase *et al.* 1979) and the unique survey-based research on the demand for money by sector by Cramer and Reekers (1972) date from the mid-1970s. Since then additional studies have appeared at regular intervals. The analysis of the payment pattern and the turnover rate of currency is the ultimate consequence of the profound interest in the velocity of circulation, rooted in the work of Holtrop (1928) and Koopmans (1933) and elaborated by Zijlstra (1948). More recently this tradition has been given some empirical foundations by the studies of Cramer and research performed in the 1980s at the Nederlandsche Bank on the use of currency and banknotes and on payment flows and payment patterns. The present study widens the scope by extending the available theoretical and empirical findings with both micro-economic and macro-economic evidence, applying newly developed methodologies and using unique data sets.

Outline of the book

The above-mentioned elements also show up in the outline of the book. Chapter 1 gives an overview of the relevant macro and micro-economic theory of the demand for money as well as of the available empirical evidence. The chapter also includes an empirical analysis of the applicability of the theory to currency demand in the Netherlands since 1955, explicitly dealing with the effects of financial innovations and with the currency velocity. In Chapter 2 we analyse the appropriateness of notably the transactions theory by means of a micro-econometric analysis of cash management and payment behaviour, on the basis of four surveys held between 1983 and 1990. These results, which partly rely on earlier work coauthored with Fase, provide unique information on the cash management and payments behaviour and the effect of automated teller machines and plastic money.

Both the macro-econometric approach in Chapter 1, and the micro-econometric approach in Chapter 2 point toward a substantial degree of hoarding of currency. This theme is elaborated further in Chapter 3, which, by way of an intermezzo, deals with the theory of hoarding, the methodology of its measurement and with the empirical results for the Netherlands. This chapter also partly relies on earlier work. Thus far, the study is Dutch-oriented.

Chapter 4 widens the scope to the international level by providing a pooled cross-section analysis of the demand for currency in 15 countries, explicitly paying attention to the effect of alternative payment media. This analysis focuses on the demand for currency by the public as well as on the currency holdings of the banking system, the composition of the currency circulation with regard to notes and coin, and a number of characteristics of the note circulation. The final chapter provides, by way of summary, a synthesis of the main results and sets out a number of implications regarding future currency use and payment patterns.

1 THEORY AND EMPIRICAL EVIDENCE

1.1 Introduction

We focus on the money demand theories which are of particular relevance to the analysis of the demand and use of currency. Most of these theories relate to M1 (sometimes referred to as cash in this chapter), including currency and demand deposits, or even broader money concepts. At least part of their findings, however, equally hold for the demand for currency as such. A few studies deal explicitly with the demand for currency, in a spectrum of other financial assets and payments media. Besides, a number of studies on currency in relation to demand deposits are of relevance, though they focus primarily on the ratio of both money components, as an element of the money multiplier 1).

The next two sections give an overview of the relevant theory. After a short impression of the main streams in the aggregate money demand theory, we deal in more detail with the specific, micro-economic theories about the transactions, precautionary and speculative demand for money, which are of special interest in the context of this study 2). Sections 4 and 5 summarize the empirical evidence from earlier studies and our findings for currency demand in the Netherlands, respectively. In section 6 we draw the main conclusions.

1.2 Macro-economic theory

The aggregate demand theory most narrowly connected with money as a means of exchange is Fisher's *quantity theory*, being indissolubly connected with the equation of exchange MV = PT, with M the stock of money, V its circulation velocity, P the price and T the volume of total

1) In the early 1980s the ratio received also interest as indicator of the growth of the black economy. See Tanzi (1982), Boeschoten and Fase (1984) and Fase (1984), who applies the currency ratio method for estimating the size of the black economy in the Netherlands.
2) Thus, we do not deal here with the question of simultaneity and exogeneity or the buffer stock approach, which seem less relevant in this context. See for extensive reviews on the demand for money Goldfeld (1973), Judd and Scadding (1982), Laidler (1985), and Goldfeld and Sichel (1990).

transactions. In Fisher's original view, M is determined independently of any of the three other variables and can at any time be taken as given. The velocity, albeit not immutable over time because of its dependency on the state of the payments system and the production structure, is assumed to have a more or less constant equilibrium value in the short run. T is also exogenous at the long run equilibrium at full-employment levels of income. The price level follows from the interaction of the other three variables. In terms of money demand, though not stated as such by Fisher, the theory implies the nominal money balance being proportional to the value of transactions, the constant fraction being the reciprocal of the transactions velocity of money (Laidler, 1985). There is, however, no necessary connection, as Fisher's position indicates 3).

Contrary to the theories, which shift the scene to the demand for money and allow for various motives for holding money, the equation of exchange considers money purely as a means of exchange in the tradition of the 'motion theory' (Holtrop, 1929). The work done by money follows from the velocity of circulation V = PT/M, *i.e.* the number of times the amount of money in circulation is used to effect the total transactions value PT. It is the difficulty of measuring the total amount of transactions that has been a major obstacle to this approach. Thus, Jevons (1875) already recognizes the importance of the concept, but concludes that the data are wanting. After Fisher's efforts and pioneering activities in the estimation of the velocity of cash, it is Keynes (1930) who shows that shifts in the composition of the money demand can cause movements in the velocity, and that turnover figures can be a valuable indicator for economic activity. Since then the attention for the turn-

3) Indeed, in the simple model used by Fisher (1922, p 84) to illustrate the effect on velocity of a shift in the payment period, individuals do not use the alternative financial assets and therefore hold an average cash balance equal to one-half of each income receipt, implying proportionality of cash balances to income. On the other hand he argues elsewhere: 'It seems to be a fact that, at a given price level, the greater a man's expenditure the more rapid his turnover ... . We may therefore infer, that, if a nation grows richer per capita, the velocity of circulation of money will increase. This proposition, of course, has no reference to nominal increase of expenditure.' (Fisher, 1922; p 167).

over figures, however, flawed with a few exceptions 4), also because the return from the velocity of circulation to the income velocity of money.

The *Cambridge approach*, as represented in the work by Pigou (1917), results in the money market equilibrium condition $M_s.1/k = M_sV = PY$, with Y the real level of income, M_s the supply of money and k the reciprocal of the, *ceteris paribus* constant, income velocity of money. The velocity is no longer determined by the technical need for money to carry out a certain volume of transactions. What really matters is the amount of money an individual wishes to hold, given the desire to conduct these transactions, which basically is in the tradition of the 'cash balance theory' (Holtrop, 1929). The demand for money is an element of the general demand theory, with constraints (wealth), opportunity costs (interest rates) and individual tastes and expectations being additional factors, besides the volume of transactions. Instead of being more or less constant, the velocity may vary quite significantly over short periods. Another important, though in the literature less emphasized difference is the exchange of the volume of transactions by income, and thus the transactions velocity by the income velocity. In spite of Keynes' (1930, 1936) warnings that the income velocity is a hybrid conception having no particular significance and that it has led to nothing but confusion, it has become a common point of reference in mainstream monetary and money demand studies.

Keynes (1936), in the Cambridge tradition of treating the problem of the demand for money as one of choice-making behaviour, focuses on the motives for holding money, explicitly dealing with the role of uncertainty. Apart from the transactions demand for regular planned payments, he distinguishes the precautionary demand. These balances serve to fill the gap between receipts and irregular unplanned payments, stemming from unexpected bills, purchases at unexpected favorable prices etc. Both types of 'active' balances depend, by and large, on the level of income.

4) *Cf.* Snyder (1934), Selden (1956), Garvy and Blyn (1969), Cramer (1981, 1986b), and Kerr (1985) who finds a close relationship between US debits and GNP, as well as Verrijn Stuart (1935) and Fase (1986) for their discussion on the MV-index.

Although Keynes considers them by no means as technically fixed to national income, he does not stress the role of interest rates here (Whalen, 1966). The speculative balances, however, are sensitive to expected interest changes (compared to the normal interest rate) and wealth, with as the most striking implication the liquidity trap doctrine, suggesting an infinite interest elasticity at very low interest rate levels. The relationship between speculative demand and wealth is not a stable one, as it depends on the level of the interest rate. The speculative demand may dominate the total demand for money so that the explanation and prediction on the basis of transactions motives alone may be inappropriate and misleading.

The *modern quantity theory*, as presented by Friedman (1956), places the demand for money, like the Cambridge approach, in a general theory of demand, treating money as a durable good rendering services, and taking into account the marginal rate of substitution. Thus besides a wealth or permanent income variable and one or more representative interest rates, the demand function contains the expected rate of interest as a measure of the expected capital gains and losses from holding other assets. The expected percentage change of the price level shows up representing the expected own (negative) return on money holding. The magnitude or importance of these relationships, especially with regard to the interest rate, is open to empirical testing. Thus Friedman and Schwartz (1963) defend a wealth or income elasticity of money greater than unity, seeing money as a luxury good whose demand increases more than proportionally to income. Meltzer (1963) departing from the same theory adheres, however, to a wealth elasticity of unity. It may be clear that this approach, with its micro-economic foundations, is closely linked to the micro-economic approach of the demand for money.

The *portfolio-approach*, based on the work of Markowitz (1952) on rules of rational behavior for investors, and its application to economic theory by Tobin (1958), is also rooted in the general demand theory, but makes explicit allowance for uncertainty and risk. Here the money holdings are part of a portfolio of all kinds of financial and possibly real assets. The return of the portfolio is maximized given the return rates of the various assets and their risk of capital gains. The resulting demand for money, being one component of the whole system, basically depends on the return rates and risk of all other assets, that have been considered. For the rest the resulting specification is rather similar to the specification of the modern-quantity theory, wealth playing a central role as scale variable.

1.3 Micro-economic theory

Although the macroeconomic theories give an inventory of the factors that may affect the money demand, and provide knowledge on the expected signs, they do not precisely predict the order of magnitude of the effects. A major step in this direction is the rationalisation of Keynes' theoretical concepts of the transactions, precautionary and speculative motives for holding money in the 1950s and 1960s. Since then the refinement and elaboration of these theories and their empirical verification has gone on until the late 1970s. The waning interest of the economic profession in later years, apart from the cash-in-advance models and the utility function approach, may indicate that at least from a theoretical point of view most of these issues are considered to have been settled.

1.3.1 The transactions demand

The theory of the cash holdings needed for the payment of regular transactions is rooted in the inventory theoretic approach as presented by Baumol (1952). The model departs from a predetermined value of transactions T, with an interest rate r and a fixed transfer cost, or 'broker's fee', b, of transferring funds between earning assets and cash 5). The precise nature of this transfer cost will vary depending on the context in which the model is being applied, but in all cases it is to be interpreted as including both the direct expenses of effecting the

5) Ordinarily, this cost is called transactions cost. Following Miller and Orr (1966) we shall refer to it, however, throughout as transfer cost, reserving the terms transactions and transactions cost for the receipts and payments, which are exogenous to the original model.

transfer, such as postage or bank service charges, and the opportunity costs, such as time spent waiting at teller's windows or in making and communicating decisions about purchases and sales of portfolio assets. Likewise the interest rate must be considered to include the risk of loss and theft, or the costs of protection against such risk. The individual chooses equally spaced withdrawals of an amount C to minimize total holding cost of cash. This cost is $bT/C+r(C/2)$, where $C/2$ is the average money holding and $r(C/2)$ is the opportunity cost of holding it. This total cost is minimized, if C is continuous, when

$$C = \sqrt{(2bT/r)}\,, \tag{1.1}$$

in which case the average money holding is $M = C/2 = \sqrt{(bT/2r)}$. This 'square root law' implies an elasticity with respect to transactions and transfer costs of 0.5 and an interest elasticity of -0.5, and homogeneity of the first degree in prices. A doubling of all prices, including the broker's fee, is like a change in the monetary unit, and may be expected to double the demand for cash balances. The resulting 'economies of scale' in the transactions balances reflect the fact that the proportional increase in the interest yield foregone if the increment in income is held in the form of cash balances, induces a reduction in the length of time between successive cash withdrawals. As a result there is a decline in the average amount of cash holdings. As Baumol already stated, the model may suggest larger economies of scale than are actually involved. Equation (1.1) requires that the average transactions velocity of circulation varies in proportion to the quantity of cash ($V=T/(C/2) = rC/b$), so that a doubling of the stock of cash will *ceteris paribus*, just double velocity.

Since its early appearance the inventory approach has been elaborated by relaxing the restrictions and by taking into account various interdependencies. Most of the refinements have a fragmentary character in the sense that they deal with one or more special elements of the theory. A synthesis of the refinements soon becomes intractable. For the sake of clarity we have, however, summarized the main extensions of the inventory model in Table 1.1. Baumol (1952) already showed that the optimal

Table 1.1 Amendments and refinements on inventory model

Author(s)	Amendment/refinement	Object, level of aggre-gation	Elasticity of money with respect to				
			income/ transactions	variance of net cash flow	interest rate	transfer cost	inflation
Transactions demand (deterministic net cash flow)							
Baumol (1952)	-	individual	½	-	-½	½	-
Tobin (1956)	integer constraint	individual	.	-	-½	½	-
Brunner and Meltzer (1967)	cash receipts from sales spending after receipt	firm	$\frac{1}{2} \le \eta_y \le 1$ a)	-	.	.	-
Sprenkle (1969)	decentralization	firm	> ½	-	.	.	-
Feige and Parkin (1971)	commodity inventories	household	≥ ½	-	≈ -½ b)	≈ ½ b)	-
Barro and Santomero (1972)	currency versus demand deposits real value of time productivity of transfers	household	. c)	-	-½ d)	< ½	-
Dutton and Gramm (1973)	real value of time	household	> ½	-	. e)	.	-
Karni (1973)	real value of time	household	≥ ½ f)	-	$-\frac{1}{2} < \eta_r \le 0$	.	-
Santomero (1974)	currency vs demand deposits commodity inventories transactions costs	household	= ½ b)	-	≈ -½ b)	≈ ½ b)	≈ ½ b)
Barro (1976)	integer constraint aggregation	aggregate aggregate	$\frac{1}{2} \le \eta_y \le 1$	-	$-\frac{1}{2} \le \eta_r \le 0$ c)	.	-
Ahmad (1977)	see Brunner/Meltzer (1967)	firm	$\frac{1}{2} \le \eta_y \le 1$ g)	-	$-2 \le \eta_r \le -\frac{1}{2}$ g)	.	-
Akerlof and Milbourne (1978)	integer constraint/aggregation accumulation savings in cash	household	$\frac{1}{2} \le \eta_y \le 1$	-	$-\frac{1}{2} \le \eta_r \le 0$ h)	.	-
Buiter and Armstrong (1978)	risk with repect to r	economic agent	≥ 0 i)	-	.	.	-
Whitesell (1989)	transactions costs diffe-ring per payments medium	household	.	-	$\eta_r < 0$ j)	.	-
Precautionary demand (stochastic net cash flow)							
Whalen (1966)	costs of illiquidity	firm	.	1/3	-1/3	1/3 k)	-
Miller and Orr (1966)	thriftless net cash flow two-parameter threshold model	firm	$1/3 \le \eta_y \le 2/3$ l)	$1/3 \le \eta_{\sigma^2} \le 2/3$	-1/3	1/3	-
Miller and Orr (1968)	proportional transfer cost	firm	$\frac{1}{2} \le \eta_y \le 1$	$\frac{1}{2} \le \eta_{\sigma^2} \le 1$	-½	½	-
Frenkle and Jovanovic (1980)	stochastic and deterministic part in net cash flow one parameter threshold model	firm/ individual	$0 \le \eta_y \le \frac{1}{2}$	$0 \le \eta_{\sigma^2} \le \frac{1}{2}$	$-\frac{1}{2} \le \eta_{\sigma^2} \le -\frac{1}{4}$	½	-

Explanatory note: a point denotes that no explicit value is mentioned.

a) η_y approaches 1 when transactions tend to infinity or transfer costs to zero.

b) linear combination of square root functions in income, interest, transfer costs and share of currency in total transactions.

c) indeterminate because of ofsetting effects of real value of time and productivity advance.

d) regards differential between marginal return rates on adjacent assets, r_c(currency; including costs possible losses and storage costs), r_d(demand deposit), r_s (saving deposits).

e) indeterminate (dependent on portfolio), negative in empirical elaboration.

f) for elasticities with respect to real wage rate and hours worked: $0 \le \eta_w \le 1$, $0 \le \eta_{tw} \le 1$.

g) η_y and η_r approach ½ and -2, respectively, for small transactions values and/or large transfer costs.

h) positive thrift in cash balances raises interest elasticity.

i) could well exceed unity in case of risk aversion.

j) in case of uniform distributed transactions $\eta_y = -\eta_r$; ambiguous effect transfer cost on currency.

k) with respect to cost of illiquidity.

l) under and upper limit if change in sales at constant frequency, or at constant amount, respectively. Wider ranges when increase is accompanied by increase in transaction frequency, or vice versa.

cash holding remains basically unchanged, if a part of the broker's fee varies in proportion to the quantity of cash handled. Only in the case of complete proportionality are there no economies of scale, because it then pays to hold zero cash balances. Lumpy but foreseen payments and receipts of cash, with sufficient foresight, can make for economies in the use of cash, *i.e.* higher velocity. This may, however, not affect the rate of increase in transactions velocity with the level of transactions. Brunner and Meltzer (1967) argue that the model does not imply important economies of scale when, along the lines that Baumol sketches, the firms are permitted to receive money from sales or payments from accounts receivable. In this amended form the elasticity of money holdings with respect to total transactions is dependent on total transactions T and approaches one for increasing T.

A first refinement concerns the *integer constraint* and its possible consequences for aggregation and the resulting money demand elasticities. As Tobin (1956) shows, the restriction to integer values implies that, at the individual level, the transfer frequencies would not react continuously to such changes as interest variables and cost of transferring. Basically, up to the point where it pays to make two transfers, all receipts are held in the form of cash, cash increasing in direct proportion to the volume of transactions, being insensitive to changes in the interest rate. Between the jump-points at which discrete changes take place, cash balances are unit elastic with respect to the volume of transactions (Brunner and Meltzer, 1967). Due to the jumpy response at the individual level, on an aggregate level the interest elasticity is likely to be much closer to zero, while the income elasticities may vary between 0.5 and 1.0, also depending on the prevailing income distribution (Barro, 1976). Including the use of cash to accumulate savings does raise the interest elasticities, though to absolute levels still substantially below 0.5 (Akerlof and Milbourne, 1978).

A second refinement regards the *mutual dependency* of the volume of transactions, the rate of interest, and the cost of cash withdrawal. In the case of a change in the overall income level, there is likely to be an accompanying change in the value of time, implying an increase in the transfer cost, to the extent that transfers require the expenditure of a certain amount of time. Due to the simultaneous effect of the wage rate on the transfer costs the individual's income elasticity may vary between 0.5 and 1 (Karni, 1973, 1974). On the aggregate level the elasticity is unity if the transactions costs is entirely a time cost and if the value of time is proportional to income (Barro, 1976). Since the value of time may increase even faster than transactions volume, diseconomies-of-scale (money being a 'luxury') is quite compatible with the inventory approach.

As argued by Barro and Santomero (1972), transfer costs may rise less than time valuation, insofar as the process of conducting transactions is subject to some real productivity advance. For example, the time involved in transfers, and thus the average transfer costs, would decrease with an increase in the number of bank branch offices, the introduction of banking-by-mail or an increase in the number of types of accounts available. If this type of technical advance occurs sufficiently rapidly, the effect of increased value of time would be offset and real transfer costs would remain unchanged or possibly even be reduced, implying an income elasticity of money of 0.5 or even less.

Likewise an interest rate change may influence not only the opportunity costs of holding cash, but also real income and consumption. Taking into account these simultaneous effects results in smaller interest effects on the money holdings. The interest elasticity might range from -0.5 to zero, compared to the fixed value of -0.5 in the original model (Karni, 1973). This result does, however, not hold for changes in the nominal rate of interest that result from changes in the expected rate of inflation, as they only affect the opportunity cost of holding money and not real income.

A third elaboration of the original inventory model concerns the distinction between the cash management behaviour of *firms and households*. In principle the transactions model holds for both sectors. The size of the effects of the determining factors may however differ between both types of economic agents. Thus Wilbratte (1975) argues that only in the case of firms is the amount of money involved large enough for interest earnings over very short investment periods to exceed the broker's fee. Furthermore, firms often have branches, which has consequences for the cash management behaviour 6). Sprenkle (1969) shows that in the case of decentralization, each of the branches having separate accounts, the optimal cash holdings will be considerably greater than under complete centralisation. The non-optimality of the decentralized accounts stems from the fact that the square root law for cash balances only holds if the volume of transactions is large enough and/or the frequency of receipts is small enough to ensure that it is profitable to buy and sell securities during the period. Thus, rather than a square root law, we may find that average cash balances increase more than proportionately with firm size because the degree of decentralization and the spread of non-optimized cash balances (special accounts *etc.*) may rise substantially with firm size.

Contrary to the studies on firm demand for money, a number of theoretical models on the household demand explicitly consider the *use of currency versus the use of debitable accounts*, and thus do justice to the fact that demand deposits and currency possess distinct characteristics that should be explicitly considered. In fact, this distinction is the fourth direction of elaboration of the transactions demand model. The deterministic inventory-type optimization model of Barro and Santomero (1972), that explicitly reckons with the movements between currency, demand deposits and savings deposits and the involved 'going-to-the-bank' cost and check-cashings, basically gives the same results as the Baumol-model. The households' currency holdings depend on the cash transactions and the cost of check-cashing with an elasticity of 0.5 and on the demand deposit rate with an elasticity of -0.5, but is insensitive to the interest rate on savings deposits. Moreover, the ratio of currency to total money holdings is independent from income, but depends on the (exogenous) share of expenditure that is paid by currency, as opposed to a check, with an elasticity of 0.5.

6) The fact that firms are confronted with a greater degree of uncertainty, especially with respect to their receipts, will be dealt with in the section on the precautionary demand for money.

The introduction of *costs for the purchases of goods* and the inclusion of *commodity inventories* as proposed by Feige and Parkin (1971) and Santomero (1971) implies a finite instead of an infinite number of trips of goods purchases. As shown by Santomero this extension per se may raise the interest rate effect, the elasticity on an aggregate level ranging between -0.5 and -0.8. Santomero (1974) further refines the model incorporating the interaction of currency and demand deposits and taking into account the effect of inflation upon commodity and money holdings. Thus the yields on commodities consist of the negative yield connected to both the cost of storage and depreciation of the item, as well as the yield gained through the expected changes in the price level. The demand for money is inversely related to the cost of goods purchase. The higher, relatively, these transactions costs, the less frequently 'shopping trips' are made and the higher the average level of commodity inventories maintained, at the expense of the monetary asset. Likewise, a rise in the rate of price increases will *ceteris paribus* raise the demand for goods inventory, at the expense of money. The resulting elasticity can, however, no longer be presented by a point value. Only if the cost of shopping trips using either form of the medium of exchange is zero, will money demand be at the level suggested by previous inventory models. If these costs are larger than zero, then money demand will be lower than traditional theory has suggested.

A final refinement of special interest for the underlying study is the explanation of different *costs of using alternative assets* for commodity purchases, *i.e.* the fact that the transactions costs differ by payments mechanism, depending on the value of the commodity purchase. Without such differentials, one monetary asset would dominate others based on 'own rate' considerations, disregarding the risk aspects. Thus, also the share of currency payments in total payments is endogenized. The elaboration becomes however so complicated that no analytical results of fixed elasticities result as in the original model. Elaborating the earlier model of Santomero (1979), Whitesell (1989) shows that, when transactions costs differ between currency and checks, and the difference depends on transactions size, the interest elasticities of an individual's demand for currency are themselves functions of the interest rate and the income level, rather than constants as in the simpler inventory models. Moreover, a reduction in the brokerage fee on withdrawals increases the frequency of withdrawal here, as is standard in the inventory models, but it may also lead to higher currency holdings because currency is substituted for alternative payment methods.

In the context of the present study it may be of some interest to summarize the main assumptions and results, starting like Whitesell (1989) with the use of debitable accounts as opposed to the use of currency. Payment from a debitable account imposes fixed costs, u, and variable costs (in relation to the costs of paying by currency). If the variable costs are assumed to be proportional to the monetary value, with ν the cost coefficient and T the transaction size, the total cost of transacting a purchase of size T then is $C = u + \nu T$. Basically, the debitable account will not be used for small transactions because of the fixed cost u. If F(T) is the value of spending on all transactions of size T during the period (implying the number F(T)/T transactions of size T), and λ the size of the largest transaction which is optimal to pay with currency, then in case of a uniform distribution the optimization problem reduces to choose λ and the number of withdrawals, n, so that the cost function

$$nb + \frac{r}{2n}\int_0^{\lambda} F(T)\,dT + \int_{\lambda}^{\infty} F(T)\left[\nu + \frac{u}{T}\right]dT \tag{1.2}$$

is minimal with b being the brokerage fee connected to withdrawals and r the interest rate on the deposit account. Abstracting from integer constraints, the first order conditions with respect to λ and n are

$$b - \frac{rS}{2n^2} = 0, \text{ and } \frac{rF(\lambda)}{2n} - F(\lambda)\left[\nu + \frac{u}{\lambda}\right] = 0 \tag{1.3}$$

with S the total amount that is paid with currency ($S = \int_0^{\lambda} F(T)dT$). The first condition corresponds to the Baumol-Tobin condition that the brokerage fee is just equal to the interest lost on the marginal withdrawal of currency. The second condition states that the marginal opportunity cost of holding and using currency for the marginal size transaction must equal the extra cost of transacting alternatively through the account. According to the comparative static signs higher fixed or variable costs of paying from deposit accounts increases the size of the largest transaction paid with currency as well as the number of withdrawals n ($\delta\lambda/\delta u>0$; $\delta\lambda/\delta\nu>0$; $\delta n/\delta u>0$; $\delta n/\delta\nu>0$). A higher brokerage fee has the opposite effect. A higher interest rate decreases the largest currency transaction size, as well as the total amount paid with currency ($\delta\lambda/\delta r<0$; $\delta S/\delta r<0$). The effect of the interest rate is ambiguous: higher interest rates imply more frequent withdrawals to economize on interest foregone, but on the other hand total currency spending falls ($\delta n/\delta r = n/2r + \delta S/\delta r.n/2S$). From the resulting demand for currency

$$C = S/2n = nb/r = b/2[\nu + u/\lambda] \tag{1.4}$$

it follows that the currency demand increases with the account-use threshold and decreases with the interest rate ($\delta C/\delta\lambda>0$; $\delta C/\delta r<0$). Thus with respect to the interest elasticity and the effect of the brokerage fee on the number of withdrawals the results correspond with the original model, albeit that, due to nonlinearities, the resulting elasticities are much more complicated. The model also shows that the demand for currency, as given by (1.2), is increasing in the costs of using the debitable account. However, (1.5) shows that, unlike simpler inventory models, the effect of the brokerage fee on currency is
ambiguous, as $\delta S/\delta b<0$.

$$\frac{\delta C}{\delta b} = \frac{n}{r} - \frac{b}{r}\cdot\frac{\delta n}{\delta b} = \frac{n}{2r} + \frac{1}{4n}\frac{\delta S}{\delta b} \gtrless 0 \tag{1.5}$$

On the one hand, higher fees imply fewer and larger withdrawals and thus larger average currency holdings. On the other hand a higher brokerage fee implies that the debitable account will substitute for currency as a payment method for some transactions (λ falls), thereby reducing currency holdings 7).

7) It is basically this second effect, which is not included in Paroush and Ruthenberg's (1986) analysis, that concludes to a negative effect of the use of automated teller machines on the demand for currency, under rather strict assumptions on the cost functions and given a fixed total of currency and demand deposits.

An alternative to the standard single-equation approach of the transactions demand for money is the inclusion of money in a general *microeconomic consumer analysis*, thus emphasizing the importance of interaction among goods. The consumer maximizes a utility function subject to a budget constraint. Money is held because of the utility it provides. The monetary variables used are the real flow of monetary services provided by monetary assets, not the simple sum of real stocks of money. The explanatory variables in the demand system are the amount available for spending and the prices of these goods. The basically unobservable quality of liquid assets can be included by means of a dual cost function (Barnett, 1978). The implicit utility considerations of narrow money can be supplemented by a partial measure of its performance, the services rendered following from the amount of payments effected, proxied by the volume of transactions. Despite its different approach the estimates for the income and the 'price' elasticity, as found by Fayyad (1986) for the United States correspond closely to their theoretical value following from the inventory approach. A similar foundation has the inclusion of money in the *production function of firms*, besides production factors as labour and capital. Restrictions on the demand function emerge from the functional form of the utility function and from the way in which money balances are included in the utility function. In the Cobb-Douglas production function case, as considered by Coates (1976), transactions and interest elasticities of 1 and -1 result, respectively.

A rather different approach to the transactions demand is the *cash-in-advance models* which place the demand for money in a general equilibrium context. They consider the institution of money as arising from frictions that prohibit trade in a full range of Arrow-Debreu contingent (Hamilton, 1989). In the version of Lucas and Stokey (1987), two categories of goods are assumed, those that must be paid for with cash, with volume C_{1t}, and those where trade is permitted on the basis of credit, C_{2t}. Households maximize the expected utility from both categories of goods, subject to the cash-in-advance constraint $P_tC_{1t} \leq M_t$, P_t being the price level. The problem can be solved by linear programming techniques. Changes in inflation, output, or the payments technology effect changes in the income velocity of money through their influence on the proportion of income that consumers choose to devote to cash goods. The eventual effects, in general, correspond with those of the more traditional theory. Thus, higher inflation increases the velocity. The income velocity is, however, constant for output changes, unless the marginal rate of substitution decreases with the scale variable. An increase in the relative cost of credit goods leads to a reduction in equilibrium velocity. In the non time-invariant case, the velocity will be a function of income price level and the change of the payments technology, and all information that is useful in forecasting these variables.

1.3.2 The precautionary demand

The precautionary demand may be interpreted as the transactions demand that stems from uncertainty. According to Keynes (1936) precautionary cash balances are those which are held 'to provide for contingencies requiring sudden expenditure and for unforeseen opportunities of advantageous purchases, and also to hold an asset of which the value is fixed in terms of money to meet a subsequent liability in terms of money'. However, precautionary balances not only apply to fortuitous expenditures but also to the unpredictability of receipts (Whalen, 1966). Thus the rationale for the holding of these balances is the need to retain a certain amount of cash to meet the possibility of an excess of disbursements over receipts 8).

In Whalen's (1966) extension of the Baumol's transactions model the optimal size of the precautionary cash balances depends on the cost of illiquidity, the opportunity cost of holding cash balances and the

8) Alternatively, the precautionary balance may be defined as the additional cash balance arising from an increased degree of uncertainty. Although theoretically more correct, empirically this definition is difficult to handle. Thus Sprenkle (1967) and in his comment also Resek (1967) show that the precautionary cash balances of large economic units may be negative, due to differences in the costs (interest foregone plus transfer costs) of being wrong with respect to the occurrence of payment rates in one direction or the other.

average volume and variability of receipts and disbursements. Basically, the cost of illiquidity has its counterpart in the transfer cost in the Baumol-model. Likewise, the opportunity costs of holding precautionary balances are very similar to those of holding transactions balances. The essential difference is the role of uncertainty. The precautionary balances M depend on the probability distribution of the net disbursements. By using Tchebycheff's inequality, it can be shown that the total costs of precautionary cash management ($E = M.r + p.c$) are minimal if

$$M = \sqrt[3]{(2\sigma^2 c/r)}, \tag{1.6}$$

where r stands for the opportunity cost rate, p for the probability that net disbursements will be greater than precautionary cash balances, c presents the fixed cost per occurrence of insufficient cash, and σ is the standard deviation of the distribution of net disbursements. This result suggests an elasticity of 1/3 with respect to σ^2 and the cost of illiquidity and an interest elasticity of -1/3 with respect to the interest rate. The elasticity with respect to the average volume of receipts and disbursements depends on their relationship with σ^2.

Miller and Orr's (1966) model of the optimal cash management of firms under uncertainty reaches, along different lines, similar conclusions. They develop an optimal two-parameter control-limit (z, h) policy over any finite planning horizon, which takes into account that the cash balance of firms fluctuates irregularly and to some extent unpredictably over time in both directions. In the case of a prolonged building-up a point is reached at which the firm decides that funds should be transferred to earning assets. In the other direction, after a prolonged net drain, a level (put at zero for the sake of simplicity) will be reached at which the firm will restore the cash balance to an adequate working level. Under the assumption of a stationary random walk of the net cash flows the optimal average precautionary money balances depend with an elasticity of 1/3 on the variance of the daily change in the cash balance and the marginal cost per transfer, and with an elasticity of -1/3 on the average yield of the managed portfolio of liquid assets.

As in Whalen's model, the variance of daily net cash flows serves as the transactions variable in the money demand function. The relation between total sales and this variance is a loose one. The difficulty in specifying the sales elasticity stems from the fact that even with unchanging prices sales may change in any of several ways, each with a different impact on the firm's need for cash. If the increase of sales is due to a doubling of each separate receipt and expenditure invoice, than the elasticity is 2/3. However, if the increase is due to an increase in the frequency of transactions, the elasticity is 1/3. The range of elasticities, of course, becomes even larger when increases in the transactions magnitude are accompanied by decreases in transactions frequency, or vice versa. Basically, the results appear to be rather robust with respect to the assumed stochastic process, the two asset environment and the lumpiness of the transfer cost (Miller and Orr, 1968). However, in case of proportional instead of lumpy transfer costs the elasticities become -1/2 and 1/2. The latter elasticity implies that the elasticity with respect to transactions may vary between 0.5 and 1.

Frenkel and Jovanovic (1980) provide a synthesis of the transactions and the precautionary motive assuming both a deterministic and a stochastic component in the expression for the cash flow changes. If the variance of the money holdings approaches zero, Baumol's square root rule results. On the other hand, in the absence of any deterministic drift in the net disbursements, the elasticity with respect to the interest rate is -1/4 and 1/4 with respect to the variance. In general the transactions elasticity is thus positive and smaller than 1/2, increasing with the volume of transactions, and decreasing with the interest rate and the standard deviation of net disbursements. Likewise, the interest elasticity varies with the volume of transactions, from -1/2 when the volume of transactions approaches infinity, and -1/4 as the volume of transactions approaches zero. All these results are, however, conditional on the assumption of minimizing the present value of the cost of cash management. The solution to the problem obtained by minimizing the steady state cost function, which was adopted by Miller and Orr (1966), would in Frenkel and Jovanovic's approach result in the original Baumol-case, which only contains the deterministic transactions cost motive.

1.3.3 The speculative demand

While the precautionary demand is primarily concerned with uncertainties regarding the pattern of receipts and disbursements, the speculative demand is more directly concerned with uncertainties regarding interest rate and capital gains and losses. Basically, the speculative motive may be expected to be of rather limited importance for the demand for cash and especially currency under present day conditions. As securities of very short maturity are always readily available, most speculation on a fall in interest rates would take the form of shortening the maturities structure of the portfolio rather than of building up cash holdings. Furthermore, Miller and Orr's (1966) suggestion, that the optimal cash holding might be affected indirectly by speculation, to the extent that the prospect of speculative gains are reflected in the value of the interest rate, may be of limited importance in this context. We will therefore focus only on the main points of the micro-economic foundation of the speculative balances and their inverse relationship with the interest rate.

Speculative cash balances may be defined as that part of investment balances - balances which do not have to be turned into cash for transactions purposes - that is kept in cash, mainly because of expectations or fears of loss on other assets. In the view of Keynes (1936) the individual speculative demand is a zero-one decision. Either all the investments balances are kept in cash or they are held in the alternative interest bearing asset (bonds), depending on the current interest rate and its deviation from the expected normal interest rate. The lower the current rate, the higher the expected losses, and thus the greater the probability that an individual holds his balances in cash. The smoothness of the aggregate money demand function follows from the differing individual opinions on the normal interest rate.

The logically more satisfactory foundation for the liquidity preference is the theory of risk-avoiding of Tobin (1958), based on the portfolio selection theory as presented by Markowitz (1952). An individual will hold part of his asset portfolio in cash because of his risk aversion.

The individual investor bases his action on the probability distribution of the future capital gains and losses on interest bearing alternative assets. The eventual portfolio composition is the consequence of the trade off between of the expected return and the accompanying risk. Under the assumption of risk aversion (implying a concave indifference function of return and risk) a rise in the interest rate may raise the terms on which the investor can obtain greater expected return at the expense of assuming more risk (opportunity locus) and thus lowering the cash balances. Due to the ubiquitous conflict between income and substitution effects the effect is however not unambiguous. Thus for high interest rates, and especially for individuals whose estimates of the riskiness of the earning assets is low, the demand for cash may be an increasing, rather than a decreasing, function of the interest rate. Even then the ultimate relationship may be inverse, insofar as this (income) effect is mitigated by the reduction of the value of the investor's total portfolio. On the other hand, the riskiness of the earning asset, reflected in the variability of the interest rates, will lower the asset holdings and thus raise the cash holdings.

The theory focuses on the effect of the interest rate and the choices among monetary assets, which bear comparable risks, are marketable, are fixed in money value and free of default risk. Thus the scale variable, being the total of monetary assets, is the result of the portfolio selection at a higher level of aggregation, where also choices on investment and consumption in particular are of concern. Liquidity preference theory takes as given how much wealth is to be invested in monetary assets and concerns itself with the allocation of these amounts among cash and alternative monetary assets. Consequently, wealth may be considered a relevant scale variable, which may in the short run and where the elasticities are concerned, come to income. In principle, the portfolio theoretic approach can be incorporated in the inventory theoretic approach. By treating the interest rate as a random variable Buiter and Armstrong (1978) show that in the case of risk aversion, the income elasticity of the demand for money balances could well exceed unity. Only when the economic agent aims at maximization of the expected return will the income elasticity always be one-half.

1.4 Empirical evidence from earlier studies

As appears from the former two sections, the theory for the demand of money provides a great number of possible determinants and wide ranges for the size of their effect, depending on the underlying motives (transactions or speculative), the type of economic units (households or firms) the pattern of receipts and disbursements (deterministic or stochastic) and the cost structure of transfer and transactions costs and so forth. Moreover, it has been argued that in a number of cases the assumptions are not satisfied, so that the inventory approach will not be appropriate at all. Consequently, the predicted elasticity of the demand for money with respect to transactions or income varies from 1/3 to over unity, while the interest elasticity may range from 0 to -0.5. After all, the answer is up to the empirical evidence.

We will first give an impression of the empirical evidence on the demand for the total of currency and demand deposits (denoted in the following as M1 or simply as money), insofar as they are relevant in the context of the demand for currency. A main point of interest here is whether the inventory theory, be it in its deterministic or its stochastic version, is supported by empirical evidence, and to what degree the successive extensions of the model find empirical support. Although basically relating to a wider monetary aggregate, the results may have also some validity to the demand for currency apart. The second sub-section deals with the much more scarce empirical evidence on the demand and use of currency and gives our results for the Netherlands.

1.4.1 The demand for money (M1)

Despite Laidler's (1985) conclusion that, contrary to the earlier years, the more recent years show some clear *economies of scale* in the demand for money holdings, a common result of many studies is still an income or transactions elasticity around one 9). Also, recent estimates using

---

9) See the surveys by Fase and Kuné (1975), Feige and Pearce (1977), Boorman (1980), Laidler (1985), Goldfeld and Sichel (1990) and Klovland (1983) for surveyed evidence from data prior to World War II.

econometrically more advanced methods, like the error correction mechanism, do not provide clear-cut evidence to the view of agents economizing on money balances relative to income as income rises (Fase and Winder, 1990; Boughton and Tavlas, 1991). Moreover, where economies of scale are observed, these may ensue from financial innovations and technological change. Obviously an increase in the availability of high interest bearing near moneys and short term investment opportunities for idle funds leads to lower money balances and increase pure financial transactions. But also the increased use of credit, better synchronization of receipts and expenditure, reduced mail float, and more efficient payments mechanisms, like wire transfers, will tend to decrease money demand. This results in a (temporarily) lower income elasticity, which may be erroneously considered as a reflection of economies of scale. Those money demand studies which include a measure of technological change such as the currency-demand deposit ratio (Bordo and Jonung, 1987 and Klovland, 1983), or a simple time trend (Lieberman, 1977) show significant improvements of the explanatory power of the money demand equations 10).

Also the studies on the firm behaviour on a cross-sectional basis, which exclude the effect of financial innovation and value of time effects, do not clearly support the presence of economies of scale 11). These results may, however, be distorted, mainly due to aggregation, denying the necessity of splitting money into transactions and liquidity balances and, in case of aggregation on a firm level, hiding the influence of the distribution of firms within the industry (Vogel and Madalla, 1967). These distributional impacts may be significant if there are substantial economies of scale or if firm size influences such things as cash management practices and the access to financial markets. In particular, the fact that the cost of credit is very likely higher for smaller borrowers, could be a reason that most cross-section studies do not or hardly find any economies of scale in the money holdings of

10) Lieberman's results suggest that technological change has reduced money demand in the US in 1947-1973 by about 1.5% to 2.5% per year.
11) *Cf.* Meltzer (1963), Whalen (1965) and Falls and Nattke (1988), who also mention a number of more recent cross-section studies on the firm demand for money.

firms. Moreover, the compensating balance requirements and the segregation of cash into various accounts may confuse the picture. As shown by Wessels (1982) for Dutch firms, also overdraft facilities may play a role.

The absence of clear economies of scale does not necessarily mean that the inventory approach is not appropriate. Thus the findings of Karni (1974) and of Dutton and Gramm (1973) for the US suggest that, at least for M1, an income elasticity which includes time valuation effects needs not necessarily be less than unity for confirmation of the economies of scale in money holdings predicted by the inventory models. The absence of any observable economies of scale may also be due to the use of income as transactions variable. Lieberman (1977) and Persson (1979), using total debits instead of income as transactions variable, come to substantial economies of scale in the money holdings in the United States and Sweden, with transactions elasticities of about 0.3 and 0.5, respectively. This may, however, be the result of a more than proportional growth of pure financial transactions, including shifts between different accounts, which are of no or minor importance to the demand for money per se. Cramer (1986b) circumvents this problem for the Netherlands by using transactions figures computed from the national accounts, finding a transactions elasticity that is only slightly less than the income elasticity of 0.74.

The conclusion of the various amendments, that the *interest elasticity* of money balances may in general be considerably smaller (in absolute terms) than the value of -0.5 of the original Baumol-model, is confirmed by the empirical evidence. The same holds for the conclusion of Miller and Orr (1968) that it is basically the highest alternative return rate, mostly the long-term interest rate, that matters (*cf.* Fase and Kuné, 1974, 1975; Laidler, 1985 or more recently Boughton and Tavlas, 1991). In most money demand studies the elasticity with respect to the interest rate is (in absolute terms) significantly less than -0.5. Moreover, it is likely that the interest rate coefficients reflect not only the opportunity cost of holding money but also, to some extent, the induced improvements in technology, which tend to reduce money demand. This relation is explicitly incorporated by Hall *et al.* (1989) in their money demand study for the UK. There is, on the other hand, no clear-cut empirical evidence for the hypothesis of Gurley and Shaw (1960), that a proliferation of money substitutes may increase the interest elasticity of money demand (Hafer and Hein, 1984).

The empirical evidence on the household demand for M1 is rather scarce, partly due to data problems. The monetary data employed are flow of funds series or data constructed on an ad hoc basis at rather strong assumptions on currency holdings. In general the results do not confirm any significant economies of scale in households' money holdings and suggest some interest sensitivity. Thus Hamburger (1966) finds the real demand of households for M1 in the United States to be statistically different from total demand. The elasticities with respect to the long-term interest rate and the yield on equity are both about -0.15. He fails, however, to find any influence of either wealth or income. Barro and Santomero (1972) find for 1950-1968 an income elasticity of 1 and an elasticity of -0.5 with respect to the earlier mentioned interest rate differential. The interest sensitivity of money demand with respect to the level of interest rates may therefore, in fact, be small. Wilbratte (1975) finds that, contrary to firm demand, the household demand for M1 in the US over 1952-1971 is rather stable with an income elasticity of 1.2 and an interest elasticity of -0.5. For the Netherlands, Fase and Winder (1989) conclude for the households demand for cash to a long-term income elasticity of unity, the long-run interest elasticity amounting to -0.4.

An alternative type of empirical evidence on the validity of the inventory models is that, at the prevailing interest rate and income levels, these models substantially underpredict actual balances. Thus Akerlof and Milbourne (1978) show that their slightly changed inventory model predicts only about 30% of the actual cash balances. Probably part of this is due to the hoarding of currency, and the use of currency for illegal transactions and tax evasion and the holding of buffer stocks to deal with uncertain flows in expenditures and receipts. Likewise Sprenkle (1969) shows that only 3% of the cash balances of 500 very large firms is explained by the simple Baumol-Tobin model with complete centralisation and that cash holdings seem to increase approximately linearly with respect to sales. Neither can the missing part be explained by the necessity for branches. In Sprenkle's view, the actual level of balances of firms can only be explained by the fact that firms pay for bank services by leaving deposits rather than by paying.

1.4.2 The demand for currency

Worldwide many currency demand functions have been estimated and are still being estimated. The relevant results are, however, rarely published in the current journals. Most of this kind of work nowadays is performed at central banks, either in view of the importance of currency as part of the monetary base, as in the case of Switzerland and the UK, or for the sake of the prediction of currency needs in the future. Especially the latter category of studies, because of their ultimate goal, often put forecasting power ahead of theoretical foundation or elegance. As it is, we have summarized the long-term characteristics of a number of available currency demand studies in Table 1.2. In view of the fast changing external factors, particularly the payments systems, we focus on the more recent studies. We leave aside equations which were estimated as part of large-scale econometric models and which are therefore mostly limited in the degree of detail of their specification.

The results suggest a sometimes considerable degree of economies of scale in the currency holdings. Even by country the results may, however, vary substantially, as for instance in Switzerland, where the income elasticity varies from 0.5 to 1.0. Moreover, as shown by the Finnish results, the conclusion may be quite sensitive to whether the equation is specified in real or in nominal terms 12). Although all theoretical models of the demand for money postulate that the demand for real balances should be independent of the price level and most money demand studies simply impose that condition from the outset, a number of

12) It goes without saying that in the case of economies of scale and a price elasticity of one, a nominal specification will raise the income elasticity and thus understate the actual degree of economies of scale.

Table 1.2 Long-term elasticities of currency or banknote demand in a number of currency demand studies

Country	Income/ consumption nominal	Income/ consumption real	Price level	Inflation	Interest rate elasticity	Interest rate semi-elast.	Other explaining variables		Estimation period	Source
Belgium a)	-	0.09h	1	0.66	-0.03*	-0.003	ln (number of check-transactions):	-0.03	1981:5-1988:12	Dombrecht (1989)
							ln (number of ATM-transactions):	0.061		
							ln (number of POS-transctions):	-0.11		
							ln (real estate registration rights):	0.059		
Canada a)	-	1.23	0.71	-	-	-			1961-1985	Cloutier (1986)
Finland a)	-	0.58c	1	-1.68	-0.08*	-0.01	credit card transactions/consumption:	-1.06	1973:III-1988:IV	Virén (1989)
a)	0.94c	-		-	-0.07*	-0.01		-1.78		Virén (1989)
a)	0.92c	-		-	-0.07*	-0.01		-0.90	1970:II-1988:IV	Virén and Kokkola (1989)
	-	0.43c	1	-0.03	-0.25*	-0.03	ln (real credit card transfers):	-0.09	1974:I-1988:IV	Kokkola (1990)
							number of ATMs:	0.84		
Germany a)	0.99/0.68yb)		-	-	-	-			1950-1975	Fase and Van Nieuwkerk (1977)
Ireland a)	-	0.64r	1	-	-0.34*	-0.03	dumEMS:	0.033	1967:I-1980:I	Browne (1981)
		0.46r	1	-0.05	-	-	dumEMS:	0.020		
Italy a)	1	-	-	-	0.24*	-0.02	ln (bank branches):	-0.610	1973:I-1986:II	Banca d'Italia (1988b)
Japan	0.72y				-0.006	-0.001*	ln (real estate):	0.262	1980:I-1989:IV	Bank of Japan (1990)
							ln (stock turnover):	0.004		
Netherlands a)	-	0.70y					cross-section analysis		1960	Nieuwenburg (1977)
	1.05/0.48y b)		-	-	-	-			1950-1975	Fase and Van Nieuwkerk (1977)
	1.05y	-	-	-	-	-	income-elasticity 1967-72:	0.60	1955-1984	Fase (1986)
	-	0.92c	1.08	-0.004	-0.07*	-0.007	ln (volume checks/consumption):	-1.02	1956-1990	This study
							ln (number of accounts per capita):	-0.24		
	1.01c	-	-	-	-0.07*	-0.008	ln (volume checks/consumption):	-0.25		
							ln (number of accounts per capita):	-0.25		
Norway	-	0.66y	1	0.04	-0.55*	-0.05	tax rate: 0.015;consumption/income:	0.011	1952-1978	Isachsen *et al.* (1982)
Sweden	-	0.63y	1	0.08	-0.40*	-0.04	tax rate: 0.009;consumption/income:	0.023	1952-1978	Klovland (1980)
Switzerland a)	0.84/0.73y b)		-	-	-	-			1950-1975	Fase and Van Nieuwkerk (1977)
	0.79c	-	-	-	-0.15	-0.03*			1959-1978	Galli (1980)
	-	0.50y	1	-	-0.24*	-0.07			1959-1983	Kohli (1984)
- large notes	-	1.05c	1	-	-0.10	-0.02*	trend d) 72-80(+) 80-85(-):	0.0045	1962-1988	Ettlin (1989)
- small notes	-	1.17c	1	-	-0.06	-0.01*	trend 1962-88:	-0.0050		
- all notes	-	1.07c	1	-	-0.10	-0.02*	trend 1962-88; 72-80: -0.003;	0.0027		
United Kingdom c)	-	0.93c	0.83	-1.63	-0.12*				1964:I-1981:IV	Trundle and Temperton (1982)
	0.84c	-	-	-	-1.51	-0.11*				
		1c	1	-	-	-	cumulated interest rate:	-0.0013	1969:III-1986:IV	Hall *et al.* (1989)
		0.88c	1		-0.10*	-0.01	ln (numbers of hours worked p/capita):	0.421		
United States	-	0.972w	1	-	-0.03	-	ln (property income)	0.069	1919-1968	Karni (1974)
a)	0.64y	-	-	-	-	-			1950-1975	Fase and Van Nieuwkerk (1977)
22 countries (14 industrial)	-	0.70	1	-	-0.18	-0.035	ln (share agriculture in GNP):	-0.171	1952-1961	Perlman (1970)
							presence of giro system:	0.244		
							risk (volatility of price level):	161		
Large industrial countries e)	-	1.15	0.53	-	-0.33	-			1950-1968	Lewis and Breen (1975)
Small industrial countries f)	-	0.80	0.84	-	-0.14	-				
Developing countries g)	-	1.74	0.20	-	-0.13	-				

c private consumption; h consumption in hotel and catering industry; pt current transactions; r retail sales; y income; w real wage rate; * computed from (semi)elasticity
a) banknotes only; b) before and after introduction of guaranteed cheques; computed on basis of marginal income quotes of banknote denominations; c) estimates of Hall et al. relate to M0; d) trend because of administrative measures against foreign money (1972-1980); e) France, UK, Italy, Japan, US; f) Sweden, Switzerland, Canada, Australia', Denmark, Belgium', Netherlands, Ireland', South Africa, Norway; g) Turkey, India, Costa Rica', Portugal, UAR', Pakistan Ceylon; (countries demoted by an ' deviate by one or more values, due to a deviating adjustment-parameter).

the studies considered here give preference to a nominal specification, probably in view of the forecasting quality. As far as homogeneity is not assumed *a priori*, the results suggest a price elasticity of less than unity.

One possible reason is that price indices may be inadequate proxies for the aggregate of prices by which agents implicitly deflate money holdings. Moreover, at least in the short run, there may be money illusion or at least non-instantaneous reaction to the change in price level due to the fact that after all economic agents adjust nominal balances. To some extent the results are in conformity with the recent findings of Boughton and Tavlas (1991) which only partly confirm the unit price elasticity of M1 in five large industrial countries. Inflation appears to influence currency demand only in a limited number of cases. This may be due to the moderate rates experienced in most of the estimation periods. Besides, the direction of the effect is not equivocal. The negative effect conforms to the basic economic view of inflation representing the opportunity cost to money holders. The positive sign may stem from the non-instantaneous reaction to the change in the price level (Koskela and Virèn, 1990).

The findings for the interest elasticities support the predictions of the elaborated inventory model, ranging from zero to about -0.5. In general, as most of the amendments of the original transactions model predict, the elasticities are fairly close to zero. The only exception is the much stronger effect for the UK. The relevant interest rate variable is, however, primarily thought to reflect innovations in financial management, which are more lucrative in periods of high interest rates. The low interest sensitivity may be explained from the fact that in the majority of countries no or very little interest is paid to the closest substitute for currency, demand deposits.

Some studies have tried to approximate the effect of changes in the financial system and the use of alternative payments media. Thus, Fase and Van Nieuwkerk (1977) find a significant drop of the income elasticity of the demand for banknotes, especially the lower denominations, in Germany, the Netherlands and Switzerland due to the introduction of guaranteed checks. In Italy the increase of the development of the financial system, proxied by the number of bank branches has considerably slowed down the growth in the currency demand. Likewise the use of check and credit cards has slowed down currency demand growth in Belgium and Finland. In both countries the use of cash dispensers and automated teller machines (ATMs) appears to have a positive influence on the demand for currency. This would mean that the negative effect of a more efficient cash management due to lower transfer costs, is more than compensated for by the increase of the share of cash payments. This contradicts the findings of Paroush and Ruthenberg (1986) for Israel. According to their results, not shown here, a 1% increase in the share of ATM-debits in total debits increases demand-deposit balances by about 0.2%, which would imply a decrease of the demand for currency if, as they assume, the total transactions balances remain constant. Moreover, a number of studies provide evidence for the importance of secular changes for the currency demand as reflected in the share of consumption, the demand for currency in view of real estate transactions and stock turnover as well as black market transactions (proxied by the tax rate).

Finally, the results of the multinational study by Lewis and Breen (1975) also support that income elasticities are greater than one-half and generally closer to or even greater than one in industrial countries. The elasticity of considerably more than one in the developing countries may reflect the effect of monetization, as suggested by Bordo and Jonung (1987). The price level elasticities are significantly less than unity in equations specified in real terms, suggesting a remarkably high degree of money illusion. The interest elasticities are not significantly different from zero in the developing countries but are significantly negative elsewhere with elasticities ranging from -0.33 to -0.14. In general the currency demand adjusts rapidly to changes in these variables.

1.5 The demand for currency in the Netherlands 1955-1990

1.5.1 Empirical evidence from demand function

In order to test to what degree currency demand in the Netherlands broadly fits the theory, we have estimated a currency demand equation, explicitly taking into account recent financial innovations. On the basis of the theory and of preceding empirical findings for the Netherlands and abroad we formulate the following currency demand function:

$$\text{Ln CV/P} = a_0 + a_1 \ln \text{CONS/P} + a_2 r_l + a_3 \dot{P} + a_4 \ln \text{NACC/POP} + a_5 \text{VCHECK/CONS} + a_6 \text{dum83} + a_7 \text{dum87} \quad (1.7)$$

CV	average currency circulation (millions of guilders)
CONS	private consumption (millions of guilders)
P	deflator of private consumption
r_l	long-term interest rate
$\dot{P}$	rate of inflation (%)
NACC	number of holders of checkable deposits
POP	population of sixteen years and older
VCHECK	guaranteed check transactions (millions of guilders)
dum83	dummy variable Slavenburg affair (dum83 = 1 from 1983 onwards)
dum87	dummy variable for tax reporting (dum87 = 1 from 1987 onwards)

Consumer expenditure has been preferred to income as scale variable, as most of the currency transactions are related to consumer purchases. There is, however, hardly any difference in the results with respect to the key elasticities. Besides, we have also considered the total current transactions PT_c as an alternative transactions variable (see Annex II for its construction). The share of the guaranteed check transactions in consumer expenditure and the number of debitable-accounts per head reflect the effect of their use on the demand for currency. As Figure 1.2 shows, both media have been widely introduced among the public since 1967, especially in the first ten years. In that period the currency ratio shows a substantial decline from about 10% to less than 6% of gross national product, the slight subsequent rise being mainly due to the increasing demand for the Fl. 1,000 and Fl. 250 banknotes (Figure 1.1).

Figure 1.1 Currency ratio and the share of currency in M1

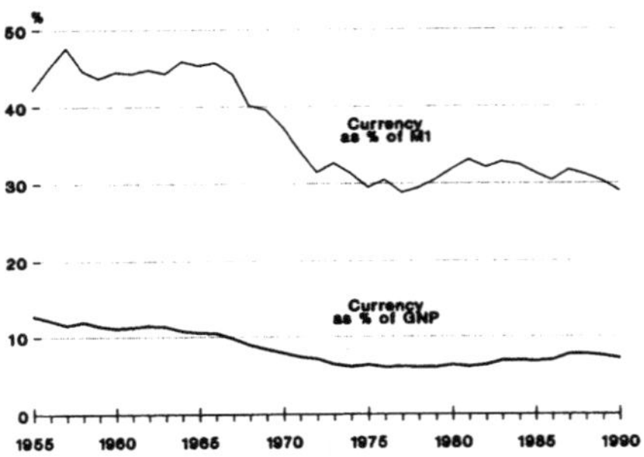

Figure 1.2 Importance of alternative payments media

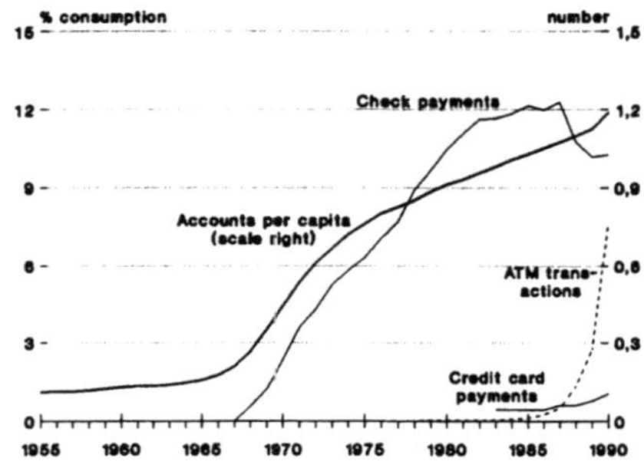

The credit card and point-of-sale transactions, which amount to 1% of the total consumer expenditure at maximum, and the ATM transactions are of too limited importance and too short a date, respectively, to have any statistically identifiable effect on the currency circulation. The dummy-variables represent the effects of fiscal rumours on the banknote circulation, which both resulted in a circulation which was about 10% higher (see Chapter 3). Basically, the relation is loglinear. For the interest rate and inflation we preferred, however, a semi-elasticity, while for the check variable, due to zero values before 1967, taking a logarithm was no option. Although (1.7) reads in real terms, we also consider a nominal specification, as applied by Fase and Van Nieuwkerk (1977) and Fase (1986) in modelling the demand for banknotes.

The estimation results in Table 1.3 do not confirm any economies of scale in the currency demand, none of the consumption-elasticities being significantly different from unity. Only when we would exclude the number of debitable accounts and the check payments variable from the equation, the consumption elasticity drops to 0.75 and 0.69, respectively. These lower elasticities reflect, however, the effect of financial innovation rather than the presence of economies of scale. As far as the equations are concerned, the interest rate coefficient gets the wrong

Table 1.3 Estimation results currency demand in the Netherlands 1956-1990

	ln CV						ln CV/P	
	(1)	(2)	(3a) long term	(3b) short term	(4)	(5)	(6)	(7)
$\ln CV_{-1}$	-	-	-	-	-	0.48	-	-
						(8.5)		
ln CONS	0.98	1.01	1.02	0.87	-	0.53	-	-
	(25.2)	(21.0)	(21.9)	(13.5)		(9.5)		
ln CONS/P	-	-	-	-	-	-	0.82	0.97
							(6.1)	(11.4)
$\ln PT_c$	-	-	-		1.02	-		
					(19.5)			
ln P	-	-	-	-	-	-	0.22	-
							(1.5)	
r_1	-	-0.006	-0.009	-0.005	-0.007	-0.001	-0.005	-0.005
		(0.9)	(1.5)	(1.3)	(0.8)	(0.4)	(0.8)	(0.7)
$\dot{P}$	-0.001	-0.004	-	-	-0.002	-	-0.005	-0.004
	(0.4)	(1.4)			(0.8)		(1.6)	(1.5)
ln NACC/POP	-0.25	-0.26	-0.28	-0.10	-0.22	-0.15	-0.21	-0.24
	(7.4)	(6.4)	(7.5)	(1.7)	(5.6)	(6.7)	(4.3)	(5.2)
VCHECK/CONS	-0.84	-0.61	-0.45	-1.50	-0.54	-0.54	-2.22	-0.61
	(2.1)	(1.3)	(1.0)	(2.2)	(1.2)	(2.6)	(1.9)	(1.5)
dum83	0.18	0.1	0.1	0.1	0.16	0.09	0.1	0.1
	(7.8)	(-)	(-)	(-)	(5.0)	(4.7)	(-)	(-)
dum87	0.10	0.12	0.12	0.06	0.13	0.04	0.10	0.12
	(4.4)	(4.6)	(4.9)	(3.2)	(5.3)	(2.8)	(3.8)	(4.9)
Constant	-0.30	-0.48	-0.55	-	4.29	-0.32	-3.97	-4.78
	(1.1)	(1.3)	(1.5)		(24.6)	(1.9)	(4.2)	(6.1)
$Res_{stat_{-1}}$	-	-	-	-0.42	-	-	-	-
				(3.8)				
$\bar{R}^2$	0.998	0.998	0.998	0.594	0.998	0.999	0.974	0.973
SE	0.029	0.034	0.034	0.018	0.033	0.015	0.033	0.034
DW	1.18	0.91	0.70	1.29	1.18	1.70	0.76	0.93

Explanatory notes: t-values within parentheses. Durbin's-h of equation (5) is 0.938.

sign unless we assume lagged adjustment (estimate 5), use the current transactions as transactions variable (estimate 4), or put the value of the coefficient of dum83 at the *a priori* estimated effect of 0.1, or lower (estimates 2 and 3). There is a clear trade off between both coefficients, which probably ensues from a structural shift in the demand for the Fl. 1,000 banknote (see Chapter 3). The rate of inflation has a fairly weak and statistically insignificant negative influence on the currency holdings.

The fairly robust coefficient of the number of debitable accounts suggests that without the large scale introduction of salary accounts since 1965 the currency circulation in 1990 would have been about Fl. 20 billion higher. As a percentage of national product this would correspond to the level of 1965. The measured effect of the value of check transactions is considerably less robust. The coefficient value of about 1 implies a circulation velocity of about 9 per year, which corresponds with the actual transactions velocity of active cash balances 13). Both payments alternatives have reduced the demand for banknotes of Fl. 100 and Fl. 25 in particular (Boeschoten, 1991). Apart from the consumption elasticity, the price elasticity is also not significantly different from unity, which means that the assumption of price homogeneity is not rejected. Consequently, the results for the real specification are similar to those for the nominal specification.

Although quite appealing from the economic point of view, the estimation results are affected with rather low values of the Durbin-Watson test statistic. As is well known, the presence of serially correlated error terms is likely to inflict a serious downward bias on the ordinary least squares estimates of the standard errors. Moreover, although the OLS coefficient estimates are unbiased, their sampling variances may be high compared to those obtainable from more efficient estimation methods. As argued by Klovland (1983), long-run demand-for-money equations are very

13) At a coefficient α_4 of 1, a Fl. 10 billion increase in the check transactions (Fl. 30 billion in 1990) reduces the circulation (Fl. 35 billion in 1990) by 3.3% or Fl. 1.16 billion. This comes to an velocity of about 9 times a year, compared to a velocity of 10.5 that follows from the total currency payments of about Fl. 170 billion in 1990 and the circulation, excluding hoarding of Fl. 16 billion (see Chapter 3).

likely to be plagued by autocorrelated residuals, because of the difficulties inherent in modelling the changes in payment patterns and financial structure over time. Although we explicitly took them into account, we still may have failed to capture all their effects on currency demand. The conventional method of correcting for serial autocorrelation may then be illegitimate, as the effects of omitted factors of the economic model, operating through the disturbance terms, are all supposed to decay exponentially with time and at the same rate. This implicit assumption does not seem to hold for such omitted factors as changed institutional features of financial markets. More probably the possible effects of these factors will persist into the future without decay. Therefore, we did not apply any correction for autocorrelation.

In all cases the exogenous variables as well as the endogenous variable are first order non-stationary, *i.e.* integrated of the order 1. Thus as far as their Durbin and Watson statistic is not less than about 0.8, the estimated relationships may still be considered a valid representation of the long-term demand for currency 14). We investigated some of the short-term characteristics by means of the error correction methodology (Davidson *et al.*, 1978). After rewriting specification (1.7) the long-run specification into first differences and including the one period lagged residual of the long-run relationship as exogenous variables, we have estimated the short-run elasticities given the long equilibrium path 15). The, apart from the low DW-statistic, fairly acceptable results under (estimation 3b) suggest slightly smaller effects of the transactions and the interest rate on the short run as compared to the long-run. The effect of the more structural changes in the payment pattern is, insofar as the number of salary accounts is concerned, in the short term considerably smaller than in the long-run.

---

14) The critical values of 0.78 and 0.69 at a significance level of 5% and 10%, respectively, apply to a sample size of 50 (Engle and Yoo, 1987; and Engle and Granger, 1987) and are therefore lower in the underlying case of 35 observations. On the other hand, these critical values concern the situation of one exogenous variable, while the cointegration theory is based on asymptotic theory. Thus the DW-statistic may not have much power in the underlying case of 35 observations.

15) The alternative method of estimating the long-term and short-term relationship simultaneously by means of non-linear least squares did not provide any useful results, probably due to the low number of degrees of freedom which are left.

1.5.2 Empirical evidence from turnover figures

As the elaborations of the inventory approach show, apart from the interest rate and the brokerage fee, the demand for currency depends on the ratio between currency payments and payments from debitable accounts. Therefore, in this section we will more closely deal with this ratio by estimating the relevant turnover figures for the Netherlands.

Payments from demand deposits are either officially published, as in the United States and the United Kingdom, or can - with some efforts - be derived from banking statistics, as in the Netherlands. They are, however, mostly distorted by financial transactions with tremendously high velocity figures. The elimination of these financial transactions, which is not free from a certain degree of subjectivity, may strongly influence the ultimate turnover and velocity figures. As it is, the estimates of the check and transfer payments for current transactions vary over countries and over time between 25 and 60 times a year (Table 1.4). As far as the Netherlands is concerned, the estimates of Boeschoten and Fase (1984) suggest an upward trend from 40.2 in 1965 to 43.3 in 1982, the last available annual period (Annex II). The slight increase between 1965-1982 conceals a considerable drop in the years 1965-1975, probably due to a shift of part of the household cash balances from currency into demand deposits (Boeschoten, 1984). This confirms Keynes' (1930) observation that the velocity of individual balances is essential rather than the form in which they are held.

The currency payments, as a matter of fact, leave no paper trail and have to be estimated indirectly. Fisher (1909) suggests that the value of currency payments can be roughly approximated by the total deposits by deposit holders plus the wages paid to non deposit-holders (at that time in the US nearly all wage earners). He argues that most of the deposits and wages received are used for one net payment before they are returned to the banking system 16). Thus he comes for the United States

16) The net payments concern the sums of money expended for goods and services, and not individual notes and coins, which may remain in circulation for a long time without returning to a bank, because used in change.

Table 1.4 Estimates of velocity of circulation

Country	Year	Velocity of circulation			Source
		currency	demand deposits	total	
Netherlands	1977	15.7	25.5	22.7	Cramer (1981)
	1980	15.2	46.6	36.7	Boeschoten and Fase (1984)
	1984	25	-	-	Feige (1987)
	1982	5.3	43.3 a)	31.5	this study
United Kingdom	1927	12.5 b)	60	51.5	Keynes (1930)
United States	1896	18.4	36.2	31.8	Fisher (1909, 1911))
	1909	21.5	47.6	47.6	Fisher (1911)
	1923	15 c)	25.8	-	Keynes (1930)
	1967	36	-	-	Laurent (1970)

a) on the basis of Boeschoten and Fase (1984), exluding central government transfers and payments to foreign countries; b) currency holdings of wage earners, including 17% hoarding; c) active currency holdings of wage earners, excluding hoarding.

in 1896 at a velocity of 18.4 times a year and an average cash loop, *i.e.* number of transactions resulting from a deposit, of 1.6.

More recently Cramer (1979) has re-used the method to estimate the currency turnover in the Netherlands. By assuming a cash loop of 2 he arrives at a velocity of 15.7. Under the same assumption Boeschoten and Fase (1984) find a slightly lower but surely comparable estimate of 15.2. However, if we take into account Cramer's (1988) later finding that a cash loop may be as low as 1.05, and a downward adjustment of the cash withdrawals by over 35%, we arrive for 1982 at a velocity of 5.3 (Table 1.4) and for 1990 at a velocity of even 4.5. This velocity is considerably lower than is often assumed. The low figure is due to the presence of inactive balances, such as the rarely used notes of Fl. 1,000 which account for more than half the circulation. Velocities of 25 as applied by Feige (1987) only hold for the active currency balances, particularly of households 17).

17) Our velocity estimate of about 5 is supported by the observation that banknotes, which account for about 95% of the currency circulation, return in terms of number and of value, on average, about two times per year to the Nederlandsche Bank. At a velocity of circulation of 5, the banking system must redistribute at least 60% of the currency deposited, which seems to correspond to the actual situation. A velocity of 25 would, however, imply an implausibly high redistribution percentage of over 90%.

The development of the currency payments over time was estimated from an index series constructed on the basis of banknote figures by weighting the denominations by their intensity of use. The intensity of use of the various denominations was derived from their life, *i.e.* the average time between their issue and destruction. The estimation on the basis of note life figures was applied originally by Laurent (1970) for the US, be it in a slightly different way. Uyttewaal (1981), Boeschoten and Fase (1984) and Feige (1987) have applied the method to the Netherlands. The methodology of the variant applied here is basically the same as that applied in Chapter 3 and provides for estimating the hoarded, or non-active part of the currency circulation, which is, as a matter of fact, not used for payments. Besides, we also derived an index series from the amount of banknotes, which are returned yearly to the central bank. Both series were transformed to a series of cash payments by putting the value in 1987 equal to the cash payments which follow from the cash withdrawal figure, obtined from the banking sector, assuming a cash loop of 1.05 which is the minimum value mentioned by Cramer (1988).

The resulting series for the Netherlands for 1955-1990 are given in Annex II. Both estimates show an obvious decline in the importance of currency payments between 1965 and 1975, due to the large-scale introduction of debitable accounts (Figure 1.3). The size of the decline between 1960 and 1975 is, however, considerably larger in the case of the estimation on the basis of the life of notes. After 1975 their pattern is rather similar and in line with the pattern of the cash withdrawals, presented in Annex II. The discrepancy between the development of the two series before 1972 may be explained from a fall in the length in the cash loop, which is implicitly included in the note life method but not in the note return method. The discrepancy suggests a fall in the cash loop length of 0.2 in the years 1960-1975, which is rather plausible in view of, among other things, the shift in salary payments from cash to transfers. Therefore, we prefer the estimations with the note life method, which include the effect of the decreasing cash loop on the volume of payments. The development of the transactions velocity of currency resulting from the two estimation methods is shown

Figure 1.3 Cash payments in relation to gross national product

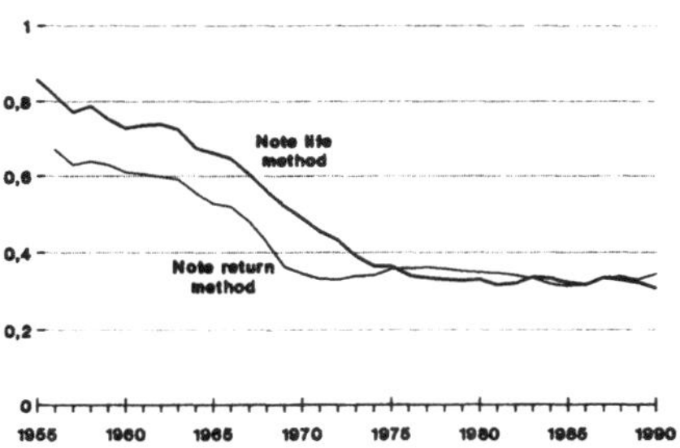

Figure 1.4 Transactions velocity of currency

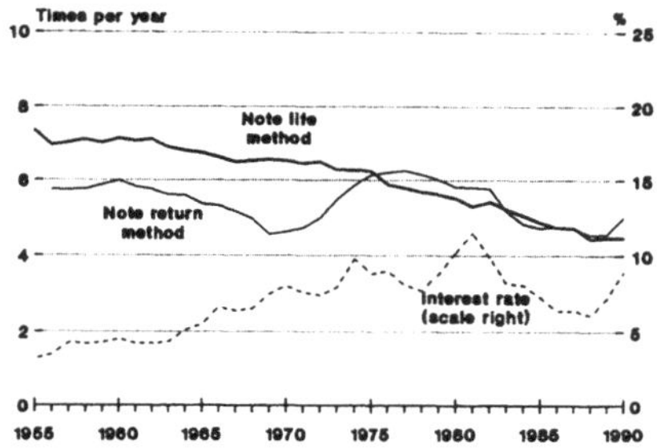

in Figure 1.4. The decline of the velocity in the 1960s and the subsequent rise, according to the note-return method, could indicate a shift of the more active transactions balances into demand deposits, and a subsequent economizing on the cash balances due to the increasing interest rate.

Whatever may be the truth, both estimates show a clear decline of the share of currency payments in total payments, *i.e.* currency payments plus debits, in the period 1965-1980 (Figure 1.5). According to the use the note-life estimation the importance of currency payments in relation to total payments dropped by 50%. The share of currency in M1 decreased in the same time by about 30%. This suggests that part of the relative smaller need for currency for payments has been compensated by an increasing use of currency as a store of value, despite the rising interest rates (see Chapter 3). This conclusion also holds when we approximate the total payments from the transactions side, thus trying to avoid possible distortion of the debit figures by financial transactions 18). In the case of the note-life estimation the share of currency

18) See Annex II for the computed figures and a short evaluation of their approximation and their usefulness.

Figure 1.5 Cash payments as percentage of total payments and transactions

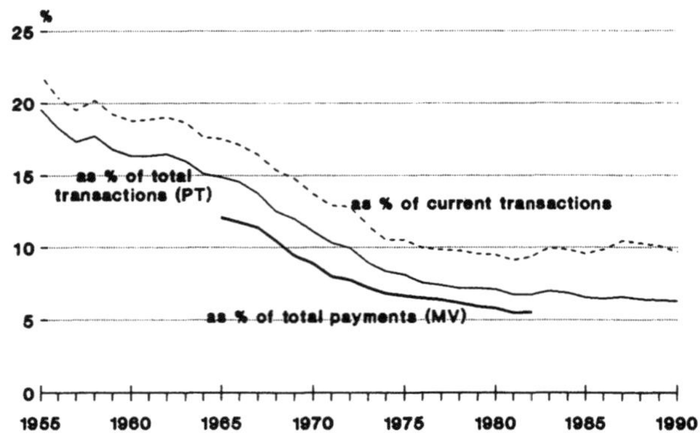

payments falls in 1965-1982 by 45% up to 50%, dependent on wether we consider current transactions only or include also income transfers and capital transactions.

1.6 Conclusions

The theories for the aggregate demand for money provide a number of explanations and corresponding variables for the demand for money. The broader the concept of money, the more fundamental the differences between the theories. Thus the discussion regarding the stability of the money demand, the choice between income, permanent income and wealth as the appropriate scale variable, and the simultaneity and aggregation problem mainly ensue from the presence of various motives for holding money. These motives deviate more from the transactions motive, as the money concept is broader. The explanation of the demand for currency, the most narrow money concept, primarily boils down to its use as a medium of exchange, *i.e.* the transactions demand, though other motives should not be neglected. Unfortunately, the elegant solution provided by Baumol in 1952 with his inventory-model, turned out to be too restrictive, inducing a great number of amendments and refinements in the following thirty years. The result is that the original point elasticities of the transactions demand with respect to income and the interest rate of 0.5 and -0.5, respectively, are replaced by wide ranges of possible values. Thus the income elasticity may range from 1/3 up to over 1 and more. Likewise the value of the interest elasticity may range between -0.5 and zero.

The empirical results for currency demand correspond more or less to the findings for the broader money aggregates, especially M1. The economies of scale in the money holdings, predicted by the original transactions and precautionary models, receive some empirical support, be it more than in the case of M1. These economies of scale may, however, equally well ensue from financial innovations and the use of alternative payments media. The degree to which the currency demand is influenced by other economic variables, like the interest rate and inflation varies by country. Our findings for the Netherlands do not suggest any economies of scale, and rather small effects for the interest rate and inflation, but a substantial reduction of the currency demand by financial innovation.

The framework for the analysis of the work money really does, *i.e.* effecting payments, is basically still the equation of exchange. The theoretical and empirical elaboration of this framework has been very meager. Nevertheless the relevant theories clearly formalise that the demand for currency as opposed to demand deposits, is mainly dependent on the relative share of money components in the total payments. The results of our analysis of the payments and transactions figures show indeed, that the fall of the relative importance of currency as compared to demand deposits in the Netherlands since 1965 ensues from the changes in the payment pattern. The decline of the importance of currency payments does, however, not fully show up in the demand for currency due to an increasing demand for currency as a store of value.

2 THE USE OF MONEY IN A MICRO-ECONOMIC PERSPECTIVE

2.1 Introduction

Although ample empirical evidence is available on the demand for money at the macro-economic level, major gaps exist in the knowledge of how money is acquired and used in the economy. The paucity of information on these issues is possibly due to difficulties of measurement. The national statistics on the turnover figures and debits are, insofar as published, distorted by financial transactions, with tremendously high transactions velocities (Garvey and Blyn, 1969). Thus, according to estimates for a number of countries, total payments per year vary from 10 to more than 200 times GNP, mainly depending on the relative importance of the country's financial sector (Annex I). Cash payments are, as a matter of fact, not registered. For these payments only rough indirect estimates are available, either on the basis of cash withdrawals, on the assumption of a certain cash loop (Fisher, 1909; Cramer, 1986), or on the basis of figures on the circulation of banknotes and their life length, as used in Chapter 1. The information at the level of financial institutions, as published in the Netherlands by the Bankgiro Centrale and a number of large banks, is not representative for the overall development, insofar as their shares in financial intermediation are shifting. On an individual basis too, this information is biased, insofar as individuals use financial services of more than one institution with changing intensity.

Surveys, containing questions on cash management, purchases and the way they are paid for can provide part of the missing knowledge on the use of means of payment. This is illustrated by the underlying chapter which deals with the micro-economic analysis of the use of money by households in the Netherlands on the basis of three surveys held for the Nederlandsche Bank in 1983, 1984-1986 and 1990. Comparison of the results of these surveys, which have different lines of approach, provides information about the development of the use of cash, albeit that prudence is required because of differences in the design of the surveys. We describe the general methodology as well as the results and their implications for the Netherlands. The methodology applied deals not only with the state at present and in the recent past, but also provides an insight into expectations on the future development. We start with the analysis of cash management, *i.e.* the acquisition of cash and the holding of cash balances. Subsequently, section 3 deals with the payment pattern in general, considering also the use of payments media other than cash. Section 4 gives some general conclusions.

2.2 The cash management of households

2.2.1 *General framework of analysis*

The methodology used for the survey-based analysis of the cash management of households for 1983 and 1990 relies heavily on the inventory-theoretic transactions approach to the demand for money 1). To use cash for transactions, individuals maintain an inventory of cash which they deplete by making payments and replenish periodically by acquiring more cash. In time the individual's cash inventory follows the well-known sawtoothed pattern, with each tooth representing one cash acquisition occasion (Figure 2.1). The distance between teeth, t, follows from the frequency of cash acquisitions, f, and the size of each tooth is determined by the amount, C, obtained on a representative occasion. On average, individuals will replenish their cash inventory before running completely out of money. Thus, we assume a bottom inventory, B. The

Figure 2.1 Cash inventory of individuals over time

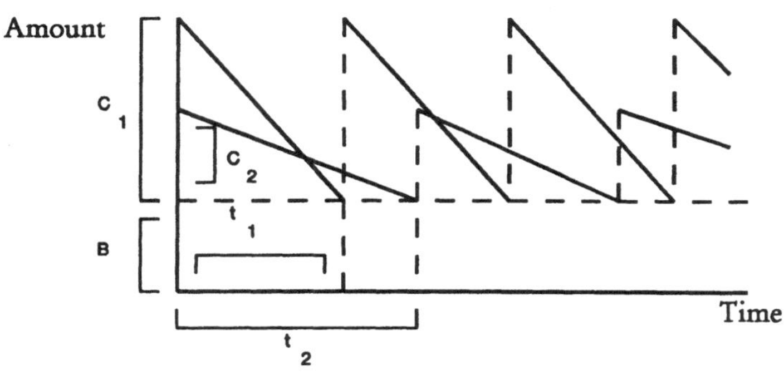

1) Avery *et al.* (1986, 1987) have applied an analogous framework of analysis for measuring the cash management behaviour of households in the United States.

total inflow of cash per month is acquired either by means of withdrawal with a frequency of f_1 per month and an average amount of C_1 per disbursement or is acquired otherwise, for instance from employers, with a frequency of f_2 per month and an average amount C_2. If we ignore the growth of the circulation, and depositing of cash at banks or saving banks, the individual's total cash turnover or transactions value per month, T, is

$$T = f_1 . C_1 + f_2 . C_2 \qquad (2.1)$$

If we assume, for the sake of simplicity, a uniform distribution of the payments between the cash acquisitions, the individual's average cash holding is

$$\overline{C} = C/2 = (C_1 + C_2)/2 + B \qquad (2.2)$$

and the turnover rate or transactions velocity per month is

$$V = T/\overline{C} \qquad (2.3)$$

The methodology enables us to measure the average transactions cash holdings of households without directly asking for their size. This line of approach is especially valuable insofar as respondents do not give correct answers to direct questions on the size of their cash holdings. The cash management variables, mentioned above, were quantified by incorporating a number of questions for the Nederlandsche Bank in two surveys among households, which are described in more detail later on. In both surveys the questions were specially designed by the author. The questions asked in the first survey, an omnibus survey held in 1983, focused solely on cash management. The questions included in the second survey, a script-panel survey held in 1990, had a comparable line of approach, but with a much more comprehensive design. Apart from questions on the cash management this survey also contained direct questions on the cash holdings, on the payment pattern and on expectations with respect to future developments.

The respondents were asked about their typical behaviour, thus avoiding distortion by isolated factors which may arise when questions concern the most recent behaviour. Basically the estimates following from these approaches represent different statistical concepts (Avery *et al.*, 1987). The previous-time behaviour represents a random selection from the behaviour possible for that person. If respondents are randomly selected, the estimates based on most-recent behaviour are proper estimates of population statistics, at least in large samples. The 1983 sample may, however, be too small to give a proper presentation of the distribution of the rare behaviour in the population and thus may be unduly sensitive to outliers. The reported typical behaviour is likely to represent most common, rather than average, behaviour. Although typical behaviour should be more resistant to distortion by outliers, it may not adequately reflect rare, or even less-common, behaviour. Because estimates based on both types of responses could be flawed, it is not clear which is to be preferred. The results of Avery *et al.* (1986, 1987), who asked for the typical behaviour as well as for the behaviour on the most recent occasion of obtaining cash, indicate, however, that in general the estimates following from the two measures are rather similar.

In the next sections we will present the main results of the surveys of 1983 and 1990, compare these results and deal with the findings on the future development of the cash management.

2.2.2 Results of the survey in 1983

In 1983, we included nine questions on cash management in surveys, held in the period late January-early March as part of the NIPO (Netherlands Institute of Public Opinion) weekly public opinion poll. The other thirteen questions included for the Nederlandsche Bank regarded the appraisal of the new banknote series (*cf.* Den Butter, 1985). To mitigate possible distortions by external factors, the surveys were spread over four successive Mondays and Tuesdays, except the carnival week. The NIPO survey comprises weekly about 2,000 interviews among persons of eighteen years and older, who are randomly selected after stratification on the basis of the relative number of dwellings per municipality or district. As the number of dwellings is only 0.6% less than the number of households, this means basically that the reference population from which the sample was drawn is the total of Dutch households. Per stratum the addresses are randomly selected from a complete set of 4,850 addresses. In case of non-response, the neighbour next door is interviewed. At an average recall rate of three times, the non-response is about 35%. The non-response with respect to the questions on the cash management behaviour varied from 1% to 6%. The weekly survey is made up of 20, likewise random representative samples of 100 interviews each, which can be cumulated. The underlying survey covered in total 1,999 respondents, compared to an average population of eighteen years and older in 1983 of 10,455 thousand. The sample was not reweighted 2). In 1983, the use of cash dispensers and automated teller machines was quantitatively negligible and therefore not considered in the survey.

Nearly 85% of the respondents regularly obtained cash by means of withdrawal. According to Figure 2.2, withdrawing cash each week, or 4.3 times per month, is by far the most popular frequency. The average frequency is 2.96 per month, which comes to 10.3 days between two withdrawals and agrees rather well with the average of 12 and 16 days (median 8 days), which Avery *et al.* (1987) report for cash acquisitions in the US in 1984 and 1986 respectively. The most popular amount per withdrawal is Fl. 200, followed by Fl. 500 and Fl. 300 (Figure 2.3). Apart from their computational ease the high frequency of these amounts may have to do with the maximum amounts to which checks are guaranteed. Especially Giro-checks and the Giro cashing checks (at that time the main means of withdrawing cash from Postgiro checking accounts) were guaranteed up to an amount of Fl. 200 and Fl. 500 respectively. The bank-check and the Eurocheck were guaranteed up to an amount of Fl. 100 and Fl. 300, respectively, but these checks are seldom used for cash withdrawals. Nearly 80% of the total amount of cash was acquired by

2) The composition of the underlying survey was 979 masters and 887 mistresses of the house, 91 sons, 23 daughters and 10 male and 9 female 'other members' of the household. The average population of 18 years and older in 1983 amounted to 10,455 thousand.

Figure 2.2 Distribution of frequency of cash withdrawals in 1983

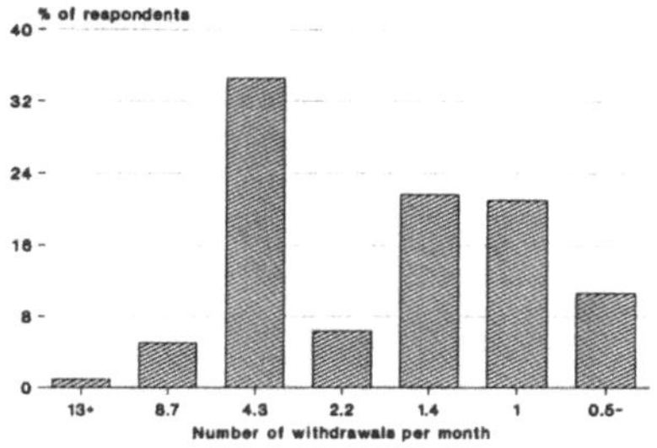

Figure 2.3 Distribution of amount per cash withdrawal in 1983

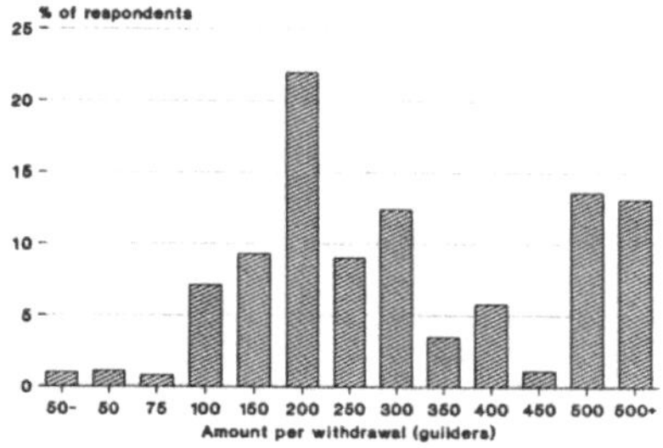

means of withdrawing from checking or savings accounts (Table 2.1). For the total population of adults of eighteen years and older this comes to an amount of Fl. 90 billion, which is Fl. 5 billion more than the estimate of the total cash withdrawals by households in 1983 of Fl. 85 billion on the basis of the withdrawal figures of a number of large banks 3).

The average amount withdrawn by the respondents amounts to Fl. 375. The over-all average is Fl. 290. The difference between the two averages stems from the weighting factors. The former is the weighted average of the average amount withdrawn per respondent. In the latter 'over-all' average, the average amounts withdrawn are weighted by their over-all frequency. Macro-economic estimates of the average amount withdrawn run to an average of Fl. 537 in 1983 (Annex II). However, this amount includes the withdrawals by stores and business enterprises, which involve considerably larger amounts than withdrawals by households. According to the survey 20% of the cash is acquired in ways other than withdrawals, that is from employers, business enterprises, stores etc. Avery *et al.* (1987) reported 14% for the US in 1986, excluding cash obtained from family or friends. About 25% of the respondents are involved. On average they acquire an amount of Fl. 406 at a frequency of

3) According to figures provided by the banking system for 1982 about 75% of the total cash withdrawals are accounted for by households, which, at a total amount in 1983 of Fl. 114 billion (see Annex II), comes to Fl. 85 billion.

Table 2.1 Acquisition of cash in 1983

Frequency	Cash withdrawals			Other cash acquisitions		
	percentage of respondents	amount per withdrawal	amount per month	percentage of respondents	amount per acquisition	amount per month
(nearly) daily	0.4	213	4,667	0.8	47	933
3x per week	0.6	163	2,113	0.5	250	3,250
2x per week	5.0	235	2,115	2.6	227	1,967
1x per week	34.5	237	1,027	28.1	289	1,251
3x per month	6.3	281	839	3.1	192	575
2x per month	21.6	384	768	11.9	462	924
1x per month	21.0	606	606	26.5	603	603
less often	10.6	515	258	26.5	365	183
Average		375	866		406	756

Explanatory note: Results for withdrawals on the basis of 1,448 respondents; for 336 (17%) not applicable; the remaining 175 respondents did not mention an amount (153), frequency (16) or either of the two (6). Results for other cash acquisitions on the basis of 388 respondents; for 1,499 (75%) not applicable; the remaining 118 did not mention an amount (97), frequency (9) or either of the two (6).

2.3 times per month. This comes to an over-all average amount per acquisition of Fl. 316. On a yearly basis, the total amount of cash acquired in 1983 (withdrawals and otherwise) comes to over Fl. 110 billion.

The estimated average amount of cash individuals had in hand before they obtained more was about Fl. 75. If we add this bottom inventory to the average transactions balances which follow from the cash withdrawals and other cash acquisitions, a sample average of cash balances of Fl. 269 results. For the total Dutch population this comes to Fl. 2.8 billion, being 12% of the amount of currency held by the public at that time. Apparently only a small part of the currency circulation can be explained from the transactions balances of households. We will deal more extensively with this result in section 2.2.4 of this chapter. According to relationship (2.3) the results imply a turnover rate of cash balances of 3.4 times per month or about 40 times per year.

An interesting question is whether the data fit the inventory approach to the transactions demand for money. According to its original form, at

Table 2.2 Optimal cash disbursements in 1983
In guilders

Interest rate (%)	Cost of withdrawal (guilders)					
	0.25	0.5	1	2	5	10
1	721	1,019	1,442	2,039	3,224	4,559
2	510	721	1,019	1,442	2,279	3,224
3	416	589	832	1,177	1,861	2,632
4	360	510	721	1,019	1,612	2,279
5	322	456	645	912	1,442	2,039
10	228	322	456	645	1,019	1,442
15	186	263	372	526	832	1,177
20	161	228	322	456	721	1,019

Explanatory note: On the basis of average monthly cash turnover of Fl. 866. Interest rate on yearly basis.

transactions T, an interest rate of r per period, and a fixed brokerage fee of b, being the overall costs of withdrawing cash, the most economical amount per withdrawal, C^*, follows from the square root formula $C^* = \sqrt{2bT/r}$. The model assumes that the process governing net disbursements is deterministic, which may be not too far from reality as far as households are concerned and the questions are related to typical behaviour. According to the computations in Table 2.2 on the basis of the average amount of cash withdrawals of Fl. 866 per month, the average disbursement of Fl. 375 can only be explained by the square-root formula at rather low costs per withdrawal or very high interest rates. At the actual interest rate of 5% per year, the average disbursement of Fl. 375 implies costs per withdrawal of less than Fl. 0.50. In fact, as Baumol (1952) already argued, the meaning of the interest rate must be extended to include the costs of possible loss or the value of protection against loss, fire or theft. Apparently this motive plays a dominant role. According to the survey reported on by Avery *et al.* (1986), 87% of the public in the United States agreed that they carry only small amounts of currency for this reason. Likewise, Mot and Cramer (1990) identify the risk of loss or theft as the major cost of using currency. Besides, from the inventory theory's point of view, uneconomically low cash balances - and thus unduly high deposits - are not necessarily suboptimal, if households pay for bank services by leaving deposits rather than paying fees 4).

As was shown in Chapter 1, according to the original square root law, in the case of deterministic net disbursements, the optimal average cash holdings increase with the square root of the transactions value, implying a transaction elasticity of 0.5. In the case of uncertainty this elasticity can be as low as 0.3. Regression analysis on the basis of data of the 1983 survey on cash acquisitions and the bottom inventory shows an elasticity of nearly 0.4 (equation 2.4), which suggests economies of scale in the transactions demand for money of households and some element of uncertainty. If we focus solely on the cash disbursements (as we will also do with respect to the results for 1990, ignoring the cash acquisitions from other sources and the bottom inventory), then the elasticity amounts to 0.42 with a t-value of 25.

$$\ln(\bar{C}) = \underset{(21.9)}{2.93} + \underset{(18.9)}{0.38} \ln T \qquad \bar{R}^2 = 0.22; \quad SE = 0.61$$

Number of observations: 1,278 (2.4)

Stated differently, the regression results confirm the consequence of the square root law that the velocity of circulation increases with the cash holdings or the transaction volume ($V = T/(C/2) = r\,C/b = \sqrt{2rT/b}$). The velocity of circulation increases with the turnover rate with an elasticity of about 0.6, thus supporting Fisher's (1922) proposition that the rich have a higher rate of turnover than the poor.

2.2.3 Design and results of the survey in 1990

Design of the survey

The survey performed in 1990 has a much broader design than the 1983 survey, paying special attention to the effects of new payments media on the demand for and use of cash. The specially designed questions, totalling eleven, were included by the author for the Nederlandsche Bank in a much broader script-panel survey of AGB-Attwood, which is described in

4) Sprenkle (1969) uses this argument to explain the unduly high demand deposit holdings of large firms in the United States (see section 2.4.1).

more detail below. The survey contains three strongly interrelated parts. In the first part the respondents were asked about their cash management behaviour. The second part regards the money kept in purses and at home for transactions purposes, as well as balances held for purposes other than every-day expenses. The third part, to be analysed in section 2.3.2, concerns the payment pattern at twelve quantitatively important or representative places of spending. The respondents were asked not only about their present-day typical behaviour, but also about their expected behaviour in a hypothetical situation where plastic money, *i.e.* credit cards, point of sale terminals and access to cash dispensers and automated teller machines (ATMs), are widely available. The questionnaire defined this future situation as follows: 'In all shops and business enterprises payment is possible by means of so-termed POS-terminals, also called electronic payment. Each consumer with a checking account has a debit card with a PIN-code. By means of this card and by inputing the PIN-code, all expenses can be paid for, without mediation of cash. Moreover, at most bank and post offices cash dispensers have been placed. Withdrawing of cash is possible at many places 24 hours a day'. Comparison of the results of the three parts of the survey enabled us to check consistency. The knowledge of the personal characteristics of all respondents such as age, sex, social status, level of education *etc*; as well as a number of typical features regarding their access to and use of various media of the payment system, provides the possibility for further analysis.

The AGB Script-panel survey "Payment behaviour and plastic money in the Netherlands", in which the questions were included, was held first in 1989. Apart from a number of questions on the possession and use of payments media, the basic questionnaire, which is accessible to all participants, contains a number of qualitative questions about the opinion of the respondents on the future of plastic money. The questions additionally included for the Bank by AGB-Attwood in consultation with the author aimed to acquire more quantitative information on the withdrawal and the payments behaviour of the respondents now and in the future. The survey is conducted in writing. The original survey comprised 9,808 persons of 18 years and older, being representative for

Table 2.3 Composition of 1990 survey with respect to use of media

User category	Total per category		Number of respondents (also) using			
	number	percentage of respondents	ATMs	checks	credit cards	point of sale
ATMs	2,344	20.2	1,544	424	83	469
Checks	1,853	20.0		1,280	65	245
Credit cards	237	2.6			110	38
Point of sale	746	8.0				161

Explanatory note: On the basis of a frequency of use of at least once a week (checks, credit cards, POS) or 'most often used means of acquiring cash' (ATMs). The numbers on the diagonal regard respondents who use solely one medium.

the relevant population in the Netherlands. The 578 cases of non-response were replaced by fresh participants. Deviations of the final sample population from the population relevant for the analysis were corrected by using sampling weights. 534 cases could not be used because of insufficient response, which brings the total non-response to about 10%. Thus, finally, 9,274 respondents remained. For these remaining cases, the data were edited and all missing values were imputed for individual or family questions by taking the most relevant average of the other respondents 5). The results were weighed by means of the AGB MiniCensus 1988. In the case of the cash holdings at home, the unit of observation is the family, the reference population being all 5.98 million Dutch families. In the part of the survey on cash acquisition and payments, the unit of observation was the individual respondent rather than the family, because respondents were expected to have more accurate knowledge of their own cash transactions and payments than of the transactions and payments of other family members. Thus the reference population for this part of the survey was made up of all Dutch residents of eighteen years and older, totalling 11.56 million. The non-response with respect to the specific questions on the cash management behaviour now and in the future varies strongly by question,

5) A more sophisticated approach is to impute the missing values by iteratively estimating the distribution of variables that are missing, conditioned on the set of variables observed for a given case (Avery *et al.*, 1985), or to use observed information in a way that respects accounting identities and preserves the randomness of the original sample data (Kalton, 1983).

Figure 2.4 Distribution of frequency of cash withdrawals in 1990

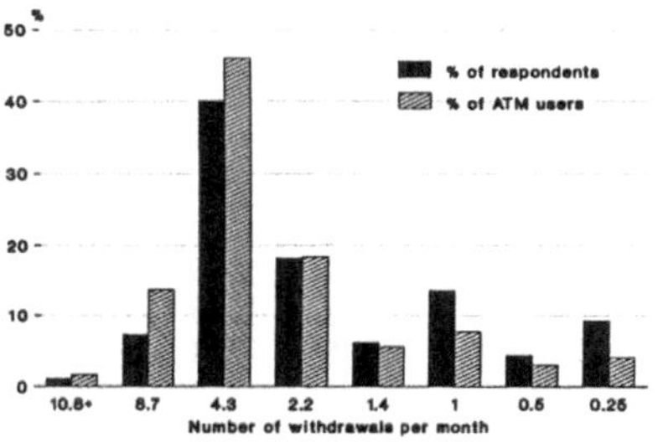

Figure 2.5 Distribution of average amount per withdrawal in 1990

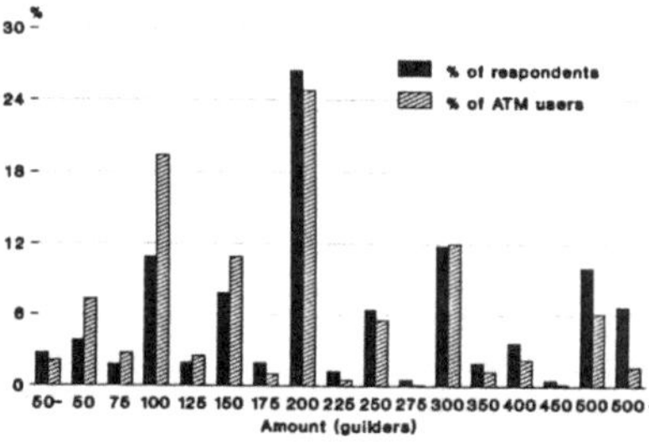

but never exceeds 10% (see Table 2.4). The percentage of respondents who did not answer all the relevant questions on payments behaviour is on average about 30%, but is on average less than 12% per separate question. Table 2.3 gives the composition of the survey with regard to the use of the most important payments media. The possession of, or access to, a medium appeared to be too weak a criterion. For instance, more than 50% of the respondents having the possibility to pay at POS-terminals with a debit card made use of that possibility less than once a month. So we consider only those respondents who use cheques, credit cards (including retailer cards) and POS at least once a week as users of these media. We consider all those respondents who said that they withdrew their cash most frequently from ATMs as users of this medium. As appears from Table 2.3, the use of the various media overlaps, especially in the case of the users of ATMs and POS-terminals; this may stem partly from respondents who mistook POS-terminals for ATMs. If we take into account the overlapping, it appears that about 45% of the respondents use at least one of these alternative payments and withdrawing facilities at least once a week.

Results on cash disbursements

On average the respondents withdraw cash 3.15 times per month (Table 2.4). This comes to 9.7 days between acquisitions and is somewhat more often than the 10.3 days following from the 1983 survey. Withdrawing

Table 2.4 Cash withdrawals and cash holdings according to 1990 survey

	All respon-dents	Use of ATMs		Users of		
		users	non-users	checks	credit cards	point of sale
Cash withdrawals						
Distribution of frequency (%)						
2x per week or more	8.3	15.4	5.9	12.8	10.9	24.4
1x per week	40.1	46.0	37.8	49.4	31.0	47.7
1x per 2 weeks	18.3	18.4	18.2	19.2	17.5	12.7
1x per 3 weeks	6.1	5.5	6.4	4.5	7.4	3.3
1x per month	13.6	7.7	15.7	7.3	10.9	6.7
less than 1x per month	4.4	3.0	4.9	2.9	5.7	2.2
less often	9.2	4.0	11.1	3.9	16.6	3.0
	100	100	100	100	100	100
Average frequency per month	3.15	3.94	2.87	3.86	3.00	4.69
Average amount per time	285	208	313	245	269	202
Average amount per month	759	739	765	861	753	837
No cash withdrawals (%)	1.9	0.0	2.5	0.5	4.1	0.5
Frequency unknown (%)	4.2	2.0	5.0	2.5	1.2	2.4
Amount unknown (%)	6.8	3.5	7.9	3.7	6.6	4.8
Cash holdings (amount)						
in purse	98	88	102	96	124	88
at home for housekeeping	189	146	203	161	184	144
as means of saving	341	316	374	325	386	327

Explanatory note: Amounts in guilders; the frequency figures include respondents who reported the frequency of withdrawals but no amount (see bottom line). Results for balances at home on the basis of heads of households. The percentage unknown for the three types of cash balances was 7, 5 and 9, respectively.

cash each week, is clearly the most popular frequency (Figure 2.4). As in the 1983 survey withdrawing cash more often than two times a week is not very common. The same holds for the option of once per three weeks (frequency 1.4 per month). On average the respondents acquire an amount of Fl. 285, the amount of Fl. 200 being the most popular. As mentioned before, the peak at Fl. 300 (Figure 2.5) may stem from the fact that checks are guaranteed up to this amount and that people minimize the efforts or costs of withdrawing money (a number of banks have limited the number of free checks to 50 or 60). The same holds for the amount of Fl. 500, which is the maximum amount of the cash-checks of the Postbank; these are used relatively often by elderly people. Apart from computational ease the peak at Fl. 200 may be the aftermath of the maximum of

Fl. 200 up to which checks were guaranteed until 1990. The average amount of Fl. 285 equals a dollar value of about $ 140, which agrees remarkably well with the average amount acquired in the US of $ 150 in 1986 (Avery, *et al.*, 1987). The average amount of cash acquired per month by means of withdrawal is Fl. 759. This figure is in line with the scarce information available from the banking system. According to the survey Dutch households acquired Fl. 101 billion of cash in this way in 1990. The average amount per withdrawal of Fl. 285 implies cash balances of the total population of Fl. 1.6 billion, which comes to 4.6% of the average currency circulation of Fl. 35.2, compared to 6.6% for the relevant cash holdings in the 1983 survey. As may be expected from the cash-inventory model, because of widely available and easier withdrawing facilities, users of ATMs obtain cash with an over 35% higher frequency and at a nearly 35% lower amount than non-users. The same holds, however, to a certain extent for the users of checks. A proper assessment of the effects of the relevant effect requires a multivariate analysis.

To model the influence of the ATMs on cash management behaviour we take the amount of cash withdrawn per month T_1 as given. Basically this amount is equal to the total amount paid in cash, T, minus the amount of cash acquired by means other than withdrawing, T_2, not considered here. In this view the amount paid in cash is the resultant of the payment pattern (which of course itself may depend on the use of ATMs) and not of the cash management. Given the amount withdrawn (per month) either the average amount per withdrawal or the frequency has to be explained.

Most of the variables representing the personal characteristics in the regression analysis have already been described or speak for themselves (see Table 2.5). The content of the remaining variables is as follows:

Sex	dummy variable (female = 1; male = 2)
Income	classes ranging from 1 up to 5
Education	classes ranging from 1 (special school) up to 7 (university)
Occupational status	dummy (= 1 if working; = 0 otherwise)
Urbanization	ranging from 1 (less than 5,000 inhabitants) up to 8 (850,000 inhabitants)
Type of employer	dummy (= 1 if self-employed; = 0 otherwise)
Number of accounts	number of salary accounts

Table 2.5 Regression results for individuals' cash withdrawals in 1990

Explanatory variable	Amount per withdrawal			Frequency	
	linear	loglinear		linear	loglinear
Amount withdrawn per month	0.16 (40.3)	0.375 (66.0)	0.387 (65.0)	0.002 (61.9)	0.625 (110.0)
Age	3.92 (19.7)	0.015 (31.2)		-0.036 (22.7)	-0.015 (31.2)
Sex	8.86 (1.6)	0.005 (0.4)		-0.274 (6.2)	-0.005 (0.4)
Income	9.27 (3.2)	0.025 (3.4)		-0.080 (3.4)	-0.025 (3.4)
Education	-1.48 (0.7)	-0.003 (0.5)		-0.007 (0.5)	0.003 (0.5)
Occupational status	11.58 (2.0)	0.150 (10.6)		-0.248 (5.5)	-0.150 (10.6)
Size of family	-1.44 (0.7)	0.025 (4.8)		-0.104 (6.3)	-0.025 (4.8)
Urbanization	1.45 (1.1)	-0.007 (2.2)		0.032 (2.9)	0.007 (2.2)
Type of employer	28.25 (2.5)	0.110 (4.0)		-0.387 (4.4)	-0.110 (4.0)
Number of accounts	9.68 (2.3)	0.027 (2.7)		-0.021 (0.6)	-0.027 (2.7)
Use of ATMs	-60.20 (9.8)	-0.196 (12.9)		0.597 (12.2)	0.196 (12.9)
Use of checks	-69.38 (11.2)	-0.183 (12.0)		0.587 (12.0)	0.183 (12.0)
Use of credit cards	-6.94 (0.4)	-0.006 (0.2)		0.096 (0.8)	0.006 (0.2)
Use of POS	-45.00 (4.6)	-0.165 (6.8)		0.799 (10.3)	0.165 (6.8)
Constant	30.13 (1.3)	2.42 (36.2)	2.97 (79.0)	3.41 (18.9)	-2.42 (36.2)
Mean dependent variable	289	5.39	5.38	3.21	0.832
SE	223	0.55	0.62	1.76	0.549
$\bar{R}^2$	0.275	0.477	0.337	0.407	0.656
Number of observations	7,991	7,991	8,329	7,991	7,991

Explanatory notes: In the loglinear specification the amount per withdrawal and the amount withdrawn per month read in logarithms; t-values within parentheses.

As in the case of the 1983 survey, the estimation results largely support the cash-inventory model. The implied transactions elasticity for cash holdings of 0.38 is lower than Baumol's value of 0.5, but agrees to some extent with the findings of Miller and Orr (1969) that the elasticity may be as low as 0.33 in the case of uncertainty. The elasticity of about 0.4 also results when we run the regression - as in the case of the 1983 survey - solely with the transactions variable T.

Generally speaking, the coefficients of the other explanatory variables following from the regression analysis are also plausible from an economic-theoretical point of view 6). They clearly support, for instance, the hypothesis of the value of time effect. Thus people from higher income classes withdraw money in higher amounts at a lower frequency; this can be explained from the higher value of leisure time and thus higher transfer costs. The same argument holds for respondents with a job, the self-employed, higher-aged respondents and - at least to some extent - heads of larger households, who all withdraw higher amounts at a lower frequency. Likewise, the higher the degree of urbanization, the more widely available the withdrawing facilities and the lower the transfer costs, the higher the number of disbursements at a lower amount. Males appear to withdraw somewhat higher amounts than females. The use of ATMs results in significant economizing on the cash holdings, a phenomenon which is also mentioned, though not quantified, by De Leeuw (1989). According to the linear equation it diminishes the average amount withdrawn by Fl. 60, meanwhile increasing the frequency by 0.60. The loglinear specification gives comparable effects for the average point (Fl. 57 and 0.63, respectively). The use of checks and POS-terminals lowers the average cash holdings by somewhat less than 20% at the same transactions value. The result for the checks is an overestimate as far as the cashing of checks is involved, while the relatively strong effect of the use of POS-terminals may to some extent stem from respondents mistaking ATMs for POS-terminals. On the whole these findings indicate that users of alternative payments media pay the same amount of cash with 20% lower cash balances, probably mainly due to the

---

6) For the sake of convenience, we present the loglinear specification for both the amount withdrawn and the frequency, although they are basically their own reflection.

lower need for precautionary balances. The linear and the loglinear specifications give comparable results. The only exceptions are the coefficients of the family size and urbanization, which are statistically significant with the correct sign only in the case of the loglinear specification. Moreover, also from a statistical point of view the loglineair specification, taking the log of the amount per withdrawal and the amount withdrawn per month, is to be preferred. Taking logs of the other explanatory variables, insofar as relevant, gives no further statistically significant improvements. The rather low values of coefficient of determination $\overline{R}^2$ could probably be increased by explicitly modelling the preference of individuals for amounts equalling a multiple of Fl. 100 and for a weekly or two-weekly frequency. As they are the values of $\overline{R}^2$ are, however, by no means exceptional for this kind of cross-section approach (*cf.* Cramer, 1964).

The application of the regression model seems adequate for the analysis of the amounts. The number of classes is relatively high, while they generally correspond with the possible alternatives. Moreover, the amounts above the highest class are explicitly mentioned. In the case of the frequency, the number of classes is rather low, but this probably also holds for the possible answers, the frequency of withdrawal clearly not being a continuous variable. Therefore, application of the *count data model* (*cf.* Cameron and Trivedi, 1986), developed for comparable, but continuous data, does not seem a sensible alternative. A more promising approach would be the *ordered response model* for ordered categories (Madalla, 1983), which may give some further improvement in the already quite satisfactory explanation of the frequency of withdrawal.

Results on cash balances

The cash holdings of households are made up of transactions balances, *i.e.* cash kept in the purse or at home, and of balances for purposes other than transactions which we will call savings balances. The average amount people have in their purse is Fl. 98. About 85% of the respondents who report their cash holdings have Fl. 150 or less in their

Figure 2.6 Distribution of amount in purse in 1990

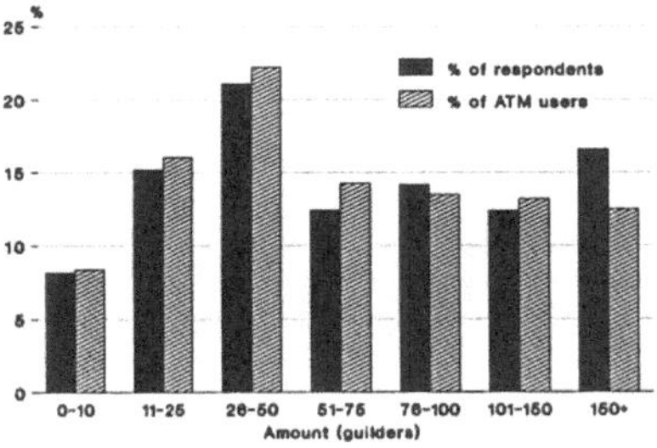

Figure 2.7 Distribution of amount kept at home for housekeeping in 1990

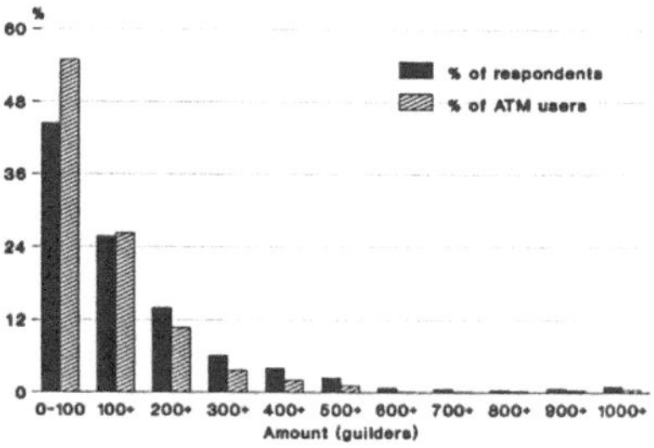

purse, with a peak at amounts between Fl. 25 and Fl. 50 (Figure 2.6). Additionally, they have on average Fl. 189 at home for transactions purposes (Figure 2.7). For other reasons, mainly saving, they hold on average Fl. 341, the amounts being highly skewed. According to Table 2.4, heads of households or their partners keep on average an total amount of Fl. 287 in their purse or at home for transactions purposes. On average, the transactions balances which ATM users keep in their purse or at home are lower by nearly 14% and 28% respectively, than the transaction, balances of those who do not use these machines. For the use of alternative payments media, such a two-dimensional analysis also suggests a negative influence on the size of the transactions balances.

Table 2.6 gives the results of a multivariate analysis of the cash holdings, analogous to that in the previous section for the average cash holdings following from the cash disbursements. A number of the results from the analysis of the cash management return. Again, the cash holdings increase with age. Females keep relatively less money in their purse and more at home, which is plausible from the point of view of their higher risk of being robbed. For the total transactions balances for 12 out of the 14 explanatory variables the coefficients have the same sign, while for the majority the order of magnitude is also the same. Exceptions are the negative effect of the family size and the positive effect of the use of credit cards on the transactions balances kept in the purse and at home. The latter result, which is not very

Table 2.6 Regression results for (ln) households' cash balances

Explanatory variable	Amount of cash in purse		Transactions balances at home	Total transactions balances	Savings balances
ln (amount withdrawn per month)	0.214 (19.0)	0.263 (24.5)	0.094 (8.4)	0.135 (12.5)	0.014 (1.7)
Age	0.011 (11.5)		0.013 (14.9)	0.012 (14.2)	0.002 (2.4)
Sex	-0.178 (6.4)		0.135 (5.2)	0.104 (4.21)	0.009 (0.5)
Income	0.015 (1.0)		0.037 (3.1)	0.032 (2.8)	-0.009 (1.0)
Education	-0.006 (0.6)		-0.034 (4.1)	-0.025 (3.1)	-0.016 (2.6)
Occupational status	0.044 (1.6)		0.041 (1.7)	0.035 (1.5)	0.066 (3.6)
Size of family	-0.080 (7.9)		0.022 (2.7)	-0.010 (1.3)	0.008 (1.4)
Urbanization	-0.014 (2.1)		0.006 (1.2)	-0.007 (1.4)	0.008 (1.9)
Type of employer	0.301 (5.5)		0.141 (3.1)	0.166 (3.7)	0.010 (2.9)
Number of accounts	0.075 (3.7)		0.052 (3.1)	0.068 (4.3)	0.027 (2.2)
Use of ATMs	-0.048 (1.6)		-0.110 (4.4)	-0.102 (4.2)	-0.006 (0.3)
Use of checks	-0.012 (0.4)		-0.142 (5.9)	-0.102 (4.4)	-0.012 (0.7)
Use of credit cards	0.238 (3.0)		0.065 (1.0)	0.121 (1.9)	0.138 (2.9)
Use of POS	0.017 (0.4)		-0.046 (1.2)	-0.049 (1.3)	0.002 (0.1)
Constant	2.57 (20.8)	2.44 (35.9)	3.78 (31.6)	4.10 (35.6)	5.38 (61.6)
Mean dependent variable	4.08	4.08	4.98	5.47	5.66
SE	1.07	1.09	0.65	0.61	0.452
$\bar{R}^2$	0.122	0.070	0.135	0.144	0.016
Number of observations	7,734	8,054	4,199	4,090	3,799

Explanatory notes: t-values within parentheses; the last three columns regard heads of households only.

plausible at first sight, may be caused by the fact that this variable is strongly connected to the income variable, as also appears from the t-values of about 50 in a separate logit analysis. Thus the credit card variable may pick up some of the income effects insofar as not reflected by the income variable, due to the rather rigid specification applied here. In general, the effects of the alternative payments media on the cash in the purses are larger than on the cash kept at home.

The estimated transactions elasticity is, however, considerably lower. For the balances in the purses it lies between 0.21 and 0.26, depending on whether other explanatory variables are included in the equation. This discrepancy may indicate that the implicit assumption of a uniform distribution of the payments between the cash acquisitions in the square root formula does not hold, households spending a large part of the money relatively soon after its acquisition. The transactions elasticity of the balances kept at home amounts to about 0.10, so for the total transactions balances a transactions elasticity of 0.15 results. As expected, the estimates for the savings balances show that these balances are hardly influenced by the use of plastic money. The effects are statistically insignificant, as in the case of ATMs, checks and POS-terminals, or get an unexpected sign, as in the case of credit cards and the number of accounts.

2.2.4 A closer look at the survey results

Cash management

Comparison of the results of the surveys of 1983 and 1990 points to a 24% decline of the average amount of cash acquired per withdrawal, from Fl. 375 in 1983 to Fl. 285 in 1990. This outcome, which is to some extent terms confirmed by the scarce information on the actual development of cash withdrawals available from the banking system, is the more remarkable as the price level has meanwhile risen by 9% and the use of guaranteed checks, the most important substitute for cash, dropped from 11.6% to 10.2% of consumer expenditure. One explanation of the fall of the average amount per withdrawal is the introduction of ATMs. Thus, at banks heavily involved in the use of ATMs, the average amount per withdrawal dropped by more than 10% between 1988 and 1990. According to the results on the cash disbursements the average amount per withdrawal of ATM users is about Fl. 60 lower than for those who do not use these machines. However, after correction for this phenomenon a decline of nearly 20% remains. This may to some extent be the consequence of the decrease of the family size from an average of 2.7 in 1983 to 2.4 in 1990, which results in more people withdrawing, at a lower amount. This is affirmed by the rise of the percentage of respondents withdrawing cash from 85% in 1983 to 98% in 1990. Also the wider availability of withdrawing facilities and the rise of the number of accounts per head of the population of 16 years and older from 0.98 in 1983 to 1.15 in 1990 may have stimulated the withdrawal of cash by more people at lower amounts 7). Moreover, further substitution of especially transfer payments for cash payments may be of some influence. Nevertheless, a great deal of the discrepancy is probably due to differences in the design of the two surveys.

The fall in the average amount per withdrawal is attended by a rise in the average frequency of withdrawals from 2.96 to 3.15 per month. The use of ATMs plays an important role, ATM users having a monthly frequency of 3.94 compared to 2.87 for those who do not use ATMs. The overall rise of the frequency does however not fully compensate for the drop in the average amount per withdrawal. The amount withdrawn per month falls by 12% from Fl. 866 to Fl. 765. The sample average shows, however, a 3.5% increase from Fl. 720 to Fl. 745. Thus the comparison suggests that a slightly higher amount of cash is withdrawn by more people at lower amounts with a higher frequency. Despite of the differences in lifestyle and in the payments systems, our results agree remarkably well with those of Avery *et al.* (1987) for the US in 1984 and 1986 on the basis of surveys among 1,885 and 658 respondents. The frequency of withdrawal of 3.0 to 3.2 is somewhat higher than their frequency of 2.5. The dollar value of the amount withdrawn ranging from Fl. 375 in 1983 to Fl. 285 in 1990 corresponds to the amount of about $ 150 found for the US.

---

7) As a consequence the decline in the sample average of the amount withdrawn from Fl. 312 to Fl. 280 (10%) is considerably less pronounced.

Cash turnover and turnover rate

According to the survey results, the Dutch population acquired over Fl. 101 billion by means of withdrawal in 1990, compared to Fl. 90 billion in 1983. This means an increase of 12%, compared to a rate of inflation of 9% in the period considered. Thus the results suggest that the real value of cash withdrawals slightly increased by some 3% in the years 1983-1991. The increase is considerably less than the more than 40% increase of the total cash withdrawal of households and businesses according to estimates by the banking system (Annex II). The amounts are, however, of the same order of magnitude as the estimates of the amount withdrawn by households on the basis of the figures for a number of large banks in the years 1984-1989.

Besides the Fl. 90.3 billion acquired by means of withdrawal, people obtained Fl. 23.4 billion (20% of the total) by other means in 1983, *i.e.* from stores, business enterprises etc. Thus the total amount of cash acquired in 1983 comes to over Fl. 110 billion. Assuming a decrease of the share of cash acquired otherwise to 12.5% in view of the cash loop decline mentioned in section 4 of Chapter 2, total cash acquisitions by households in 1990 can be estimated at about Fl. 115 billion. Not all this money is spent on goods or services. A considerable part of it - according to rough estimates up to Fl. 15 billion - may be deposited into demand deposits and savings accounts. Moreover, part of the cash acquired by other means is received from private persons and thus stems from withdrawals by individuals, causing double counting 8). Finally, on average Fl. 1.5 billion is required for the annual growth of the currency circulation and Fl. 7 billion was in 1990 taken abroad, for the greater part by private persons (Ter Braak, 1991). From this point of view the total amount paid in cash by households is less than Fl. 115 billion. On the other hand, payments by individuals under 18 years of age are not included in the results. A rough estimate for the total cash payments by households in 1990 is Fl. 100 billion, which agrees rather well with the amount of nearly Fl. 95

8) Cash transactions within the families were excluded by asking the respondents about cash inflow from outside the household only.

that follows from the cash payments in 1986 of Fl. 80 billion (see section 3.3) taking into account the nominal consumption growth of 17%. The amount of transactions resulting from these payments is higher, as part of the cash is re-used for payments by the receivers 9).

The results for the cash turnover and the average cash balances from the 1983 survey imply a turnover rate of the household cash balances of 40 times per year, regardless of whether we include or exclude cash acquisitions by means other than withdrawal. The turnover rate according to the 1990 survey comes to 24 for the cash turnover from withdrawals and may amount to 27 if we include the cash obtained otherwise, which was not considered in the latter survey. Despite the huge growth of the use of ATMs, the turnover rate found in 1990 is lower than the rate found in 1983. This is probably due the inclusion of savings balances, which were not covered explicitly in the 1983 survey. The turnover rate of the pure transactions balances - excluding the savings balances - comes for 1990 to 46 times a year. This is not only in line with the result of the 1983 survey, but also corresponds with the turnover rate of 46 found by Avery *et al.* (1987) for the United States.

These figures on the turnover rate of the cash balances of households are not directly comparable to the macro-economic transactions velocity of currency VT = PT/M, with PT representing the total transactions value and M the stock of currency outside banks. Firstly, part of the cash turnover flows into checking and savings accounts and abroad, thus not involving any guilder transactions. Excluding this part of the currency flows the turnover rate may be about 20. Secondly, in principle M also includes money held by business enterprises, shops *etc.* This may lead to a lower overall transactions velocity insofar as the cash is kept in idle balances for some time. For instance, stores usually wait for some time before depositing their receipts of money at the bank. Thirdly, M also includes that part of currency that is kept in hoards, while the computed average transactions balances of the households do not or only

9) According to Cramer (1988) about 10% of the cash payments are re-used by the receivers (mainly shops). However, insofar these payments are paid to individuals, they are already included in our estimate.

partly (see next section). Including these hoards, which were not covered by the survey, the transactions velocity would be considerably lower.

Cash balances

According to the survey, the cash balances of the Dutch population in 1990 amounted to Fl. 4.3 billion, transactions balances and savings balances each accounting for about one-half (Table 2.7). The size of the transactions balances of Fl. 2.2 billion corresponds to the amount of Fl. 1.6 billion that follows from the cash management behaviour, if we take into account a bottom inventory of Fl. 0.5 billion (on the basis of the 1983 survey). The total balances of Fl. 4.3 billion are 12% of the actual currency circulation with the public in that year, and corresponds - despite the additional question on savings balances - to the 12% traced by the survey of 1983. Likewise, Avery *et al.* (1987) could locate only 12% of the US currency circulation in 1986 with households, while Cramer and Reekers (1972), using a budget survey among 110 households, arrived at 17% of the Dutch currency circulation with households (Table 2.7). Apart from the difference in time and method this higher percentage may partly be due to the fact that the survey was held at the end of the month, when people have relatively high cash balances. On the other hand, as Cramer and Reekers (1972) argue, the fact that the respondents were explicitly asked to count the notes per denomination may have led to certain separate cash balances being overlooked.

If we estimate, from their findings for 1971 on the basis of countings and a survey, the holdings of the business sector at 15% of the circulation, and if we add Fl. 0.4 billion in view of foreign demand, we still cannot account for 72% of the currency circulation. Thus, as Avery *et al.* concluded for the US in 1984-1986, a large percentage of the Dutch currency stock in 1990 was apparently held 'underground' for illegitimate purposes or was held in unreported hoards. Likewise Cramer and Reekers suppose that the reported cash holdings mainly concern transactions balances, and that the missing notes - in fact they did not consider coin - are kept in hoards and underground transactions balances,

Table 2.7 Estimated cash holdings outside banks

Sector	1971 Cramer/Reekers		1983 NIPO survey		1990 AGB survey	
	Amount (bln)	Share (%)	Amount (bln)	Share (%)	Amount (bln)	Share (%)
Households	1.67	17.2	2.81	11.6	4.31	12.1
transactions balances	.	.	2.81	.	2.17	6.1
- cash in purse	.	.	.	.	1.14	3.2
- cash at home	.	.	.	.	1.13	3.2
- from withdrawals	.	.	1.63	6.7	(1.6)	(4.5)
- other acquisitions	.	.	0.53	2.2	.	.
- bottom inventory	.	.	0.65	2.7	.	.
savings balances	.	.	.	.	2.04	5.7
Business sector	1.33	13.7	.	.	4.89 b)	13.7 b)
Offshore	.	.	.	.	0.4	1.1
Not considered	0.77	7.9	.	.	.	.
Unknown	5.94	61.2	21.5	88.4	26.1	73.1
Total	9.7 a)	100	24.3	100	35.7	100
Memo: Circulation						
Fl. 1,000 and 250 b)	1.97	20.3	7.4	31.9	17.6	49.2
up to including Fl. 100	7.74	79.7	16.9	68.1	18.1	50.8

a) excluding circulation with banks (estimated at 6.4% and 7%, respectively); b) on the basis of Cramer and Reekers (1972).

with relatively many notes of high denominations. Even if the underground economy would be as large as 10% of GNP - which is probably much too high a figure (Broesterhuizen, 1983) - this would, even at a transactions velocity of as low as ten, explain an additional currency circulation of less than Fl. 8 billion (Section 4.2). Apparently, at least 50% of currency in circulation is kept in unreported hoards. The fact that the two largest notes of Fl. 250 and Fl. 1,000, which are hardly used for regular payments, account for 50% of the circulation, confirms this conclusion. The apparent rise of the importance of currency hoards, as appears from the rise of the share of the Fl. 1,000 and the Fl. 250 notes from 20% in 1971 to 50% in 1990 (Table 2.7), may explain the lower share we traced with households in 1990, as compared to the findings of Cramer and Reekers. If we exclude these two notes, the share of currency with households is 22% according to Cramer and Reekers in 1971, compared to 24% in 1990 following from this study.

According to the combined results of this study and those of Cramer and Reekers, the average cash holdings of the population of 18 years and older have risen from about Fl. 200 in 1971 to Fl. 270 in 1983 and to Fl. 373 in 1990 10). For the whole period 1971-1990 this comes to a rise of 86% as compared to an increase of the price level of 140%. Consequently, the real average cash balances dropped by more than 22% between 1971 and 1990. According to the estimates, this decline took place in the period 1971-1983, which may be due to the large-scale introduction of guaranteed checks and salary accounts. Since 1983 the real cash balances show an average increase of 3.5% per year. As a matter of fact, the validity of these conclusions depends strongly on the comparability of the surveys, which because of their different designs, bear the risk of measuring different parts of the household cash balances.

2.2.5 *Expected changes in cash management*

One way to examine the possible influence of alternative payments media on the need for currency is to measure their effects on present-day withdrawal and payment pattern. An alternative approach is to ask people directly for their expectations about changes in their use and need for cash. Thus, analogously as for the present-day patterns, the survey contains questions on the expected behaviour in the hypothetic situation, where plastic money is widely available and usable, as defined in section 2.3 of this chapter. When the withdrawing behaviour was concerned the questions about the future were the same as for the present-day situation. With respect to the cash balances, people were asked for the expected changes with respect to the present-day balances. No questions were asked about the savings balances, which are assumed to be insensitive to changes in the payment pattern, with respect to the future. Table 2.8 summarizes the main results regarding the cash management behaviour. The respondents expect a clear decline of their use of cash. With respect to the withdrawing of cash, apart from a small decrease of the average frequency they expect, on average, a decline

10) The average cash holdings following from Cramer and Reekers' study of Fl. 188, concerned banknotes only and have been increased by a proportional amount of coin.

Table 2.8 Cash management and cash balances now and in the future

	Cash withdrawals			Transactions balances			Savings balances
	frequency	amount per withdrawal	amount per month	in purse	at home	total	
All respondents							
- now	3.09	288	729	98	98	196	177
- future	3.05	245	627	77	83	161	
- change	-1%	-15%	-14%	-21%	-15%	-18%	
Users of ATMs							
- now	3.94	202	735	88	75	163	163
- future	3.51	163	537	63	58	121	
- change	-11%	-19%	-27%	-28%	-23%	-26%	
Non-users of ATMs							
- now	2.79	320	724	102	106	208	194
- future	2.89	275	657	82	92	174	
- change	3%	-14%	-9%	-19%	-13%	-16%	
Users of checks							
- now	3.84	258	856	96	95	191	193
- in future	3.47	215	654	73	80	152	
- change	-10%	-17%	-24%	-24%	-17%	-20%	
Users of credit cards							
- now	2.88	251	691	124	92	216	194
- future	2.82	186	468	86	70	156	
- change	2%	-26%	-32%	-31%	-24%	-28%	
Users of POS							
- now	4.67	193	836	88	80	167	181
- future	3.81	150	546	57	60	117	
- change	-18%	-22%	-34%	-34%	-25%	-30%	

Explanatory notes: Sample averages, including respondents not withdrawing cash. The cash balances at home and for savings purposes (reported on a head of household basis) have been recalculated on a respondent basis.

of about 15% in both the amount per disbursement and the total amount withdrawn per month. The strictly transactions oriented cash kept in the purse is expected to decline more than the cash kept for these purposes at home which is probably also underlain by some precautionary motives. On average the respondents expect a drop in the cash in their purse and at home of 21% and 15%, respectively. This comes to a decline of the total transactions balances of 18%. The savings balances, making up nearly 50% of the the households' cash holdings, may be rather insensitive to developments in the payment system. Therefore, the expected decline of the total cash balances of households is 10%, which comes to about two years' nominal growth of the circulation. In general those who already use plastic money expect a larger decline of the average amount per withdrawal and of the total transactions balances of between 20% and 30%. If their opinion is more representative of future developments, an expected future decline of the total balances of about 15% results.

2.3 Manner of payment and use of currency

Our analysis of the payment pattern of Dutch households is based on two surveys of different design, held in the years 1984-1986 and 1990, respectively, for the Nederlandsche Bank. The first concerns an extensive budget survey among 1,000 households. The second survey, of 1990, is the same as used for the measurement of cash management. Focusing as it does on the quantitatively most important places of purchase, the design of the latter is less exhaustive than that of the former. On the other hand, its methodology enables us to roughly measure people's expectations regarding the future use of means of payment.

As mentioned before, statistical information on payments, including the use of cash, which is, at least in terms of numbers, by far the most important mode of payment, is fragmentary and incomplete. Exceptions are a study made at the Bank of England in the early 1980s (Trundle and Temperton, 1982) and later studies on the development of the payment system in the United Kingdom, as published by APACS (1989). The study of Avery *et al.* (1987) gives comparabele information on the payment patterns of households in the United States in 1984 and 1986. For the rest, estimates of the payments of households, especially cash payments are mostly based on heroic assumptions. Apart from this, a number of studies, like Mandell's (1972) interesting study on credit card use in the US, deal with some specific means of payment. The next section 2.3.1 discusses the results of the budget survey in 1984-1986 by describing the underlying samples, and analyzing the results in an international context. Moreover we investigate the connection between households' expenditure and the manner of payment as well as the probability distribution of payments by households and its consequences for the currency and note circulation. This section relies heavily on earlier work by Boeschoten and Fase (1989). Section 2.3.2 deals with the design and results of the 1990 survey including the expected changes in the use of payments, which are compared to the results of the cash management part of the survey.

2.3.1 Payment patterns in 1984-1986

The basic observations

The data are taken from a series of sample surveys conducted among households in the Netherlands by AGB-Intomart during 1984-1987, in which the Nederlandsche Bank participated from 1984 to 1986. In contrast to the surveys described so far, in this case no additional questions were included, but solely part of the basic questions was used. The AGB-Intomart sample survey was a continuous inquiry into family income as well as into consumer purchases, modes of payment and other financial transactions by households. The main objective it was to determine the pattern of expenditure and payment by households as well as their attitude towards different financial instruments. The conception of this panel research owed much to a similar sample survey in United Kingdom by AGB-Research, used in the studies mentioned above.

The observations were obtained from a panel of 1,000 households, covering about 2,400 persons of 12 years of age and older. The information was collected monthly by asking each household in the sample to complete diaries and detailed questionnaires, and by interviews. The survey covers individuals living in private households in the Netherlands who were additionally interviewed once a year on the more or less regular payments, like those for tax, insurance, rent, mortgages, telephone and gas and electricity, as well as on income and a number of other socio-economic characteristics. The sample covers on average 1,000 households in each survey and the sampling is designed to obtain representative samples which are homogeneous over time. The results were adjusted for

Table 2.9 Assessment of the sample according to consumer expenditure

	Total consumer expenditure (billions of guilders)			Average consumption per houshold		
	1984	1985	1986	1984	1985	1986
AGB sample	194.5	202.6	206.5	37,833	38,546	38,440
CBS, National accounts	236.8	247.7	256.3			
CBS, budget survey				34,293	35,596	36,167

fluctuations in the sample by means of weighting to maintain the sample representative. As a result differences in the composition of the panel between months are negligible. Each household in the sample reports all payments for transactions in excess of Fl. 10. In addition, a small number of the sampled households was asked to record payments below Fl. 10 as well. The size of this subset declined, however, from 122 in 1984, to 100 in 1985 and to 62 in 1986. This small and declining number may influence the assessment of the overall payments pattern, particularly because over 40% of payments concern less than Fl. 10 per transaction. The relevant results were blown up to the total sample by means of the (increasing) ratio between the total number of respondents and the number of respondents also reporting on payments of less than Fl. 10 11).

The design and purpose of the survey are highly demanding on the respondents in that an abundance of information is asked, entailing the risk of bias. To assess the quality of the survey results, we compared the sample estimates with the consumer expenditure figures recorded by the Dutch Bureau of Statistics (CBS) and with the figures on the actual use of guaranteed checks. Table 2.9 compares the results for total consumer expenditure and consumption per household with the CBS figures based on the national accounts and the national budget survey, respectively. The results for total consumer expenditure indicate a considerably lower

11) Correcting by means of blow-up factors is appropriate for the underlying analysis on total payments, if the respondents reporting all amounts are randomly selected. For studies which focus on individual spending patterns the application of a *Tobit* or *Count data model* is to be preferred (Alessie *et al.* 1990).

Table 2.10 Assessment of the sample according to modes of payments

	Share in total amount of check payments (%)			Share in total number of check payments (%)		
	1984	1985	1986	1984	1985	1986
Banking system						
Bank checks		9	8		14	13
	51			48		
Eurochecks		43	45		34	35
Postal checks	49	48	47	52	52	52
Total	100	100	100	100	100	100
Total amount/number	29.4	31.5	32.3	293.1	308.0	313.5
Sample						
Bank checks		12	10		14	13
	43			43		
Eurochecks		33	36		31	34
Postal checks	57	55	54	57	55	53
Total	100	100	100	100	100	100
Total amount/number	26.0	29.1	29.8	277.5	296.4	299.0

Explanatory note: Amounts are in billions of guilders, numbers in millions.

figure for the AGB sample over the years, mainly as a consequence of different consumption concepts. The differences between the two samples for average consumption per household, however, are fairly small and are mainly due to variations in the definition in the samples. Table 2.10 sets out the distribution of guaranteed check payments in both amounts and numbers over the different types of checks according to the reporting of the banking system and the sample considered here. The figures make clear that the sample results closely match the distribution within the population, suggesting again that the sample is representative. On the basis of these assessments, we conclude that the sample design warrants further statistical analysis of the sample outcomes.

Expenditure and manner of payment

On the basis of the sample survey, the number of payments in, for example, 1986 may be estimated at nearly 3.8 billion, corresponding to an average of two payments per household or 0.7 payment per inhabitant per day. At first sight, this would seem to be a strikingly low figure. Leaving aside the major difference in the years of observation, this number also represents a surprising result relative to comparable figures for other countries such as the United States and France. For these countries, the number was estimated at about three payments per person per day for the mid-1980s. For the United Kingdom the estimate ranges from 2.3 to 3.0 payments per person per day (Table I.1 in Annex I). Part of the discrepancy may be due to underreporting of the smaller cash payments. According to a count made by the CBS in February 1984, Dutch consumers bought about 29 billion goods and services in 1984 (*cf.* Flikweert, 1985). Combined with the number of 3.8 billion of payments following from the present survey, this amounts to an average of nearly 7.5 goods and services per purchase, which also seems rather high. Comparison of the frequency distributions of the prices and the amounts paid (see next section) suggests that the bias may be mainly located at amounts of Fl. 4 and lower, being of relatively small importance insofar amounts are involved.

As to the average amount of payment, the results in Table 2.11 show that cash, guaranteed checks and debits, including transfer, payform and preauthorized payments are by far the most important means of payment. The share in total payments of, for instance, the credit card is negligible. The payment pattern is very stable over the years 1984-1986 for which we participated in the survey (Fase and Boeschoten, 1985; Boeschoten and Fase, 1987, 1989). Cash payments account for nearly 40% in terms of amount and for nearly 80% in terms of the number of payments. This finding is in fair agreement with that for other countries and also with the rule of thumb, often used in practice, that cash payments account for about 20% in terms of amount and for 80% in terms of number. Von Schimmelmann (1985) estimated the share of cash payments in Germany at 86% in terms of number. Percentages of 83 and 90, respectively, have been reported for the United States and the United Kingdom in 1987 by

Table 2.11 Expenditure of households by in 1986

Manner of payment	In terms of amount		In terms of number		Average amount (guilders)
	billions of guilders	%	millions	%	
Cash	79.8	38.6	2924.6	77.9	27
Guaranteed check	29.8	14.4	298.0	7.9	100
Transfer	39.6	19.2	148.9	4.0	266
Payform	24.4	11.8	176.9	4.7	138
Preauthorized debit	30.8	14.9	190.1	5.1	162
Others	2.2	1.1	14.5	0.4	151
of which:					
- retention from salary	1.9	0.9	9.1	0.2	205
- point of sale	0.0	0.0	0.9	0.0	38
- credit card	0.2	0.1	2.1	0.1	95
- gift coupon	0.1	0.1	2.4	0.1	35
Total	206.6	100	3753.0	100	55

Humphrey and Berger (1990) and the BIS (1989), while, according to the survey results reported by Avery *et al.* (1986), in terms of amount American families pay 36% of their expenditure in cash (Annex I). These percentages relate solely to payments made by households and, therefore, do not include business payments. If business payments, which on average concern higher amounts and are consequently relatively more often made by transfers, are included, the share of cash payments, notably in terms of amount, becomes substantially lower. Thus, according to estimates on the basis of the results of this study and of Boeschoten and Fase (1984), cash payments account for about 6% of the total amount of payments (excluding financial transactions) in the Netherlands. The estimates for the United States, Japan and France show a comparable share in total payments (Annex I). In terms of numbers the estimated share of cash payments ranges from 80% to 90%.

During the observation period 1984-1986, the increase in the amount of cash payments was 6.7%, which is two percentage points less than the expansion of the amount of currency in circulation. On the assumption that business cash payments showed a similar development, the transactions velocity of currency thus declined slightly between 1984 and 1986. Even allowing for the fact that business transactions have been left out

Figure 2.8 Relationship between amount paid and manner of payment

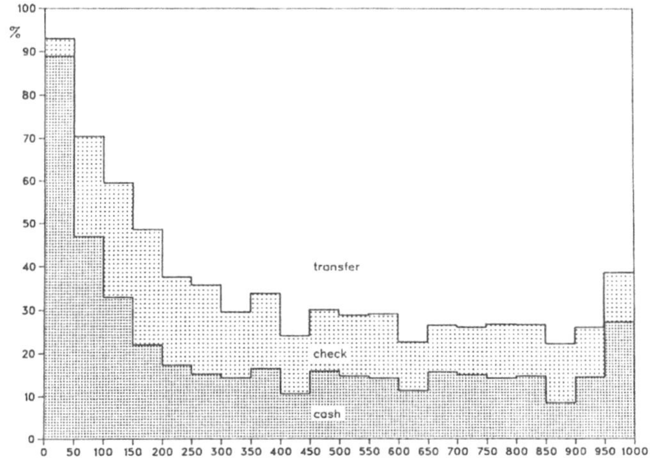

of consideration, the resulting transactions velocity of 2.8 is a strikingly low figure, which contrasts sharply with the estimations of Laurent (1970) and Feige (1979) for the United States, amounting to 25 and higher. The share of guaranteed checks in the total amount of household payments of 14% on average shows a slight increase from 1984 to 1986, resulting from a 6% rise in the average amount paid. This shift probably reflects the tendency for higher amounts in particular to be paid more often by check than by cash. Likewise, the average amount of transfers shows a 7% decline as a result of the substitution of cash and check payments by debits.

Figure 2.8 illustrates that the manner of payment is strongly correlated to the amount paid. At amounts below Fl. 50, nearly 90% of all expenditure is paid in cash. The share of cash payments declines to less than 15% at amounts of about Fl. 300, at which level most payments - approximately 70% - are made by transfers. Checks are the most important for amounts from Fl. 50 up to Fl. 200, where on average 25% of the amounts are paid in cash. Beyond Fl. 200, checks and cash payments are of approximately equal importance, checks losing part of their attractiveness because of the increasing inconvenience, when the stated amount is exceeded and consequently more checks have to be filled in (*cf.* Mot and Cramer, 1990). From about Fl. 1,000 upwards, cash regains importance as a means of payment. In 1986, 23% of the 15 million payments higher than

Fl. 1,000 was made in cash. This share appears to be rising over time, amounting to 19% in 1984 and 21% in 1985. Apart from the factor represented by the amount involved, the payment pattern depends on personal characteristics. According to a two-dimensional analysis, the share of cash payments declines with age, income, education and the number of checking accounts. Furthermore, women appear to pay more in cash than men do and those persons who have guaranteed cheques at their disposal pay less in cash than those who do not have. Each of these correlations is statistically significant at a 5% significance level, with a degree of association - expressed in Cramèr's measure of association V (see Goodman and Kruskal, 1979) ranging from 0 to 1 - of nearly 0.2. These findings are in agreement with those reported by Avery *et al.* (1986) for American families.

Since the personal characteristics may well be interdependent, the relationships established may be related as well, requiring a multivariate approach as applied by Mot *et al.* (1989) and Mot and Cramer (1990) on a random sample of about 3,000 payments from the 1987 version of the AGB/Intomart survey. According to their multinomial logit analysis, the mode of payment primarily depends on whether daily purchases, irregular purchases, transactions with prior notice or regular transactions are concerned. Within each category of transactions, the amount paid is the most important determinant of the mode of payment, as also appears from this study. As for the role of personal characteristics, their findings confirm the negative effect of education on the use of cash. The slightly differently measured possesion of checking accounts does not, however, always lead to a reduction in the use of cash. The negative influence of age and income is not found, and the negative influence of being male is only found for transactions with prior notice. Some of the differences may ensue from substantial discrepancies between the sample averages used by Mot and Cramer and those used in Table 2.11. Nevertheless, part of the effects following from the two-dimensional approach applied here may disappear when, by means of a multivariate approach, the mutual dependency of some of the personal characteristics such as income, education, sex and occupational status is taken into account.

The distribution of payments

The data from the budget survey allow the establishment of the frequency distributions of amounts paid. Figures 2.9, 2.10, and 2.11 give the distributions with different class intervals in 1986 for cash, checks and transfer payments, respectively, each covering at least 95% of the payments concerned. The class interval of Fl. 1 refers to amounts of Fl. 0.46 up to and including Fl. 1.45, Fl. 1.46 up to and including Fl. 2.45, and so forth. Likewise, the class interval of Fl. 5 refers to amounts of Fl. 4.46 up to and including Fl. 9.45, and so forth, and the class interval of Fl. 10 to amounts of Fl. 9.46 up to and including Fl. 19.45, and so forth. The distribution of the cash payments, which account for nearly 85% of all payments for amounts up to and including Fl. 100, shows marked peaks at multiples of Fl. 5. Similar peaks can be observed in the distribution of checks and transfer payments at a class interval of Fl. 1, which are not shown here for the sake of brevity.

For payments in excess of Fl. 100, notable peaks for all three means of payment occur at multiples of Fl. 100. At least in the case of cash payments, the clustering of expenses at amounts of multiples of Fl. 5 and Fl. 100 respectively could be due to reporting errors. The distribution of check payments and debits, which are recorded, show, however, the same clustering while the frequency distribution of 120,000 prices of 1,500 products, registered by the CBS in January 1984, also shows comparable peaks (Figure 2.12). Moreover, less than 25% of the reported payments in the underlying survey are rounded to full guilder amounts (Figure 2.13), which also seems to indicate that the extent to which the respondents may have resorted to rounding is limited. The distribution of the amounts of combined purchases of more than a single item do not show similar peaks at multiples of Fl. 5 and Fl. 100. Therefore, it seems unlikely that consumers arrange their combined purchases to attain totals of these amounts.

Figure 2.9 Cash payments in 1986 up to and including Fl. 100 at a class interval of Fl. 1

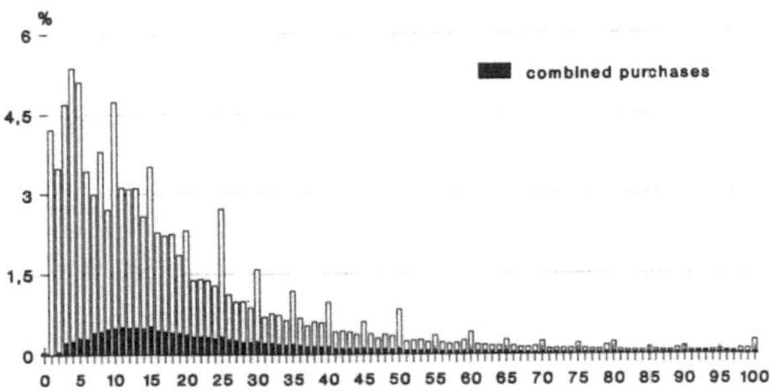

Figure 2.10 Payments by means of guaranteed checks in 1986 up to and including Fl. 250 at a class interval of Fl. 5

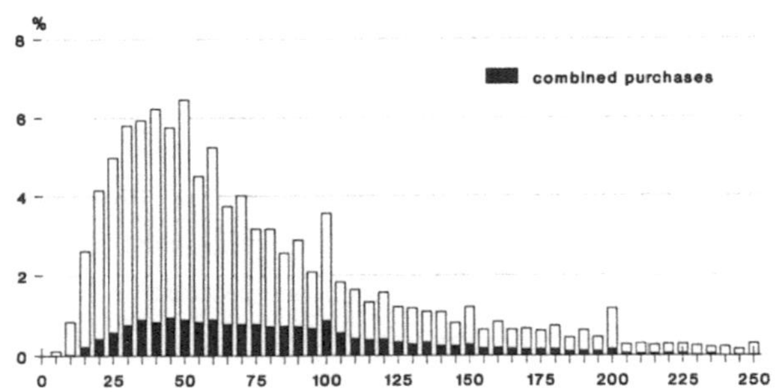

Figure 2.11 Payments by means of debits in 1986 up to and including Fl. 1,000 at a class interval of Fl. 10

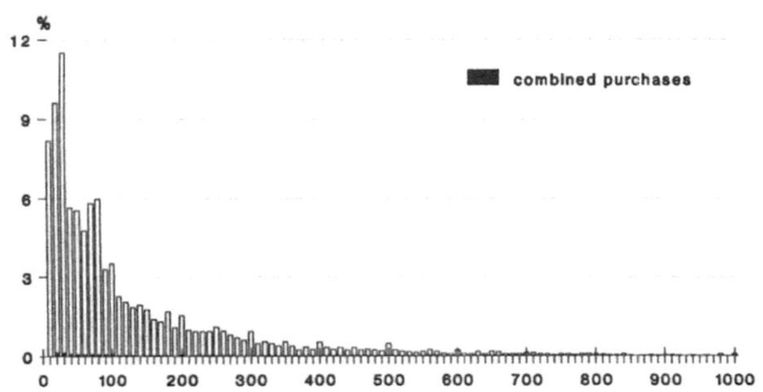

Figure 2.12 Frequency distribution of CBS prices in 1984

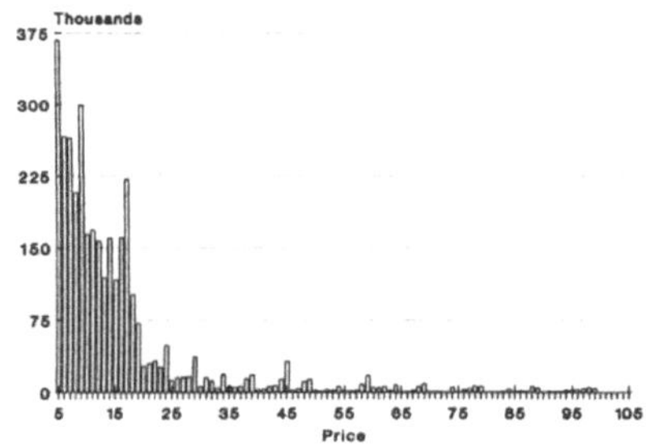

Figure 2.13 Distribution of rounding-off of payments in 1985-survey

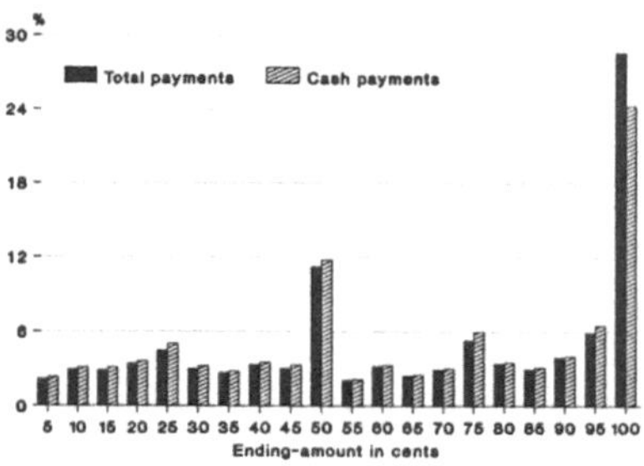

The question arises as to which probability distribution fits the observed frequency distributions satisfactorily. Besides the gamma-distribution, which was assumed by Manski and Goldin (1987), we fitted the lognormal distribution defined by

$$f(x;\mu,\sigma) = \frac{1}{x\sigma\sqrt{2\pi}} \exp[-\tfrac{1}{2}((\ln x - \mu)/\sigma)^2] \qquad x,\sigma \geq 0, -\infty \leq \mu \leq \infty \qquad (2.5)$$

According to the test statistic developed by Cox (1962), at a 5% significance level for all the three years observed, the lognormal distribution is to be preferred to the gamma-distribution (Table 2.12). As yet this empirical preference lacks a theoretical foundation. The case in question does not show clear similarity with the various applications of distribution as described by Aitchison and Brown (1957), among others. The fitted distributions turn out to be fairly stable over time. The parameters estimated for 1986 differ by an average of 1% and by a maximum of 4% from those found for 1984 and for 1985 (*cf.* Boeschoten and Fase, 1989).

With a class interval of Fl. 1 or more, the frequency distributions shown in Figures 2.9, 2.10, and 2.11 do not afford an insight into the rounding-off practices of the amounts paid. As can be seen from Figure 2.13 with the frequency distribution of the amounts behind the steps of

Table 2.12 Estimation results for lognormal distribution for 1986

Manner of payment	μ	σ	ln (L) (x1,000)	Standard deviation of residuals	χ^2 (x1,000)	ν
Cash	2.496 (0.002)	1.157 (0.001)	-2,153	31.9	79	1,049
Checks	4.153 (0.004)	0.859 (0.003)	-293	8.1	8	933
Transfers	4.258 (0.002)	1.313 (0.001)	-557	13.5	24	1,729
Total	2.871 (0.002)	1.360 (0.001)	-3,119	30.3	64	2,2027

Explanatory notes: Standard deviations are put in parentheses; L is the value of the likelihood function; ν indicates degrees of freedom

5 cents nearly 25% of all cash payments concern full-guilder amounts and 12% are rounded at 50 cents 12). The results of our analysis suggest that rounding off increases significantly with the amount paid. In case of amounts in excess of Fl. 1,000, however, the majority, that is more than 80%,is in full guilders or is not rounded.

Because of combined purchases, the peak of the frequency distribution for payments is considerably more to the right than for prices of the individual goods and services (Figure 2.13). According to the count made by the CBS in 1984, more than 85% of the prices of the goods and services bought by consumers amount to less than Fl. 5, the prices between Fl. 0.50 and Fl 1.50 accounting for more than 35%. The average price of all goods and services in 1984 was about Fl. 4.8, compared to an average amount per payment of Fl. 56. The total turnover that follows from the frequency distribution of prices as registered by the CBS comes for 1984 is Fl. 138 billion, compared to our estimate of transactions of about Fl. 110 billion for cash and check payments. The discrepancy of Fl. 28 billion probably ensues from debits.

12) Since 1982 when the Fl. 0.01 coin was abolished as legal tender, the Fl. 0.05 coin has been the lowest coin. Prices of goods are, however, still expressed in cents. In case of cash payment, the final amount to be paid is rounded to the nearest multiple of 5 cents.

Application to the use of denominations

The probability distribution of cash payments mentioned before allows assessment of the households' need of currency for payments. For the currency-issuing authorities, it is important to know to what extent they succeed in meeting the need for currency efficiently by means of the denominational mix. Moreover, an insight into the use of currency as a means of payment and as a means of hoarding is essential for forecasting the need for currency.

Following Cramer (1983a), the frequency distribution enabled us to simulate the theoretically most efficient manner of payment, each payment involving a minimum of notes and coins. Therefore, the number of notes and coins required for each amount x_i

$$n(x_i) = \sum_j \mid n(j, x_i) \mid \tag{2.6}$$

must be minimized under the restriction that

$$\sum_j n(j, x_i).v(j) = x_i \tag{2.7}$$

where v(j) represents the face value and $n(j,x_i)$ the number of notes of denomination j used for the payment of amount x_i. If change is received in return, the $n(j,x_i)$ integers are negative. Although the solution to this problem can be obtained by means of the technique of integer linear programming, for reasons of computational ease the use of the heuristic search procedure proposed by Cramer is preferable. In this procedure combinations of various denominations increasing in size are checked until all amounts have been covered. First the amounts that can be paid with one note are traced and blocked. Next, this is repeated with all amounts that can be paid with two notes, and so forth. The procedure is continued until all amounts considered have been blocked. When the amounts x_i can be paid efficiently in more than one manner, say K, the average frequency $a(j,x_i)$ of denomination j for amount x_i is computed as

$$a(j, x_i) = \frac{1}{K} \sum_{k=1}^{K} \mid \hat{n}_k(j, x_i) \mid . \tag{2.8}$$

Thus for each amount increasing by Fl. 0.05 the minimum number of notes, required $\hat{n}(x_i)$, is computed, as well as the corresponding frequency of the denominations involved. Combination of these results with the frequencies $f(x_i)$ of the amounts paid, as shown in Figure 2.9, gives the total number of notes required for those payments and the total frequency per denomination j as followes

$$a(j) = \sum_i f(x_i).a(j,x_i) \tag{2.9}$$

In addition, by way of sensitivity analysis, the computations were repeated by assuming, successively, payment with the exact amount - that is efficient but without change - payment with the next higher denomination, change being returned in an efficient way; and a combination of these two payment forms in which for each amount the minimum number of notes and coins is taken. All these alternatives, also considered by Flikweert (1985), can be seen as particular cases of the efficient manner of payment described above.

According to the results, set out in Table 2.13, efficient payment would have meant that in 1986 households needed 9.5 billion notes and coins for their 2.9 billion cash payments, or on average 3.3 notes and coins per payment. In the case of exact payment, *i.e.* efficient without change, and in the case of payment with the next higher denomination, these numbers would be 35% and 70% higher, respectively. The payment pattern appears to affect the need for coins in particular. Payment with the next higher denomination involves nearly two times as many coins, but only 25% more notes than efficient payment. The shares of the denominations in the number of notes and coins needed differ rather strongly, depending on the assumed manner of payment. As expected, in the case of exact payment, the share of the lower and in case of payment with the next higher denomination, the share of the higher denomination is relatively larger. In the case of efficient payment, the shares are somewhere in between. In all of the simulated payment patterns, the actual shares of the higher denominations are considerably larger and those of the lower denominations considerably lower than the computed

Table 2.13 Currency circulation and households' computed need for currency in 1986

Description	Currency (end of year)	Manner of payment			
		efficient (1)	efficient without change (2)	with the next higher denomination (3)	minimum of alternatives 2 and 3 (4)
	Composition (in %)				
Notes					
Fl. 1,000	3.6	0.4	0.3	0.3	0.2
Fl. 250	2.0	1.1	0.7	2.0	0.7
Fl. 100	35.4	3.6	2.3	5.3	3.6
Fl. 50	5.4	8.4	6.0	10.5	7.6
Fl. 25	19.0	22.1	16.0	24.9	20.3
Fl. 10	18.8	38.2	44.2	35.2	38.7
Fl. 5	15.8	26.2	30.5	21.8	28.9
	100	100	100	100	100
Coins					
Fl. 2.50	5.7	15.1	12.4	9.6	11.6
Fl. 1.00	19.0	34.1	32.7	30.5	34.9
Fl. 0.25	15.7	21.5	28.8	24.0	27.9
Fl. 0.10	23.2	15.9	18.8	29.7	16.6
Fl. 0.05	36.4	13.4	7.3	6.2	9.0
	100	100	100	100	100
	Number (millions)				
Notes	350	3,620	3,641	4,596	3,680
Coins	3,211	5,917	9,0921	1,446	7,677
Total	3,561	9,5371	2,7331	6,0421	1,357
	Value (millions of guilders)				
Notes	30,341	90,957	73,182	134,632	81,191
Coins	1,561	4,701	6,642	7,975	5,596
Total	31,902	95,658	79,824	142,607	86,787

shares. This means that the higher denominations are actually used much less frequently than the lower denominations (Table 2.14). The physical velocity - that is the number of times a note changes hands in a year - increases from 1 for Fl. 1,000 notes to about 20 for Fl. 10 and Fl. 5 notes, with a coefficient of correlation between the face value of the denominations and their physical velocity of -0.65. This finding corresponds to what two other indicators of the intensity of use of banknotes suggest. Thus, the return rate, that is the average number of times a note returns to the central bank in one year, decreases with the face value of the four largest notes 13). Likewise, the average life of a banknote increases with its face value. The coefficients of correlation of the computed intensity of use with these two indicators amount to 0.25 and -0.75, respectively.

To the extent that the physical velocity is an indicator of the intensity with which a denomination is used in payments, this confirms the presumption formulated earlier that especially higher denominations are used not only as a means of payment, but also as a means of hoarding (see Fase, 1985a). From the discrepancy between the computed use of denominations and the actual circulation, the share of Fl. 1000 notes in circulation that are hoarded is estimated at more than 90%. This figure, however, may overstate reality because business cash payments, which may involve relatively many Fl. 1,000 notes, have not been taken into account. Besides, these notes are also used in the shadow economy. Moreover, the simulations of the payment pattern ignore the fact that when withdrawing cash people prefer the higher denominations, especially the Fl. 100 notes, regardless of the expenditure they intend to make. Besides the undeniable presence of hoarding, this phenomenon may explain a good deal of the remarkably low physical velocity of the Fl. 100 note as computed in Table 2.14. The relatively high velocity of the Fl. 250 note probably ensues from the fact that the circulation of this note had not yet reached full maturity at end-1986, the first year of its introduction. Nevertheless, the estimations indicate a hoarding percentage of at least 70% of this note.

Contrary to expectations, the physical velocity of coins is considerably lower than the velocity of notes. According to the assumed payment pattern they change hands one to three times a year. Moreover, this

---

13) The low return frequencies of the Fl. 10 and Fl. 5 notes stem from the fact that the incentive to the banks to return them to the central bank is relatively low because of the low opportunity costs (interest forgone by not returning), compared to the transportation costs.

Table 2.14 Frequency of use and average frequency per payment in 1986

Denomination	Computed frequency of use (per year)				Average frequency per payment	
	efficient (1)	efficient without change (2)	with next higher denomination (3)	minimum of (2) and (3) (4)	this study	Cramer (1986)
Notes						
Fl. 1,000	1.1	0.9	1.1	0.6	0.01	(0.38)
Fl. 250	5.7	3.6	13.1	3.7	0.01	0.85
Fl. 100	1.1	0.7	2.0	1.1	0.04	0.51
Fl. 50	16.1	11.6	25.5	14.8	0.10	0.30
Fl. 25	12.0	8.8	17.2	11.2	0.27	0.38
Fl. 10	21.0	24.5	24.6	21.6	0.47	0.51
Fl. 5	17.2	20.1	18.1	19.2	0.32	0.30
Total	10.3	10.4	13.1	10.5	1.22	.
Coins						
Fl. 2.50	4.9	6.2	6.0	4.9	0.31	0.35
Fl. 1.00	3.3	4.9	5.7	4.4	0.69	0.74
Fl. 0.25	2.5	5.2	5.4	4.2	0.43	0.57
Fl. 0.10	1.3	2.3	4.6	1.7	0.32	0.53
Fl. 0.05	0.7	0.6	0.6	0.6	0.27	0.40
Total	1.8	2.8	3.6	2.4	2.07	.

Explanatory note: Average frequency per payment on the basis of efficient payment.

velocity declines with the coin value, as opposed to that of banknotes, with a surprisingly high coefficient of correlation of 0.97. This is possibly caused by the disappearance from circulation of the low denominations in particular as a result of loss, destruction, saving, and collecting (see Laurent, 1974; Goldin, 1985).

The turnover rate, which is the amount of currency needed for all payments over the year divided by the amount of currency outstanding, and which equals the weighted average of the frequencies of use with the value shares of the denominations as weights, ranges from 2.5 times a year for efficient payment up to 4.5 in the case of payment with the next higher denomination. The former turnover rate compares to the transactions velocity, as known from monetary theory. All other turnover rates also include currency needs for giving change, and thus are higher. As a consequence of the skewness of the distribution of

Table 2.15 Computed need for banknotes at various banknote ranges

	Need for banknotes at bank note range as at 1986	Need for banknotes at banknote range as at 1986				
		excl. Fl.250	excl. Fl.50	Fl. 500 instead of Fl.250	Fl. 200 instead of Fl.250	Fl. 20 and Fl.200 instead of Fl.25 and Fl.250
Number (millions)	3,620	3,658	3,856	3,633	3,615	3,570
Value (millions of guilders)	90,957	89,646	93,411	89,691	89,952	90,534

Explanatory note: The banknote range as at 1986 corresponds with the range in Table 2.13

payments, the average frequency per payment of the higher denominations is considerably lower than in the case of a uniform distribution, which has implicitly been assumed by Cramer (1983a). This means that his conclusion that the higher denominations circulate faster than smaller ones, may not hold. For the denominations of Fl. 5, Fl. 10 and Fl. 25, for which the intervals of constant average frequency are small relative to the dispersion of payments, the average frequencies per payment are, remarkably similar (Table 2.14). The average frequencies of the coins show, apart from those of the Fl. 2.50 and Fl. 1.00 coins, some clear discrepancies, mainly ensuing from rounding off and 'odd pricing' practices, as mentioned before. Besides, according to the results of simulations not shown here, the average frequency of especially the higher denominations appears to be rather sensitive to the payments pattern that is assumed.

As is evident from the bottom rows of Table 2.13, the amounts of notes and coins needed for payments do not necessarily run parallel with their number. In the case of efficient exact payment, the required amount of currency is lowest and equals the total amount of cash payments. The total number of notes and coins is 25% higher. This finding means that the manner of payment that is optimal from the point of view of the required number of notes and coins is not necessarily optimal from the economic viewpoint based on opportunity costs. A similar conclusion holds in the case of a change in the banknote range. The simulation results in Table 2.15, which are based on the assumption of an efficient payment pattern, show that a reduction in the number of notes needed for cash payments is not necessarily attended by a decline in their total value. At least theoretically, the introduction of the denominations of Fl. 50 and Fl. 250 in 1984 and 1986 permitted reductions in the number of notes by 6% and 1%, respectively. Only in the case of the Fl. 50 denomination, has this been attended by a reduction in the value of the banknote circulation, of 2.6%. In the case of the Fl. 250 denomination, the value increased slightly, by 1.5%. These results indicate that, contrary to Chen's (1976) assumption, the demand for currency does not necessarily decline with a more efficient denominational mix. Furthermore, the present banknote range appears to meet the payment needs of households rather effectively. Only a changeover from the 5-10-25 range to a more normal 5-10-20 range would yield some material advantages. The 1.4% reduction in the number of notes is for the greater part undone by an increase in the number of coins. Alternatives tested for the remainder involve an equal or higher demand for notes.

In our analysis, the frequency distribution of cash payments was assumed to be independent of the available set of banknotes and coins. It is reasonable to assume, however, that this is not entirely true and that the observed distribution is a reflection of the available set of banknotes and coins. If so, the simulation results to some extent underestimate the decrease in the demand for notes resulting from the changes in the banknote range and are consequently somewhat flattened.

2.3.2 Payment patterns in 1990 and expected changes

The standard approach to forecasting changes in the payment pattern is to use relationships, as quantified before, subject to a number of assumptions on the future development of the explanatory variables. This line of approach has to be preferred from a theoretical point of view, but involves uncertainties as regards the development of the determinants and the validity of the model in a strongly different state of the payments system. An alternative, through more qualitative, approach is to eliminate these uncertainties by measuring the expectations directly.

The main aim of this section is to develop and apply a methodology for this line of approach, special attention being paid to the effects of plastic money. After a general description of the survey design, we analyse the observed payment pattern of households in 1990 as well as the expected changes for the future payment pattern.

The survey design

For the measurement of expectations we use a more condensed survey design which is less exhaustive than the budget survey as described in the preceding sections, but which nevertheless enables us to quantify the main patterns and developments. As our interest primarily regards the substitution between various payments media and cash, we focus on those expenses that may involve cash payments. This comes to about 60% of consumer expenditure (Annex III). The remaining 40%, including medical care, gas and electricity, rents, and interest payments and redemptions on mortgages, are predominantly paid by payment by means of transfer, impayment form, standing order or direct debit. According to Mot and Cramer (1990) in terms of value more than 90% of the comparable 'regular' payments of Dutch households in 1987 were paid in this way.

From the 60% of the consumer expenditure considered, we selected twelve representative places of purchase, representing 75% of the consumer outlays potentially paid in cash. The classification inevitably contains some overlapping, especially as far as supermarkets and department stores are involved. Moreover, the category of miscellaneous goods and services accounting for nearly 20% of the expenditure considered is not directly observed, nor does it have a clear equivalent within the observed classes. The clear advantage of the approach is, however, that 75% of the over-the-counter purchases of households are captured in a rather condensed and accessible way.

Payment pattern in 1990

First, the respondents were asked for the present frequency of their expenses at the twelve distinguished spending places, as well as for the average amount paid and for the mode of payment mostly used. On average about 14% and 6% of the respondents does not know or does not mention the payment frequency and the average amount paid, respectively. These percentages are fairly alike for all the spending places considered. Besides, on average 13% of the respondents did or could not mention the way they pay, with outliers for the supermarket (23%), the bakery, butcher's shop and the clothes shop (20% each). These percentages were somewhat lower for the expected behaviour in the future. As in the case of the answers on the cash management behaviour, we adjusted for this non-response by imputing the missing values for the individual questions by taking the most relevant average of the other respondents. The resulting total payments come to nearly Fl. 120 million, which is about 75% of the total expenditure potentially payable in cash in 1990 and 45% of total household expenditure 14). Nearly 65% of the amount of Fl. 120 billion is paid for in cash and about 30% by means of guaranteed checks. The remaining 7% is paid by credit cards, POS transactions and other means of payment, mainly transfer payments.

According to Table 2.16 the purchases at supermarkets are by far the most important, followed by purchases at clothes shops, gas stations and furniture shops. The share of nearly 45% of the supermarkets is considerably higher than the share of 25% which we estimated from the budget survey of the Central Bureau of Statistics (CBS). This indicates some overestimation, which may be due to the way we corrected for the relatively high non-response for this sector. If we apply a downward adjustment to the share of the payments at supermarkets, the shares of the other spending places are much more like those that follow from the CBS budget survey. The share of payments paid in cash in supermarkets of 72.5% agrees remarkably well with the percentage of 71 reported by Zillinger Molenaar (1986) for 1985 on the basis of the AGB-Intomart expenditure survey, also used in section 3.1 of this chapter. Likewise,

14) Total expenditure of Fl. 259.4 billion is computed from the total of Fl. 229.0 billion which follows from the CBS budget survey 1987 (Annex III), assuming for 1987-1990 a growth rate of 13.3% of total private consumption, as reported in the CBS National Accounts.

Table 2.16 Payment by place of spending 1990

Spending place	Share of means of payment					Total amount		Share according CBS-survey
	cash	check	point of sale	credit card	other	billion guilders	share (%)	
Supermarket	72.5	25.2	0.0	1.6	0.7	53.4	44.8	25.3
Bakery	97.6	0.8	0.0	0.5	1.1	4.4	3.7	3.1
Butcher's shop	92.0	6.6	0.0	0.5	1.0	9.1	7.6	8.5
Licensed victualler	71.4	26.5	0.4	0.4	0.9	2.2	1.8	5.5
Department store	57.2	37.2	4.3	0.8	0.6	5.7	4.8	6.4
Clothes shop	35.6	60.2	2.6	1.1	0.6	11.2	9.4	19.7
Gas station	44.5	21.9	12.7	19.2	1.6	14.8	12.4	8.3
Furniture shop	30.2	64.2	2.5	0.6	2.6	8.1	6.8	8.2
Restaurant	43.3	47.3	8.2	0.9	0.4	5.3	4.5	7.7
Pub	95.9	1.4	0.0	0.5	2.3	2.2	1.8	2.7
Cinema	82.6	14.6	0.8	0.4	1.7	0.8	0.7	1.3
Public transport	76.6	18.6	0.0	1.3	3.5	2.0	1.7	3.3
Total	63.6	29.4	2.6	3.5	1.0	119.2	100	100

Explanatory notes: Shares in % of total amount paid. The shares according to the CBS-budget survey have been estimated from the most recent publication of 1987 (Annex III), by combining the relevant expenditure categories as far as possible.

the composition of the payments in department stores agrees closely, with a share of guaranteed check payments of 37.2% found in this study compared to 35.5% reported by Zillinger Molenaar. The slightly higher figure in this study may be the result of a further substitution of checks for cash since 1985. This probably also explains some of the difference with the share of check payments of 25% reported by Cramer (1987) on the basis of 2,312 payments in a department store in March 1986. As far as these results are concerned, the representativeness of the survey seems quite satisfactory.

Table 2.17 gives the resulting total payments, before and after conversion to the expenditure potentially payable in cash of Fl. 155 billion derived from the CBS-budget survey. By way of sensitivity analysis we apply two alternative adjustments for the missing payments. In both approaches we depart from the average mode of payment of the observed purchases. However, the first alternative is based on the distribution of the payments over the purchase places according to the survey, while the second alternative is based on the distribution as estimated from

Table 2.17 Amount of payments before and after conversion
In billions of guilders

Basis	Mode of payment					Total
	cash	check	point of sale	credit card	other	
AGB survey	75.8	35.0	3.1	4.0	1.3	119.2
Conversion to CBS survey						
- proportional	99.0	45.7	4.0	5.3	1.6	155.6
- with CBS percentages	104.5	40.1	3.2	2.9	4.9	155.6
Actual payments	.	32.1	0.9	3.1	.	.

Explanatory note: The total payments potentially payable in cash of Fl. 155.6 billion have been computed as 60% of the total estimated household expenditure of Fl. 259.4

the CBS budget survey. The resulting amount of cash payments is Fl. 100 and Fl. 105, respectively. These amounts correspond remarkably well with the amount of cash payments of Fl. 100 that has been estimated from the AGB/Intomart survey as reported in section 2.3 of this chapter. The use of checks is, however, too high as compared to the actual turnover of Fl. 32.1 billion, including payments abroad. This may be due either to overreporting of the frequency or average amount paid by check or to confusion of check and transfer payments, which may especially hold for the purchases in furniture and clothes shops. Thus the results are probably biased for some places of purchase. This conclusion also follows from a comparison of the share per place of purchase in the total cash payments according to this study and according to the results of the much more extended AGB/Intomart budget survey in 1987, reported by Cramer (1988). Nevertheless, the results can be a valuable starting point for the analysis of expectations 15). For a closer analysis of the determinants of the mode of payment we have selected five places of purchase, which are quantitatively important, and where most of the modes of payment are used to some extent. We explain the choice between the modes of payment by means of the multinominal logit model

$$P_j = \exp(\beta_j' x)/(1 + \sum_{j=1}^{m-1} \exp(\beta_j' x) \qquad (2.10)$$

15) The argument is similar to simulations of exogenous shocks with macro-econometric models. The simulated effects may still be correct despite of possible deviations of the central path from reality.

Table 2.18 Determinants of mode of payment
Effect on probability x 100

Explanatory variable	Supermarket			$\chi^2(2)$	Department store			$\chi^2(2)$	Clothes shop			$\chi^2(2)$
	cash	check	POS		cash	check	credit card		cash	check	credit card	
Amount (logarithm)	-29.50	29.29	0.21	778.0*	-3.07	2.93	0.13	116.2*	-5.75	5.35	0.40	68.8*
	(30.8)	(22.4)	(0.9)		(10.6)	(10.4)	(1.3)		(8.0)	(7.4)	(2.6)	
Age	0.01	0.00	-0.01	3.6	-0.03	-0.06	0.09	14.2*	-0.11	0.11	-0.00	4.6
	(0.2)	(0.1)	(1.0)		(0.4)	(0.9)	(3.5)		(1.5)	(1.6)	(0.3)	
Sex	-1.53	1.10	0.43	2.0	1.21	0.08	-1.30	4.0	5.43	-5.63	0.20	12.4*
	(1.0)	(0.7)	(1.2)		(0.6)	(0.0)	(2.0)		(2.8)	(2.9)	(0.6)	
Income	-2.33	1.99	0.35	10.6*	-3.37	2.94	0.43	15.0*	-7.52	7.00	0.52	73.6*
	(2.9)	(2.5)	(1.8)		(3.8)	(3.4)	(1.3)		(8.3)	(7.7)	(2.3)	
Education	-1.78	2.05	-0.27	16.0*	-1.80	0.73	1.07	25.4*	-3.19	3.03	0.16	31.4*
	(3.1)	(3.5)	(2.0)		(2.8)	(1.2)	(4.6)		(4.8)	(4.6)	(1.1)	
Occupational status	-6.66	6.56	0.10	15.8*	-10.90	9.35	1.55	35.2*	-10.21	9.35	0.87	32.4*
	(4.1)	(3.9)	(0.3)		(5.8)	(5.1)	(2.3)		(5.4)	(4.9)	(2.0)	
Size of family	-1.18	1.01	0.17	5.2	-1.28	1.35	-0.08	5.2	-1.30	1.37	-0.07	5.2
	(2.2)	(1.8)	(1.3)		(2.0)	(2.2)	(0.3)		(2.0)	(2.1)	(0.5)	
Urbanization	-1.13	0.74	0.39	26.4*	-0.34	-0.22	0.56	15.8*	0.35	-0.63	0.28	12.6*
	(3.2)	(1.9)	(4.7)		(0.8)	(0.5)	(4.0)		(0.8)	(1.4)	(3.4)	
Type of employer	17.37	-17.14	-0.23	25.2*	14.70	-15.07	0.37	16.4*	21.32	-21.10	-0.22	35.8*
	(5.5)	(4.6)	(0.3)		(3.6)	(3.8)	(0.3)		(6.0)	(5.9)	(0.3)	
Number of accounts	0.82	-1.65	0.83	17.0*	-0.53	-0.12	0.65	2.6	-2.47	1.88	0.59	10.4*
	(0.9)	(1.4)	(3.8)		(0.4)	(0.1)	(1.6)		(1.9)	(1.4)	(2.7)	
Use of ATMs	1.63	-3.01	1.38	20.2*	3.40	-3.03	-0.37	4.0-	2.76	2.60	0.16	3.8
	(1.1)	(1.8)	(3.9)		(1.8)	(1.7)	(0.6)		(1.4)	(1.4)	(0.4)	
Number of observations	3,518	1,148	59		2,594	1,192	115		1,697	2,503	47	
Maximum loglikelihood	-2,414				-2,723				-2,874			

Explanatory notes: The t-values within parentheses have been derived from the original t-values of the logit estimates using the covariance matrix concerned (see Cramer, 1991); the value χ^2-test variable is computed as -2 times the increase of the loglikelihood by including the relevant variable in the specification. $\chi^2(\alpha=0.05, n=2) = 5.99$; $\chi^2(\alpha=0.05, n=3) = 7.81$. The symbol * denotes statistical significance of the regressor for the whole model.

with P_j the probability of mode of payment j (j = 1, 2...m), x the vector of explanatory variables and β_j the vector of coefficients which differ by mode of payment j (see Madalla (1983) and Cramer (1991) for more details). For the interpretation of the effects of the regressors we use, following Cramer (1991), the derivatives computing P from the sample frequencies. As a matter of fact, for each explanatory variable

Table 2.18 Determinants of mode of payment (continued)
Effect on probability x 100

Explanatory variable	Gas station cash	check	credit card	POS	$\chi^2(3)$	Furniture shop cash	check	credit card	other wise	$\chi^2(3)$
Amount (logarithm)	-9.49	5.84	1.85	1.81	99.8*	-0.42	0.28	0.06	0.07	0.8
	(8.5)	(6.7)	(3.8)	(2.5)		(0.7)	(0.5)	(0.4)	(0.5)	
Age	0.12	0.30	-0.11	-0.31	43.4*	-0.19	0.16	0.01	0.02	5.2
	(1.4)	(4.3)	(2.5)	(5.0)		(2.2)	(1.9)	(0.5)	(0.8)	
Sex	-1.20	-1.86	3.19	-0.13	11.2*	2.82	-2.45	-0.36	-0.01	1.6
	(0.6)	(1.0)	(3.0)	(0.1)		(1.2)	(1.1)	(0.7)	(0.0)	
Income	-6.37	2.13	2.59	1.65	46.2*	-5.33	4.68	0.36	0.30	25.8*
	(6.0)	(2.4)	(4.5)	(2.2)		(4.9)	(4.3)	(1.4)	(1.0)	
Education	-1.34	0.51	0.15	0.68	3.6	-2.92	2.87	0.01	0.05	14.0*
	(1.8)	(0.8)	(0.4)	(1.3)		(3.7)	(3.7)	(0.1)	(0.2)	
Occupational status	-6.49	-0.40	3.53	3.37	16.6*	-6.34	5.52	0.06	0.76	8.0*
	(2.9)	(0.2)	(2.9)	(2.1)		(2.6)	(2.3)	(0.1)	(1.1)	
Size of family	-1.96	1.52	0.24	0.19	9.0*	-0.21	1.09	-0.41	-0.47	8.6*
	(2.6)	(2.3)	(0.6)	(0.4)		(0.3)	(1.3)	(1.9)	(1.9)	
Urbanization	-0.82	0.23	-0.66	1.25	27.0*	0.03	0.53	-0.04	-0.52	10.4*
	(1.6)	(0.5)	(2.4)	(3.5)		(0.1)	(0.9)	(0.3)	(3.1)	
Type of employer	19.67	-12.14	3.65	-11.17	41.2*	15.55	-14.53	0.55	-1.57	15.4*
	(3.9)	(3.2)	(2.1)	(2.8)		(3.6)	(3.0)	(0.7)	(1.1)	
Number of accounts	-0.85	-0.17	0.35	0.67	1.6	0.69	-2.04	0.75	0.61	8.8*
	(0.6)	(0.1)	(0.5)	(0.7)		(0.5)	(1.4)	(2.5)	(1.6)	
Use of ATMs	-3.36	-7.44	1.45	9.36	56.4*	-0.72	0.97	0.90	-1.14	5.8
	(1.6)	(3.7)	(1.4)	(6.9)		(0.3)	(0.4)	(1.8)	(1.5)	
Number of observations	1,675	879	251	492		920	1,602	35	49	
Maximum loglikelihood	-3,635					-2,001				

Explanatory notes: The t-values within parentheses have been derived from the original t-values of the logit estimates using the covariance matrix concerned (see Cramer, 1991); the value χ^2-test variable is computed as -2 times the increase of the loglikelihood by including the relevant variable in the specification. $\chi^2(\alpha=0.05, n=2) = 5.99$; $\chi^2(\alpha=0.05, n=3) = 7.81$. The symbol * denotes statistical significance of the regressor for the whole model.

$$\delta P_j/\delta x_i = P_j\{\beta_{ji} - \sum_{k=1}^{m} \beta_{ki} P_k\} \qquad (2.11)$$

the derivatives sum to zero over the considered modes of payment. The resulting derivatives, which have been multiplied by 100, indicate the change of probabilities in percentage points upon a change of the explanatory variables by one unit.

Table 2.18 summarizes the estimation results for the samples of the respondents who reported the mode of payment as well as the average frequency of purchases and the average amount spent. Basically we used the same personal characteristics as in the analysis of the cash management behaviour in section 3.2 of this chapter. With respect to the interpretation of the t-values it should be noted that in a multinominal logit model a regressor may be significant for the model as a whole, even though its separate effects on each probability are not. The statistical significance of each regressor for the model as whole was formally tested by means of the likelihood ratio test. If λ is the ratio between the restricted ($\beta_{ij}=0$, j = 1,...,m) and the unrestricted maximum of the likelihood function, then $-2\ln\lambda$ has, in large samples, χ^2-distribution with m-1 degrees of freedom. The relevant test values are mentioned in Table 2.18 for all five places of purchase considered. As in the analysis of the cash management we preferred the logarithm of the amount because of significantly better estimation results. The results confirm the findings of section 2.3.2 and of the studies of Trundle and Temperton (1982) and Mot and Cramer (1990), that the size of the transaction is the dominating determinant of the mode of payment. The larger the amount, the lower the probability that it is paid in cash. The size of this effect differs strongly by place of purchase, being by far the largest for supermarkets, where the probability of payment in cash decreases by 2.9 percentage points, if the amount increases by 10% 16). This result corresponds rather well with the effect of 2 percentage points which Mot and Cramer report for all daily purchases. The most important substitute is as yet the check. Only at gas stations, there is also a clear shift towards credit card and POS payments for the larger amounts.

A number of personal characteristics have a remarkably unequivocal effect on the payment pattern. At all spending places people with higher income and a better education pay less in cash and more with checks and credit cards. Also those who have a job or a large family pay relatively less in cash. On the other hand, self-employed people are clearly more

16) Contrary to the other effects reported, the effect of the (logarithm of the) amount paid is a quasi elasticity.

inclined to pay in cash. The - not always statistically significant - influence of age and sex and the family size is ambiguous for the various spending places, which corresponds to the findings of Mot and Cramer, who did not find a clear effect of these variables either. People who use ATMs pay relatively more with cash in supermarkets and department stores. For the other three places of purchase the effect is, however, the reverse. This may be due partly to the high correlation between the use of ATMs, on the one hand, and the use of checks and POS terminals, on the other. Furthermore, the results show that the POS terminals, which are as yet installed mainly in supermarkets and gas stations, are especially used by younger people, also using ATMs, with relatively many salary accounts, in areas with a high degree of urbanization, which clearly is a proxy of the availability of these machines.

Expectations about future payments patterns

As for their present payment behaviour, the respondents were asked for their behaviour in a future situation, where plastic money is widely available. To keep the questions within reasonable limits, the categories credit card payments and other payments (mainly debits) were combined for this purpose. According to the results in Table 2.19, based on the expectations of the respondents on their future payment behaviour, the wide availability of plastic money will reduce the demand for cash over 30%. This figure is considerably higher than the 15% to 20% lower cash holdings which result from the expected changes in the cash management behaviour. The substitution effects are the largest at those places of purchase where the availability of POS terminals is the most probable and relevant, because of the frequency of purchases or the amounts paid. Thus, the decrease in the use of cash is the largest in department stores (-52%), furniture shops (-48%), gas stations (-35%) and supermarkets (-34%). The results confirm that electronic payments are probably a closer substitute for check payments than for cash payments. Check payments are expected to drop overall by nearly 50%. The drop of the category other payments, including debits and credit card payments is even larger. The quantitative importance of these modes of payment is, however, rather low with respect to the over-the-counter payments.

Table 2.19 Expected manner of payment by place of spending in the future

Spending place	Share of means of payment				Change of amount paid (%)			
	cash	check	point of sale	other, credit card	cash	check	point of sale	other, credit card
Supermarket	47.6	12.9	39.4	0.1	-34	-49	2,408	-89
Bakery	88.5	0.9	10.5	0.1	-9	8	1,991	-94
Butcher's shop	80.5	4.2	15.1	0.2	-12	-37	3,244	-84
Licensed victualler	53.3	13.4	32.8	0.5	-26	-50	8,858	-57
Department store	27.6	24.7	46.6	1.1	-52	-34	6,550	-77
Clothes shop	20.3	33.7	45.1	0.9	-43	-44	4,661	-73
Gas station	28.8	13.4	55.3	2.5	-35	-39	1,873	-83
Furniture shop	15.7	32.4	46.6	5.2	-48	-49	8,123	3
Restaurant	35.1	26.0	37.4	1.4	-19	-45	4,054	-83
Pub	87.9	0.6	11.2	0.3	-8	-57	2,144	-86
Cinema	61.9	7.6	30.0	0.5	-25	-48	8,333	-81
Public transport	51.0	7.4	37.3	4.3	-33	-60	2,842	24
Total	44.0	15.9	39.0	1.0	-31	-46	1,054	-72

Explanatory note: Shares in %. The changes in the shares have been computed by comparing the expected composition of payments in the future with the composition in 1990 (see Table 2.16) on the basis of the total amount paid in 1990.

2.4 Conclusions

The results of this chapter show that the micro-economic analysis of survey data provides valuable additional information on the demand for and the use of money as compared to the macro-economic approach. The analysis of the withdrawing patterns and cash holdings confirm the economies of scale in money holdings and also suggest the presence of uncertainty. On the other hand, the cash management behaviour is far from optimal, unless the risk of loss or theft of currency is considered very high. However, the analysis shows that the use of ATMs clearly leads to more efficient cash management, by lowering the average amount withdrawn and increasing the frequency. The results also confirm earlier findings that slightly more than 10% of the currency circulation is needed to pay for the transactions of households (Fl. 100 billion in 1990, with a turnover rate of between 30 and 40 times per year). The rest is used by firms but probably mainly as a store of value (see also next chapter).

Cash payments still account for nearly 80% of total payments of households in terms of numbers and for 40% in terms of value. The latter figure is in fair agreement with the findings for the United States and the United Kingdom, in spite of the considerable differences between the payment systems. The - apparently lognormal - frequency distributions of the payments that follow from the budget survey enable us to compute the need for currency. Especially the need for coin is very sensitive to the way people pay with cash. Inefficient payment can easily cause a 40% higher demand. On average, banknotes change hands at least 10 to 15 times a year, the low figures for the higher denominations indicating a high degree of hoarding of these denominations. Moreover, from simulations it appears that the total amount of currency is not invariant in respect to the denominational mix, and that, contrary to what Chen (1976) has argued, a more efficient mix does not necessarily mean a lower demand for currency.

With respect to the explanation of choice by individuals of the mode of payment of daily purchases, the effects found by us are comparable with those of Mot and Cramer (1990) who analysed separate payments in 1987. The payment pattern appears to be primarily dependent on the amount paid, and moreover on a number of personal characteristics of the payor, such as education and employment. The underlying approach, however, also considers credit card and POS payments, which have become of some importance since 1987. Moreover the analysis by respondent enabled us to measure the impact of the use of ATMs on the payment pattern. Although statistically significant, its effect is not the same for all places of purchase.

Finally, we have applied a methodology to measure substitutions between payments media by asking respondents directly for their cash management and payment behaviour in a world of widely available plastic money. The results suggest indeed a considerable increase of the use of POS-payments. The main losers are the checks, showing an expected decrease of nearly 50%. The decrease of the use of cash lies between 20% and 30%, depending on wether the expected changes in the cash management or the payment pattern are representative. This concerns, however, only transactions balances. The effect of plastic money on the total currency, including the currency kept in hoards may be considerably lower.

3 THE HOARDING OF CURRENCY IN THE NETHERLANDS

3.1 Introduction

As appears from Chapter 2, the size of the currency circulation, amounting to more than Fl. 2,500 *per capita* in the Netherlands, cannot be explained from the need for transactions only. Moreover, the astonishingly large *per capita* demand for currency and especially larger banknotes is a well-nigh worldwide phenomenon, which has frequently been discussed in the literature (*cf.* Keynes, 1930, Tinbergen, 1939; Cagan, 1958; Porter and Bayer, 1984). The obvious conclusion is that the remainder functions as a store of value for speculative and precautionary purposes but especially as a means of hoarding. However, the methodology of simply ascribing the unexplained part of an economic variable to a plausible, though statistically unobserved, phenomenon involves clear risks. If other factors or structural developments also play a role, then the estimates may be biased. Thus, more direct evidence is required.

In this chapter we will theoretically and empirically underpin the hypothesis that hoarding is a substantial component of the demand for currency, using the Netherlands as a case study. The next section goes into the question whether the phenomenon of hoarding fits into any theoretical framework. Section 3 deals with the macro-economic empirical evidence on its size and development in the Netherlands, paying explicit attention to the methodology of measurement of hoarding on a macro-economic level. Section 4 deals with the empirical evidence on a sectoral level, as well as the methodology of measurement. Like section 2, this section strongly relies on Boeschoten and Fase (1991). After some observations on the empirical implications for the currency demand function in section 5, section 6 draws some general conclusions.

3.2 Hoarding in an economic-theoretical setting

As appears from Chapter 1, the demand for cash is mostly explained from the transactions motive only. However, the transactions model generally underpredicts actual cash balances, as was shown, for instance, by Sprenkle (1969) and Akerlof and Milbourne (1978) for the United States. The findings in the preceding chapter confirm the inadequacy of the transactions motive as the sole explanatory factor of cash holdings for the Netherlands.

Many authors consider the large currency circulation and especially its growth relative to the outstanding demand deposits, in spite of widespread use of currency substitutes like credit cards and checks, as an indication of a growing underground economy (Cagan, 1958; Gutmann, 1977; Feige, 1979; and Tanzi, 1982). Because currency transactions are less easily traced than transactions carried out by check, currency has a decided advantage over checks for those who wish to avoid taxes. The higher probability of detection lowers the expected yields of alternative means of payment, thus causing, according to the cash inventory approach, a higher demand for currency. The results in section 4 of this chapter indeed indicate that a considerable share of the holdings of the Fl. 1,000 note is located in illegal sectors like the drug trade and in sectors where tax evasion is most likely to occur. The cash transactions in the underground economy alone cannot, however, explain the high currency figure. Even if the underground economy would amount to 10% of GNP, and all relevant (current) transactions totalling about Fl. 160 billion in 1990 were paid in cash, at a turnover rate of cash of 20 times per year, a currency circulation of Fl. 8 billion would suffice. If all underground transactions were paid with Fl. 1,000 bills - which is not the case - they would require about 50% of the Fl. 1,000 notes outstanding, while according to the findings in the preceding chapter there is an excess of about 85%. As the turnover rate of pure transactions cash balances may even be higher than 20 and black market transactions are paid partly by check (Feige, 1979), the need for cash to finance the underground economy is, however, much lower. Therefore, as has also been concluded by Kimball (1981) and Porter and Bayer (1984) for the United States, the use of cash for transactions in the underground economy can at most explain part of the high *per capita* currency circulation in the Netherlands.

A second, and probably more important explanation for the high currency figures is hoarding. Akerlof and Milbourne (1978) point to the hoarding of currency as a major complication in explaining the size of cash holdings. Moreover, several studies (*cf.* Anderson, 1977; Kimball 1981; Whitehead 1982) provide, mainly on the basis of banknote figures, evidence for considerable currency hoarding in the United States. Also, for the Netherlands, there is already ample empirical evidence for this hypothesis (Cramer and Reekers, 1972; Fase, 1984; Boeschoten and Fase, 1989, 1991).

The question arises why households would hoard such large amounts in the form of currency with the nominal interest rate as opportunity costs and with the risk of loss, theft or destruction. The answer seems to be the unique combination of liquidity, security and privacy of this financial asset (Kimball, 1981). The lack of one or more of these qualities may cause lower yields of alternative assets and, according to the inventory model, result in higher currency holdings. Currency is extremely liquid in the sense that it can be used and changed directly and in any amount without loss of value. Thus, besides being an outstanding means of payment for transactions, it can be an attractive liquid resource to deal with unforeseen contingencies as well as with large disbursements as far as the gains in transfer costs exceed the opportunity costs. The liquidity of currency is connected with its security. Insofar as the risk perception regarding the loss of value of other assets, be it financial or real, exceeds their yields, individuals may prefer to hold wealth in the form of currency. The well-known rise of currency holdings in wartime illustrates this security aspect. The third, and in combination with the two other features perhaps most important, quality of currency as a means of hoarding is the privacy it provides. The lack of bank statements and records allows holders of currency to conceal the existence of such hoards. As pointed out by Anderson (1977), the desire for privacy can be based on solely legitimate motives. Some may simply not want anyone to know how much they have in savings. Others may be shy and feel uncomfortable in the white-collar atmosphere of banks or may dislike the prying that is involved in opening a deposit account. Still others may be classical misers.

Holding wealth in the form of currency in order to conceal accumulated earnings or wealth for tax authorities can, however, be purely economically motivated. Reportedly, the large tax evader or drug dealer frequently accumulates sizable amounts of currency in the larger denominations. These cash balances may be maintained, despite high interest rates, to avoid arousing suspicion when converting this currency into other assets. When it becomes profitable to do so, the holder may purchase a legitimate business or launder the illegal gains.

If we assume a constant expected pre-tax interest rate r_i on the alternative asset i (as opposed to currency), then the expected value of gross earnings W_o after t years in case of tax evasion and holding the total amount unreported (superscript ur) in asset i, follows from

$$W_{ti}^{ur} = (1 + r_i - p_i.\beta)^t . W_o \tag{3.1}$$

where p_i is the probability of detection in the case of holding W_o in the form of asset i, and β is the fraction of the amount outstanding that has to be paid to the tax authorities in the case of detection. From (3.1) it appears that keeping unreported or illegal income in the form of an interest-bearing asset i instead of in a cash hoard is worthwhile if and only if the expected value when kept in asset i, W_{ti}^{ur}, is greater than the value when kept in currency hoards, thus if

$$(1 + r_i - p_i.\beta)^t W_o > (1 - p_c.\beta)^t W_o , \tag{3.2}$$

which condition comes to

$$(1 + r_i - p_i.\beta) - (1 - p_c.\beta) = r_i - (p_i - p_c).\beta > 0 , \tag{3.3}$$

with subscript c indicating currency. Generally speaking the probability of detection for interest-bearing financial assets is considerably higher than for currency. Therefore, in particular for illegally acquired income, where β may be even higher than 1, the interest earnings do not outweigh the losses expected due to the higher probability of detection. But also for legally acquired income (with a lower value of

β), the high value of p_i - especially in the case of automatic reporting by banks on interest payments, as was introduced in the Netherlands in 1988 - makes it economically preferable to keep it unreported in currency hoards. Thus, moral feelings apart, currency generally has to be preferred to interest-bearing assets, when it comes to holding unreported earnings. The presence of risk aversion might even strengthen this argument.

Illegally acquired or black income, as described earlier, is by definition unreported. With regard to legally acquired income individuals can, however, weigh tax evasion in combination with keeping earnings in a cash hoard against reporting the income and holding it in the form of interest-bearing assets. In case of reporting (superscript r) and holding the gross earnings, W_o, in the form of financial asset i at a constant expected marginal income tax rate τ, the resulting value after t years follows from

$$W^r_{ti} = (1 + (1 - \tau).r_i)^t.(1 - \tau).W_o \tag{3.4}$$

Whenever the resultant of not reporting on income and keeping it in currency hoards, W^{ur}_{tc}, exceeds W^r_{ti}, it is preferable to keep W_o unreported. We assume for the sake of simplicity a probability of detection of zero for cash hoards ($p_c = 0$). The break-even time horizon t_o (in years), from where it is preferable to report income and to hold W_o in the form of an interest-bearing asset i, then follows from the identity $W^r_{ti} = W_o$. Given (3.4) this comes to

$$t_o = -\ln(1-\tau)/\ln(1+(1-\tau)r_i) \tag{3.5}$$

The time horizon indicates the attractiveness of keeping earnings concealed and hoarding them in the form of currency. According to (3.5) tax evasion combined with hoarding is the more attractive, as the tax rate is higher and the interest rate is lower. This is illustrated by the break-even points, as computed in Table 3.1. The lower the interest rate, the lower the interest earnings forgone by keeping the gross earnings unreported in currency hoards, and the longer the decision

Table 3.1 Break-even time horizons for hoarding (in years)

Tax bracket	Interest rate						
	2%	4%	6%	8%	10%	12%	14%
20%	14.1	7.1	4.8	3.6	2.9	2.4	2.1
30%	25.7	12.9	8.7	6.5	5.3	4.4	3.8
40%	42.8	21.5	14.4	10.9	8.8	7.3	6.3
50%	69.7	35.0	23.4	17.7	14.2	11.9	10.2
60%	115.0	57.7	38.6	29.1	23.4	19.5	16.8
70%	201.3	100.9	67.5	50.8	40.7	34.0	29.3

Explanatory note: The figures, computed with formula (3.5), give the time horizon in years within which it is economically more lucrative to keep earnings concealed in hoards instead of receiving interest payments but paying tax.

period must be to make it attractive to report on the earnings and keep them subsequently as interest-bearing assets. Likewise, the higher the tax rate, the longer the planning horizon must be to make it uneconomic to keep the earnings unreported in currency hoards. For instance, at a 6% interest rate, an individual in the 40% tax bracket would be as well off only after about 15 years by paying his income tax and earning 5% before tax on the remaining income.

This illustrates that at least in the case of tax evasion there can be strong incentives for hoarding currency, especially for shorter periods. Besides the evasion of income tax there can, however, especially for older people, be other economic motives to hoard currency such as evading death duties or, at least in the Netherlands, bypassing the regulation that individuals with a wealth of more than Fl. 8,000 have to pay themselves rather than the social security system for their stay in homes for the elderly. We may conclude that, in spite of the non-interest-bearing character of currency, it can still be worthwhile from an economic point of view to keep large amounts of currency in hoards.

3.3 Estimation of hoarding

For the estimation of the amount of hoarding we concentrate on the banknote circulation, which accounts for nearly 95% of the total amount of currency in circulation. According to the findings of Goldin (1985) for Israel and the recent experiences with Fl. 5 coins in the Netherlands, coin may be hoarded to an even larger extent than notes. However, in value terms, by far the larger part of idle currency is kept in banknotes. We will apply two methods to estimate the size of these hoards. Besides, we will provide some additional empirical evidence.

3.3.1 Estimation from banknote figures

The size of the share of hoarding in the currency circulation can be estimated on the basis of the life of notes, considering the average life of a note of a given denomination as a proxy for its intensity of use. In this view the often observed longer lives of the higher denominations are the consequence of hoarding. The percentage of notes of a given denomination that is hoarded is computed from the difference between the average life of that denomination and the average lives of the lower denominations, which are used for transactions only. The method bears strong resemblance to the methodology applied by Anderson (1977) and Whitehead (1982) who estimated the percentage of inactive currency on the basis of the number of redeemed notes per denomination.

First, we compute the average life of a denomination, defined as the average period of time between issuing and destroying a note, by means of the following formula 1).

$$AL_{it} = (C_{it} + C_{it-1})/(N_{it} + D_{it}) \qquad (3.6)$$

AL average note life
C number of notes in circulation (end-year figure)
N number of new notes
D number of notes redeemed from circulation
i denomination i
t period (year)

This formula reflects the actual note life correctly in a stable situation. If the circulation of a denomination changes substantially over time or if a new note or a new series is introduced, the computed

1) See De Wolff (1969) for the rationale of this formula, which, albeit in a slightly different form, was also used by Coenen *et al.* (1978) and Den Butter and Coenen (1981).

average life is influenced by these short-run fluctuations and probably distorted. For this reason, as is described below, we have concentrated on the longer-run trend in average life. Figure 3.1 gives the actual development of the average life of the various denominations and its trend for the period 1960-1990 (see Annex IV for the data).

It has been assumed that the lower denominations are used for payments only and are not hoarded. Therefore, the average life of these denominations is considered to be the normal average life. We take into account that the average life of the smaller notes is not constant, neither over time, nor over the value of the denominations by means of relationship (3.7). This relationship may reflect the more careful treatment of the higher-value denominations by the public as well as their often higher quality. Even so, a reduction of the average life of smaller notes over time can be observed, because of their decreasing real value. Failure to take this phenomenon into account would lead to over-estimation of the amount of hoarding. The relationship, chosen as semi-loglinear following Laurent (1974), was estimated by means of pooled regression on the relevant data for 1960-1990 for the denominations up to and including the Fl. 50 note.

$$AL_t = \underset{(7.0)}{0.99} + \underset{(2.5)}{0.12} \ln RD_t \qquad \bar{R}^2 = 0.05 \quad DW = 0.52 \qquad (3.7)$$

AL average note life (in years)
RD real value of denomination

The results, with t-values within parentheses, indicate that a 100%-increase in the real value of a note leads to an increment in its average life of 0.12 years.

Subsequently, we compute the normal average life for the denominations of Fl. 100 and higher by means of (3.7). Figure 3.1 shows, for each denomination, the resulting normal life. The actual life of the higher

Figure 3.1 Average life by denomination, 1960-1989

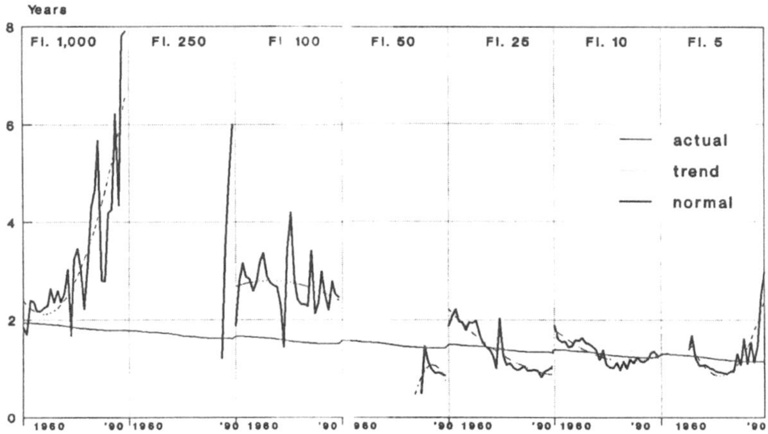

denominations clearly exceeds the normal life, notwithstanding their higher opportunity costs which, according to Cramer (1983a) and Manski and Goldin (1987), lead to higher velocities. In our view, this phenomenon reflects the dominant presence of hoarding. If opportunity costs are of importance, the degree of hoarding might be underestimated on the basis of actual note life figures. The opportunity costs play, however, a role only when the opportunity costs per note are considered as a relevant factor rather than the opportunity costs per unit value. By contrast, the opportunity costs per currency unit held are the same for all denominations.

Finally, the share of the circulation in hoards has been computed from the difference between the actual and the normal computed average life of the highest denominations, after correcting the actual average life for short-run fluctuations by imposing a linear plus quadratic trend. The percentage hoarded of each (large) denomination i follows from:

$$HP_{it} = 100.\ (AL_{it} - NAL_{it})/AL_{it} \tag{3.8}$$

HP percentage of circulation kept in hoards
AL actual average note life corrected for short-run fluctuations
NAL normal average note life

Table 3.2 Estimates of notes in hoards on basis of note life
Amounts in billions of guilders

Year	Fl. 1,000		Fl. 250		Fl. 100		Total	
	amount	%	amount	%	amount	%	amount	%
1955	0.1	9	-	-	0.7	40	0.8	19
1960	0.1	10	-	-	0.9	38	1.0	20
1965	0.1	9	-	-	1.8	40	2.0	25
1970	0.3	15	-	-	2.4	42	2.7	29
1975	1.2	33	-	-	3.7	43	4.9	35
1980	3.2	50	-	-	5.4	43	8.6	40
1985	7.7	64	-	-	5.6	41	13.3	47
1990	11.3	73	3.0	73	4.9	37	19.2	53

Explanatory notes: The estimates for the Fl. 1,000 note in 1955 are partly derived from its return rate (see Table 3.4). The last column relates the hoards of the three highest notes to the total currency circulation outside banks.

Table 3.2 presents the resulting estimates of the amounts hoarded in the Netherlands for the three highest denominations for 1955-1990. According to these estimates, the share of hoarding in the total currency circulation has grown from less than 20% around 1960 to more than 50% in 1990. There is a clear substitution of notes of Fl. 1,000 and Fl. 250 for notes of Fl. 100 as a means of hoarding. While the share of the Fl. 100 notes in hoards increased only slightly in the first half of the observation period and has dropped since 1980, the importance of the Fl. 1,000 note - and since 1986 the Fl. 250 note - has clearly increased, especially since the mid-1970s. This is in agreement with the findings of Fase (1984) on the use of the Fl. 1,000 note.

The estimations based on the lives of notes are beset with a number of uncertainties. Thus, the quality of notes may have changed during the observation period (Den Butter and Coenen, 1982) as well as the withdrawal policy, *i.e.* the standards set by the central bank for redemption of notes. The rather flat development of the life of the lower notes suggests, however, that systematic distortions resulting from these phenomena may be of minor importance quantitatively. The same holds for another possible source of distortion, the loss and destruction of notes. For only one of the banknote series redeemed since 1945 in the

Tabel 3.3 Key data for withdrawals of banknotes since 1945

	Design	First year of issue	Year of expiration of exchange period	Time of circulation (years)	Total number issued (in millions)	Notes not withdrawn as % of total issue: 5 years after expiration	Notes not withdrawn as % of total issue: end of 1987	Notes not withdrawn as % of circulation a)
Fl. 1,000	1945	1946	1960	14.4	1.8	0.23	0.12	0.30
	1956	1958	1978	19.5	9.5	0.16	0.13	0.26
Fl. 100	1945	1945	1950	4.9	17.6	0.14	0.10	0.13
	1947	1949	1961	11.7	26.9	0.16	0.11	0.12
	1953	1954	1978	23.2	258.6	0.15	0.14	0.32
	1970	1972	1986	13.6	384.2	0.35	0.47	0.99
Fl. 50	1945	1946	1960	14.5	9.7	0.23	0.18	0.45
Fl. 25	1945	1945	1953	7.3	39.3	0.16	0.14	0.23
	1947	1949	1956	7.8	36.5	0.12	0.10	0.11
	1949	1952	1961	8.8	47.1	0.17	0.14	0.16
	1955	1956	1978	21.8	408.2	0.16	0.16	0.98
Fl. 20	1945	1946	1961	15.2	25.3	0.13	0.11	0.40
	1955	1956	1961	5.1	13.7	0.11	0.08	0.16
Fl. 10	1945	1945	1950	4.9	70.5	0.28	0.25	0.39
	1945	1947	1957	9.5	75.0	0.19	0.17	0.26
	1949	1952	1957	5.3	50.0	0.19	0.15	0.16
	1943	1954	1978	23.2	612.7	0.23	0.23	2.17

a) In principle, circulation in year before the exchange. However, in the case of the Fl. 20 and Fl. 50 note, which were withdrawn completely, the years 1957 and 1953, respectively, were taken as the years of reference.

Netherlands, the loss rate was more than 1% of the circulation (Table 3.3). Although we corrected for short-term fluctuations due to, for instance, the introduction of new series, the resulting hoarding figures may still contain some irrelevant fluctuations. All in all the method is unduly crude for detecting short-term fluctuations in the amount of hoarding, as ensued from fiscal rumours in 1983 and 1988. Thus, the sharp increase in the number of Fl. 1,000 notes in circulation in response to the announcement in 1987 of the automatic reporting by the banks to the tax authorities of interest payments, which came into operation on 1 January 1988, is only slightly and with some delay reflected in the estimates given in Table 3.2.

By way of overall verification of the results, we also estimated the importance of currency hoarding on the basis of the development of the return rate of banknotes. This is the number of times that a note of a certain denomination returns on average to the central bank each year 2). The underlying thinking is that the return rate of a note of a particular denomination reflects the intensity of its use as a means of payment. If the actual numbers of notes of a particular denomination received turn out to be lower than the return rate which might be expected on the basis of use for payment transactions alone, this can be attributed to hoarding. The further estimation procedure is analogous to that based on the life figures. Again, we need a normal value, this time of the return rate, for the case where no hoarding exists. The number of notes not in active use of denomination i then follows from

$$BN^{na}_{it} = BN_{it} - BR_i / fr_{0t} \tag{3.9}$$

BN_i number of notes of denomination i
BN^{na}_i number of notes not in active use of denomination i
BR_i number of notes returned in year to central bank
fr_0 normal return frequency (BR/BN) in case of absence of hoarding

As can be seen from Figure 3.2, the average return rate does not show a comparable systematic pattern over the denominations as in the case of the lives. At the beginning of the observation period the return rate of the Fl. 1,000 note is nearly twice as high as that of the notes of Fl. 10 and Fl. 25. This may reflect, indeed, the fact that this note was at that time used relatively more intensively, but it may also be due to the high opportunity costs of keeping this note as compared to the handling costs. The high real value was a strong incentive for the banking system to return the note as soon as possible. For the same reason the very low opportunity costs of holding notes of Fl. 5 and Fl. 10 in later years have led to very low return rates of these notes, the opportunity costs of holding them exceeding their handling costs.

2) This statistic, introduced by COTOB (1976), is calculated as the quotient of the number of notes received by the Bank each year and the average number of notes in circulation for the denomination concerned.

Figure 3.2 Average return rate by denomination, 1960-1990

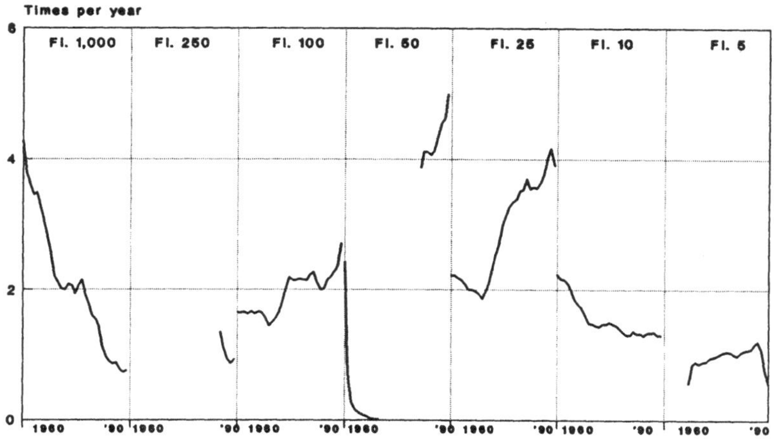

Whereas the return rate of less than once per year of the Fl. 1,000 note probably reflects a high degree of hoarding of this note, the nearly equally low return rates of the Fl. 5 and Fl. 10 notes ensue from the fact that these notes, which are used intensively in the payment system, may continue circulating in this system without regularly returning to the central bank. It is therefore not always possible to take the return rate as a measure of intensity of use. Also changes in the cash management behaviour of the banking sector, such as the economizing on their balances, the introduction of ATMs and the recent introduction of 'counting centres' by a large supermarket chain may considerably affect the return rate. For these and other reasons we were not able to ascertain a stable relationship between the return rate and the real value or the interest rate multiplied by the value, being the opportunity costs of holding the notes.

In the absence of such patterns we put the normal return rate at a constant value of 4 times per year, being the return rate of the Fl. 1,000 and Fl. 25 note at the beginning and the end of the observation period, respectively. Also, according to the estimates presented

Table 3.4 Estimates of notes in hoards on basis of return rate

Year end	Fl. 1,000		Fl. 250		Fl. 100		Total	
	amount	%	amount	%	amount	%	amount	%
1956	0.1	11	-	-	1.0	59	1.1	26
1960	0.1	13	-	-	1.3	59	1.4	28
1965	0.2	18	-	-	2.3	59	2.5	33
1970	0.9	48	-	-	3.5	62	4.3	45
1975	1.7	52	-	-	3.3	45	5.0	36
1980	3.4	60	-	-	5.4	46	8.8	41
1985	8.6	77	-	-	6.8	50	15.4	54
1990	12.5	81	2.9	76	4.2	32	19.6	54

Explanatory note: Total as percentage of currency outside banks.

in Table 3.4, there has been a clear increase in the share of hoarding, especially since 1975. The development is, however, more erratic. The higher level at the beginning of the period is largely the consequence of the choice of the return rate of 4 3). Although the return rate reacts more directly to changes in hoarding, it may give a perverse signal. Even so, the sharp increase in the number of Fl. 1,000 notes in circulation in response to the announcement in 1987 of the automatic reporting by banks to the tax authorities of interest payments, is not reflected in these estimates on the basis of the return rate. This is because this increase was attended by a very substantial additional flight of capital abroad in the form of banknotes. The consequent increase in the return rate is wrongly interpreted by the estimating method used in Table 3.4 as an increase in the intensity of use.

Figure 3.3 shows the development of hoarding according to the note life method and the return rate method and - by way of reference - the estimates that result, if we assume that the hoarding solely concerns the circulation of the Fl. 1,000 note and part of the newly introduced Fl. 250 note. This method denies, however, the hoarding of Fl. 100

3) If we take the return rate for Fl. 25 notes, which are pre-eminently used as a means of payment, as the norm in view of the possible variations of the return rate over time, we arrive at a comparable hoarding percentage of nearly 50 in 1990. However, this method gives implausible negative percentages for the hoarding of Fl. 1,000 notes for the years up to 1970, since Fl. 25 notes had a higher return rate than Fl. 1,000 notes in these years.

Figure 3.3 Hoarding as percentage of currency circulation

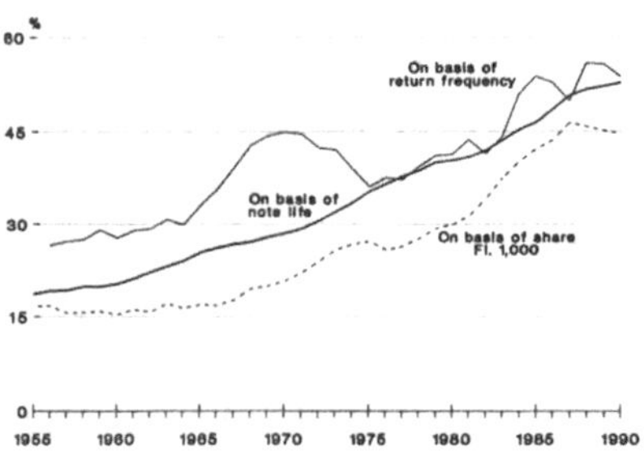

Figure 3.4 Currency including and excluding hoards as percentage of GNP

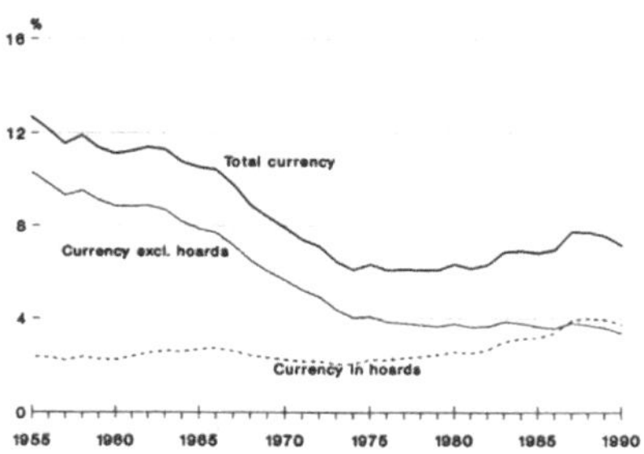

notes and neglects the possible substitution of Fl. 1,000 notes for Fl. 100 notes as means of hoarding in the earlier part of the observation period.

We conclude that estimation on the basis of the life of notes is the most useful method, from the theoretical as well as from the empirical point of view, although the results of the two methods seem to be in fair agreement as far as the considerable increase of hoarding since the mid-seventies is concerned. Most of the distortions which show up by using the return rate, are, however, avoided by using the life as an indicator of the intensity of use of notes. Therefore, we will concentrate on these estimates in the rest of this chapter. They indicate that the fall in the currency ratio during the large-scale introduction of guaranteed checks and salary accounts mainly affected the currency used for payments, the currency in hoards showing only a slight drop in the late sixties and early seventies (Figure 3.4). The estimates also show that the rise in the currency ratio since around 1975 has been due to the increasing importance of hoards, rising from about 2% of national income in the mid-seventies to nearly 4% in 1990. The currency holdings excluding these hoards show an, albeit moderate, further decline, which is in line with the increased importance of check and transfer payments since 1975. According to the estimates more than 2 percentage points of the average annual growth of the currency circulation in this period has been to hoarding.

3.3.2 Empirical evidence from circulation figures

We will add here four short observations which support the earlier hypothesis of a considerable and increasing amount of currency hoarding in the Netherlands. The first is that the circulation of the Fl. 1,000 notes shows a much more moderate seasonal pattern than the total circulation (Figure 3.5). Over the period 1983-1990, on average less than 15% of the summer peaks in the amount of notes in circulation can be ascribed to an increase in the demand for notes of Fl. 1,000. According to its share in the circulation outstanding, this should be more than 40%. This suggests that about 65% of these notes are not directly used for payments. This is probably an underestimate as part of the additional demand for Fl. 1,000 notes in the summer ensues from the fact that the holiday and peak month July is used to carry cash over the border for investment purposes. In December the contribution of the Fl. 1,000 notes to the circulation peaks amounts to nearly 35%. This higher percentage may, however, be more than completely the result of the temporary cashing of deposits for fiscal reasons. A comparable fiscally motivated shift in cash, and especially in the highest denomination, has been also observed and analysed for Switzerland (see Ettlin and Fluri, 1986).

The second observation regards the reflection of two recent fiscal rumours in the banknote circulation, and especially the circulation of the highest notes. Both the so-called Slavenburg affair around 1983, which was attended by a raid on a bank, and the announcement in July 1987 of the introduction of the automatic reporting by banks of interest income to the fiscal authorities by January 1988, caused an increase of the banknote circulation by about 10% in value terms, mainly accounted for by the highest denominations, especially the Fl. 1,000 note. In the absence of any significant dishoarding (which would have resulted in very low or negative 12-month growth rates following to the initial rise in Figure 3.6), both increases have caused a permanent rise in the circulation level.

The third observation regards the development of the circulation of notes of Fl. 100 during the withdrawal from circulation of the 'De

Figure 3.5 Banknote circulation per month (billions of guilders)

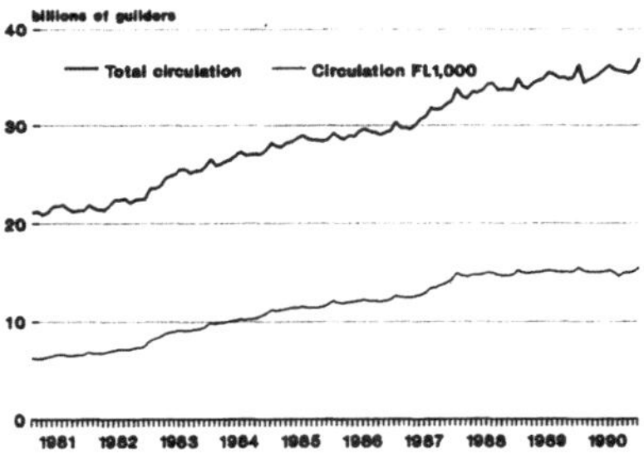

Figure 3.6 Growth of banknote circulation on a 12-month basis

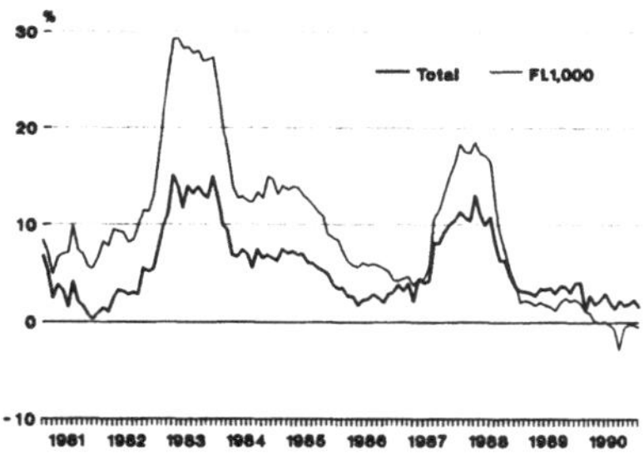

Ruyter' banknote and its replacement by the 'Snip'. The month following the announcement of the exchange on 22 October 1985 saw a marked deceleration of the growth of the number of Fl. 100 notes. In December the deceleration intensified into a decrease of 0.5%, the first since 1981, a tendency which continued in 1986. The marked slowing-down of the growth of the number of Fl. 100 notes during the last two months of 1985 suggests that not all old notes were replaced by new ones. The movements in the circulation figures of the other denominations furthermore do not point towards large-scale substitution of denominations. Apparently, the withdrawal of the 'De Ruyter' note led to dishoarding of banknotes, estimated at 2.2 and 0.7 million notes for November and December, respectively, which comes to an amount of Fl. 290 million. This amount corresponds to over 2% or the Fl. 100 circulation and nearly 1% of the total banknote circulation at that date (Boeschoten, 1986). The distortion of the figures from January onwards by the introduction of the Fl. 250 note only allows a rough guess of the total effect of this phenomenon. However, given the number of notes withdrawn in the following months, the total amount of dishoarding may be estimated at 5% of the circulation of notes of Fl. 100. Comparable autonomous declines can be observed for earlier exchanges since 1945, summarized in Table 3.3.

The fourth observation regards the shift from hoards in Fl. 100 notes to Fl. 250 notes. According to rough estimates on the basis of changes in the circulation shares of the denominations shortly after the introduction of the Fl. 250 note in 1986, about 80% of the circulation of the Fl. 250 note comes from the circulation of Fl. 100 notes. At the end of 1990 the circulation of the Fl. 250 note amounted to more than Fl. 4 billion, of which Fl. 3 billion came from the circulation of Fl. 100 notes. As, according to earlier estimates, at least 75% of the notes of Fl. 250 are kept in hoards, this means that before the introduction of the Fl. 250 note at least 17% of the notes of Fl. 100 were hoarded, but probably much more. This shift in hoards from Fl. 100 notes to Fl. 250 notes is also reflected in the recent increase of the return rate of the Fl. 100 note and in the estimates in Table 3.2.

Thus, all these four observations support the hypothesis that considerable amounts of higher banknotes are hoarded. This holds not only for Fl. 1,000 and Fl. 250 notes, but also for the Fl. 100 note, which is, however, also frequently used as a means of payment.

3.4 Cross-sectional evidence on the Fl. 1,000 note

As appears from our estimates, the upper-range note of Fl. 1,000 is the main means of hoarding, with a clearly growing importance since 1975, which cannot be solely attributed to increased transactions demand, including the effect of inflation (Fase, 1985a). At year-end 1987, the Fl. 1,000 note reached its temporary peak, accounting for almost 45% of the value of banknotes in circulation (Table 3.5). At that time, there were approximately 15 million Fl. 1,000 notes in circulation. This works out at an average of one of these notes per head of the population and over 2.5 notes per household, compared with less than one note per household just ten years earlier. Since 1986 its role has been partly taken over by the Fl. 250 note, at end-1990 accounting for 11% of the amount of banknotes in circulation.

In order to check whether some of the earlier conclusions on the basis of circulation figures are borne out by cross-sectional evidence, a specially designed non-standard survey was carried out in 1986 for the Nederlandsche Bank. The main purpose of this survey, which was designed

Table 3.5 Development in the circulation of Fl. 1,000 notes

Year-end	Circulation		Number of notes *per capita*	Percentage of value of total banknote circulation
	value in billions of guilders	as % of gross national product		
1955	0.7	2.1	0.06	16.9
1960	0.8	1.7	0.07	15.7
1965	1.3	1.8	0.11	16.9
1970	2.0	1.6	0.15	20.5
1975	3.8	1.7	0.28	26.0
1980	6.4	1.9	0.45	29.4
1985	12.1	2.9	0.84	41.4
1986	12.6	3.0	0.87	41.6
1987	14.9	3.5	1.02	44.2
1988	15.2	3.4	1.02	43.7
1989	15.5	3.3	1.04	42.8
1990	15.4	3.0	1.03	41.9

and conducted by the Centre of Marketing Analyses and Social Scientific Research (Centrum), in close cooperation with the Econometric and Special Studies Department of the Nederlandsche Bank, was to provide quantitative micro-based insight into the use of higher denominations by sector. We will deal here with the methodology and results insofar as they are relevant for this study. For more details see Boeschoten and Fase (1988, 1991), on which the following is largely based.

3.4.1 Methodology of the survey

In view of the delicate nature of the enquiries on note holding, the textbook sample approach seemed to be inappropriate to carry out the survey. Apart from a high non-response rate, direct questioning about possession and usage of Fl. 1,000 notes would in all probability have led to a considerable response bias. This hypothesis is illustrated by the fact that, in the 1963 survey of Consumer Finances sponsored by the Federal Reserve, American consumers were not even asked about their cash holdings because it was felt that accurate responses would be very unlikely. As it was, checking accounts and savings accounts, which were surveyed, were underreported by about 50% (Anderson, 1977). Likewise, the National Savings Survey 1960 of the Central Bureau of Statistics among Dutch households could locate only 6% to 7% of the total of currency and demand deposits. Taking into account the holdings of financial institutions and large firms, more than 78% of M1 remained basically unexplained and had to be ascribed to small firms (Nieuwenburg, 1969). Finally, with their survey of money demand in the Netherlands, conducted in 1971 and largely based on a written questionnaire, Cramer and Reekers (1972, 1976) could account for only 22% of the Fl. 1,000 notes in circulation, despite their very thorough survey approach. In view of these experiences a more qualitative survey was preferred, comprising elements of a Delphi approach, extended to sectors usually covered barely by surveys, if at all.

The methodology underlying the survey within the various sectors distinguishes between balances kept for payments, and those which form a store of value. Information on the cash balances is obtained by indirect questioning on the proportion of turnover in a sector paid by cash, pcash; the proportion of cash turnover paid by Fl. 1,000 notes, p1000, and the number of days that notes are kept before they are used for payments or deposited at banks, t. The value of the holdings of Fl. 1,000 notes, denoted by $V1000_i$, for transactions purposes in sector i then equals

$$V1000_i = (pcash_i \,.\, p1000_i \,.\, PT_i \,.\, t_i)/365 \tag{3.10}$$

with PT_i the value of incoming and outgoing transactions per sector, obtained from national accounts. This approach has an advantage in that the respondents are indirectly questioned on the use of cash in general and Fl. 1,000 banknotes in particular within their sector. For the more permanent holdings of Fl. 1,000 notes no such indirect approach was available. The respondents were therefore asked directly about these holdings. However, in certain sectors, like the drug trade, no clear distinction could be made between the two types of cash holdings.

The survey was carried out in three phases. The subsequent results and the number of respondents per sector are summarized in Annex V, which also contains the figures on the turnover and the number of units by sector. In the first phase, after eight exploratory interviews among specialists, 130 brief telephone interviews were conducted in order to obtain rough estimates of the above-mentioned variables. The number of respondents per sector was chosen on the basis of turnover figures and the degree of sector homogeneity. For the drug trade and the gambling sector it was preferred to interview experts in the relevant fields. On the basis of the information thus obtained, along with the data concerning the number of units and the total payment flow per sector, initial estimates were made of the numbers of Fl. 1,000 notes held in each sector. In the second phase, this initial estimate was checked in greater detail by means of 190 telephone interviews, asking the respondents not so much for their own estimates but whether they thought the estimates derived from the initial survey were plausible, or if not, what they should be. This phase, in which a further subdivision was made of the sectors concerned, led to a considerable downward adjustment of the initial estimates. The results and the reported standard deviations show a high degree of heterogeneity, even for the various sub-sectors. Because of the high non-response rate in the household sector in the first phase, in an additional omnibus survey 2,000 households were asked about the use of Fl. 1,000 notes as a means of payment and as a means of hoarding. The results confirmed, however, the findings for the 20 respondents from the first phase. In the third phase the holdings in a number of sectors not considered so far were traced by means of interviewing insiders in the relevant fields. These sectors included foreigners and caravan dwellers as well as car dealers and car-breaking yards. As for some sectors in the first rounds, especially those covering 'grey' or even illegal activities, expert interviews are to be preferred to surveying a great number of respondents. Moreover, the Fl. 1,000 notes kept by the banking sector were estimated from the figures on their till money.

3.4.2 The demand for Fl. 1,000 notes by sector

Using this sampling strategy, it was possible to trace almost 60% of the Fl. 1,000 notes in circulation (Table 3.6). According to the estimates, almost 25% of the Fl. 1,000 notes thus traced are to be found in the

Table 3.6 Estimated distribution of holdings of Fl. 1,000 notes

Sector	Centrum survey 1986 total value (millions of guilders)	Centrum survey 1986 % of notes held	Cramer and Reekers for 1971 % of notes held
1 Agriculture and fisheries	557	4.6	0.9
2 Industry	206	1.7	1.0
3 Construction	242	2.0	1.0
4 Motor trade	811	6.7	0.6
5 Retail trade	339	2.8	1.3
6 Wholesale and distributive trade	145	1.2	0.9
7 Hotel, catering and licensed trade	24	0.2	0.2
8 Real estate	218	1.8	0.1
9 Other services	169	1.4	1.0
10 Households	1,125	9.3	6.8
11 Banks and government	774	6.4	4.9
12 Foreigners	327	2.7	-
13 Caravan dwellers	353	2.9	-
14 Drug trade	1,211	10.1	-
15 Gambling community	448	3.7	-
Sub-total	6,949	57.5	18.7
16 Financial institutions	121	1.0	1.0
17 Transport	169	1.4	1.4
18 Other institutions	24	0.2	0.2
19 Abroad	85	1.0	1.0
Known holdings	7,348	61.1	22.3
Unknown holdings	4,752	38.9	77.7
Total	12,100	100	100

Explanatory note: The percentages for 1986 are expressed in terms of average number of notes in circulation in the first half of 1986. The percentages of Cramer and Reekers (1972) relate to the circulation on 31 March 1971. The percentages for the categories 16 - 18 in the 1986 survey were derived from the estimates of Cramer and Reekers.

drug trade and the partly legal, but mainly 'underground' gambling community. A further 9% of these Fl. 1,000 notes are in the hands of private households. This works out at an average of 0.2 notes per household. Other sectors which stand out are the motor trade (including scrap yards) and caravan dwellers. Not only in absolute terms but also in relation to the estimated amount of cash changing hands, the drug trade and gambling community stand out as regards the use of Fl. 1,000 notes. Then, following at some distance, come the motor trade, other services and agriculture and fisheries. According to the results, there is a clear relationship between the number of Fl. 1,000 notes kept and the degree to which illegal transactions and transactions not declared to the tax authorities are likely to occur. The only clear exception is construction. Although this is traditionally a sector where a high number of illegal transactions and tax evasion take place, our estimates indicate a remarkably low holding of high-denomination notes. The average number of notes per economic unit, incidentally, shows a picture broadly in line with the frequency of use per sector.

Owing to the qualitative nature of the survey method employed, the results are subject to a fairly large degree of uncertainty. The number of respondents per sector is often rather small, the subdivision into sectors is not exhaustive, and in a few sectors there is a certain amount of overlapping. Owing to the latter situation, the estimated proportion of the notes in circulation is perhaps biased upwards. The resulting picture, however, is in a number of respects rather similar to the findings of Cramer and Reekers (1972), which were based on logged counts by financial institutions, major companies and a large part of the retail trade as well as on a survey conducted among more than 1,500 small companies and households. The estimated percentages of notes held by the sectors industry, construction, the wholesale and distributive trade, hotel, catering and licensed trade, other services and banks are of a comparable order of magnitude despite the intervening years (Table 3.6). For the sectors agriculture, the motor trade, real estate and households, however, the estimates produced by the present survey are higher. This is at least partly due to the more indirect qualitative approach. The combined share of the first eleven sectors in Table 3.6, which are covered by both studies, totals 38% in the case of the present survey compared with 19% in the case of the Cramer and Reekers' survey. On top of that, according to the underlying survey, nearly 20% of the Fl. 1,000 notes are held by foreigners working in the Netherlands, caravan dwellers, the drug trade and the gambling community.

3.4.3 Results on the hoarding of the Fl. 1,000 note

The survey produced a number of interesting results with respect to the hypothesis of large-scale hoarding of the Fl. 1,000 note. First, for a number of sectors, together accounting for approximately 40% of the Fl. 1,000 notes in circulation, it was possible to make a very rough distinction between cash holdings for transactions purposes and for hoarding purposes. According to the initial estimates, roughly 70% of the Fl. 1,000 notes in circulation are hoarded. According to the later estimates presented here, the proportion is more like 60%. As noted before, the distinction between means of transaction and means of hoarding is, however, fairly arbitrary. Thus, for a number of sectors including the drug trade and caravan dwellers, it is not possible to draw a precise dividing-line between the two. In these sectors, Fl. 1,000 notes commonly serve the function of means of payment and means of hoarding at one and the same time.

A second intriguing result is that, despite the inclusion of a number of generally unobserved sectors and the use of a survey method which made allowances for the delicate nature of the subject, initially over 40% of the holdings of Fl. 1,000 notes could not be accounted for. Some of the untraced notes are bound to be held in sectors not included in the study. According to the estimates of Cramer and Reekers, for instance, a total of over 2.5% of Fl. 1,000 notes can be traced to the currency holdings of financial institutions (excluding banks), to the transport sector and to social institutions, churches, associations, educational establishments and local authorities. The existence of another 1.0% or so of the Fl. 1,000 notes can be explained by the flow of payments abroad using these notes, which amounted to some Fl. 2 billion in 1985. In addition, it is possible that some Fl. 1,000 notes are held abroad for speculative reasons. Finally, as appears from the loss rates of former series in Table 3.3, loss may account for 0.5% the missing notes. All told, however, only some 5% of the notes in circulation which are still unaccounted for can be explained in this way. Presumably, therefore, the holdings of notes may have been underestimated in a number of sectors. One possible reason for this is that the possession and use of

Fl. 1,000 notes is very unevenly distributed within the sectors, with many holdings of small numbers of notes and a relatively small number of holdings of large or very large numbers of notes. This possibility is confirmed, at least in the case of households, by the results of a supplementary omnibus survey, which we shall discuss later. If there is in fact a skewed distribution of this kind, then the respondents will have underestimated the true average to the extent that their answers reflect the modal value rather than the mean. If we assume, for the sake of simplicity, that the holdings of Fl. 1,000 notes follow a (negative) exponential distribution, which is in defiance of the discrete character of the distribution, but not of the data (generally the mean equals the standard deviation), the actual mean amounts to 1.44 ($= 1/\ln 2$) times the median. Correcting the estimates in this way causes the unexplained proportion of the circulation of Fl. 1,000 notes to diminish by some 12 percentage points, or 30%. If it is assumed that it is not the median but the modus which is reported when holdings are estimated at zero, the correction would be even larger. Moreover, if the skewness of the distribution curve for the holdings of Fl. 1,000 notes differs from one sector to another, this could also distort the figures for the percentages of notes held by the various sectors.

A second important reason for the high proportion of unexplained holdings is presumably the tendency of respondents to understate the numbers and amounts involved as far as the possession and use of Fl. 1,000 notes is concerned. The results of the telephone survey confirm this conjecture. For instance, a number of respondents mentioned the existence of hoarding of Fl. 1,000 notes, but denied their use in transactions, which appears rather inconsistent.

For the household sector an attempt was made to improve the initial estimates by means of a random survey technique, in this case an omnibus survey. Therefore six questions on the familiarity with and the use of banknotes of Fl. 1,000 were included in the omnibus survey, conducted by Centrum in May 1986 among 2,079 persons of 15 year and older. The sample was drawn on a household basis in clusters of three interviews per starting address from 1,000 strata with about the same number of homes. Departing from the randomly chosen starting addresses, the cluster was worked off by means of a random-walk method, with a minimum of at least five homes between two interviews. In case of 'not at home' or refusal after two recalls the household was substituted. The non-response for surveys thus constructed is about 30%. With respect to the questions on the Fl. 1,000 banknote the non-response was less than 1% except for the question on the possession of Fl. 1,000 notes, which 11% of the respondents did not answer. After aggregation according to the composition of the total population with respect to the three categories considered, the final sample was reweighed by means of a number of socio-economic variables, of which the distribution was known from the 1983 AGB Mini-Census. This led to a representative sample of 2,000.

The results of this survey show that the possession and use of Fl. 1,000 notes exhibits a highly skewed distribution. On average, the respondent in the random sample aged 15 and over, came into the possession of one or more Fl. 1,000 notes, either withdrawn from an account or received in some other way, 2.0 times a year and spent one or more of these notes 1.4 times a year. The fact that Fl. 1,000 notes are received more often than they are spent cannot be solely explained by hoarding. If the difference between issues and withdrawals and receipts of Fl. 1,000 notes is attributed exclusively to hoarding, this gives an estimate of at least 7 million for the number of Fl. 1,000 notes held in hoards in 1985, while the actual number of notes in circulation increases by only 1 million. Presumably, people spend more notes in one go than they receive or withdraw. Assuming that an average of two notes is withdrawn or received on each occasion and that they are held for an average of five days, the transactions requirement for Fl. 1,000 notes on the part of households can be estimated at 0.6 million notes, or 5% of the notes in circulation at year-end 1985 4).

4) According to the NIPO survey in 1983, mentioned in Chapter 2, an average of around ten days elapses between two consecutive cash withdrawals. Partly on the basis of this figure, the average retention time of a Fl. 1,000 note has been taken to be five days.

The present estimate of holdings for transactions purposes also agrees closely with the findings of the surveys described in Chapter 2 on the use of Fl. 1,000 notes. For instance, on the basis of results of the 1983 survey, the turnover of Fl. 1,000 notes for that year is estimated at Fl. 10 billion. The necessary holdings of notes for this volume of transactions was estimated at around Fl. 400 million or 5% of the notes then in circulation. A comparable figure can be arrived at from the information concerning cash payments by households in the years 1984-1986, also described in Chapter 2. In value terms, over 15% of the cash payments of households, amounting to Fl. 80 billion, was made up of payments of Fl. 1,000 or more. It is estimated that in paying these amounts 12 million Fl. 1,000 notes were used in 1986. Assuming a turnover rate of 20 for cash transactions balances, a circulation of Fl. 1,000 notes of just over Fl. 600 million, or 5% of the actual circulation at that time, should have been enough to meet the transactions requirements of households.

According to all three studies referred to, the holdings of households for transactions purposes therefore amount to around 5% of the total number of Fl. 1,000 notes in circulation. The closeness of agreement is remarkable. It is even more remarkable when one considers that the three random surveys were quite different in design and approach. Moreover, in two of the three surveys, respondents were not asked direct questions about their own particular use of Fl. 1,000 notes, so that the amount of distortion in the estimates is presumably small. Thus 5% of the actual circulation of Fl. 1,000 notes should presumably be enough to fund the transactions which households pay in Fl. 1,000 notes each year. No estimates are available concerning the volume of business transactions paid for in cash. On the basis of the results of the sectoral survey, however, a figure of Fl. 60 billion may be taken for 1985 as a very rough estimate, of which Fl. 20 million is paid for with Fl. 1,000 notes. At a turnover rate of 20, around 1 million Fl. 1,000 notes would therefore be needed for these transactions. This means that a total of 1.6 million Fl. 1,000 notes, or less than 15% of the notes in circulation, would suffice for the payments made by households and the business community together. On this basis, therefore, the remaining 85% of notes must fulfil a hoarding function.

In view of this, the omnibus survey also contained questions about the hoarding of Fl. 1,000 notes. According to the survey, 1.8% of the respondents held Fl. 1,000 notes as a means of saving. People aged 50 and are more inclined to do so than the younger generation. On average, they have savings of three notes. This information, when applied to the Dutch population as a whole, also gives a figure of around 0.6 million Fl. 1,000 notes, or 5% of the circulation, held by way of savings. On the basis of the omnibus survey results, the total number of Fl. 1,000 notes held by households for transactions and hoarding purposes combined therefore works out at 9.3% of the notes in circulation in 1985. This figure is not significantly different from the 9.2% arrived at in the initial phase of the survey.

The results discussed above, however, suggest that considerably more Fl. 1,000 notes may be kept in hoards by the households than they report in the omnibus survey. Suspicion of financial institutions and the desire for secrecy are important reasons for holding financial assets in this non-interest-bearing form. Thus there are plenty of reasons for assuming that people will tend to quote figures which are on the low side rather than on the high side and that therefore the share of Fl. 1,000 notes in circulation held in hoards by households is in fact very much higher than the 5% reported in the survey.

3.5 Empirical implications for the demand for currency

As the economic motives underlying the holdings of cash balances for transactions purposes differ from those for holding cash hoards, the relevant demand functions may also differ for the two types of balances. This concerns the type of explanatory variables as well as the magnitude of their effects. We test this implication empirically by estimating the currency demand function (3.11), as explained and estimated in Chapter 1 for the total circulation, as well as for its components, using the hoarding estimates from section 3.1 of this chapter.

$$\ln CV_t = a_0 + a_1 \ln CV_{t-1} + a_2 \ln CONS_t + a_3 r_t + a_4 \ln NACC_t/POP_t$$

$$+ a_5\, VCHECK_t/CONS_t + a_6\, TAX + a_7\, dum83 + a_8\, dum87 \quad (3.11)$$

CV	value of average currency circulation
CONS	nominal private consumption
r	long-term interest rate
NACC	number of salary accounts
POP	population of 16 years and older
VCHECK	value of payments by guaranteed payments media
TAX	tax and social security rate
dum83, dum87	dummy variables with respect to fiscal rumours

To avoid the need of fixing the coefficient of the dummy variable dum83 (see Chapter 1), we take the lagged adjustment specification as a starting point. As a very rough approximation of the fiscal attractiveness of hoarding we included the average tax and social security rate. The resulting estimates for the circulation excluding hoards as well as for the currency hoards and the circulation of the Fl. 1,000 notes are given in Table 3.7. As expected, the currency excluding hoarding has a considerably lower consumption elasticity than the currency in hoards. The long-term elasticities of 0.85 for the whole period and of 0.77 - not shown here - for the more recent period 1970-1990 are, however, still higher than the elasticity of 0.5 or less that follows from the basic cash-inventory model. The estimates also confirm that the currency kept as a store of value is sensitive to interest rate changes contrary to the transactions balances which even show a negligible positive effect. None of the interest rate effects is statistically significant. Their size seems, however, plausible, an interest rate increase of one percentage point causing a decline of the hoarded currency balances by at most 1.1%.

The tax and social security rate has a statistically significant effect on the demand for the Fl. 1,000 notes at a 10% significance level, a 1-percentage point increase causing a 1.7% higher demand for Fl. 1,000 notes in the long term. According to the estimation results, the transactions balances and the hoarding balances are equally influenced by the alternative payments media. This result may, however, be due to the way hoarding has been estimated and the impossibility to filter the esti-

Table 3.7 Estimation results for currency demand, 1956-1990

	Total circulation	Total excluding hoards	Currency in hoards		Circulation of Fl. 1,000	
$\ln CV_{-1}$	0.48 (8.5)	0.47 (5.7)	0.49 (10.0)	0.49 (9.7)	0.56 (7.1)	0.60 (6.9)
ln CONS	0.53 (9.5)	0.46 (6.9)	0.77 (11.1)	0.75 (9.7)	0.45 (5.2)	0.39 (3.5)
r	-0.001 (0.4)	0.001 (0.3)	-0.006 (1.4)	-0.006 (1.4)	-0.003 (0.4)	-0.004 (0.5)
ln NACC/POP	-0.15 (6.7)	-0.12 (5.1)	-0.18 (7.2)	-0.18 (7.0)	-0.02 (0.6)	-0.04 (1.0)
CHECK/CONS	-0.54 (2.6)	-0.84 (3.3)	-1.07 (4.4)	-1.09 (4.5)	0.54 (1.1)	0.36 (0.7)
TAX	-	-	-	0.25 (0.7)	-	0.68 (1.0)
dum83	0.09 (4.7)	0.06 (3.0)	0.11 (5.4)	0.11 (5.4)	0.19 (4.2)	0.18 (4.2)
dum87	0.04 (2.8)	-0.01 (1.0)	0.06 (3.7)	0.06 (3.3)	0.05 (1.4)	0.04 (0.9)
constant	-0.32 (1.9)	0.37 (1.7)	-3.37 (10.7)	-3.24 (8.8)	-1.55 (3.9)	-1.23 (2.4)
$\bar{R}^2$	0.9996	0.9993	0.9998	0.9997	0.9991	0.9991
SE	0.015	0.015	0.017	0.017	0.032	0.032
DW	1.70	1.45	1.61	1.70	1.58	1.62
Durbin's h	0.94	1.76	1.19	0.93	1.42	1.31
Long-term elasticities						
ln CONS	1.01	0.85	1.50	1.47	1.04	0.96
r	-0.003	0.002	-0.011	-0.011	-0.008	-0.010
ln NACC/POP	-0.28	-0.23	-0.35	-0.36	-0.05	-0.11
CHECK/CONS	-1.04	-1.57	-2.08	-2.15	1.24	0.90
TAX	-	-	-	0.50	-	1.70

Explanatory notes: t-values within parentheses; the circulation of Fl. 1,000 includes 20% of the circulation of the Fl. 250 note, which was introduced in 1986.

mates adequately for irrelevant short-term movements. This is at least suggested by the estimation results for the circulation of Fl. 1,000 notes which appears to be rather insensitive to changes in the payment system, check payments even showing a positive effect.

Figure 3.7 Currency and its components as percentages of M3

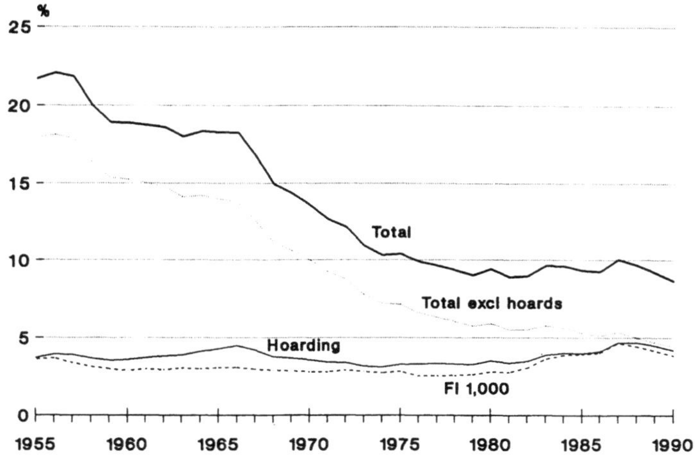

For the time being, the analysis suggests that the main difference between the two types of cash balances is the considerably higher consumption elasticity of the cash hoards. Whereas the transactions balances move in line with nominal income or consumption, with some economies of scale, the hoarded balances have to be considered to a much greater extent as a component of the portfolio of the private sector. In that sense these hoards are probably dependent on the financial wealth of the private sector, rather than on income. This hypothesis is supported by the actual development of the currency component of financial assets since 1955. The total currency declined from about 20% of the total of liquid assets and savings deposits, M3, in 1955 to less than 10% in 1990 as a result of the diminishing importance of the transactions balances. The balances kept in hoards have, however, remained at an approximately constant level of 5% of M3 (Figure 3.7). Apparently people prefer to keep a certain share of their financial wealth in currency, despite of the absence of any interest revenues. Nieuwenburg (1969) comes to a comparable conclusion for Dutch current accounts at commercial banks (as opposed to transfer accounts with the Giro institution) on the basis of cross-section data for households in 1960. He does not find such an effect for currency. This may, however, be due to the minor importance of currency hoarding in those days and the fact that the currency hoards were probably not reported.

3.6 Conclusions

We have shown in this chapter that, within the present-day financial and fiscal constellation in the Netherlands, the hoarding of currency can be meaningful from an economic point of view, especially where illegal or unreported income is concerned. Estimates on the basis of various methods confirm this phenomenon, indicating a considerable and increasing size of currency hoarding of at least 50% of the currency circulation at end-1990. The currency hoards not only contain Fl. 1,000 notes - and since 1986 Fl. 250 notes - but also a considerable number of notes of Fl. 100. Over time, however, there has been a clear shift towards the highest notes resulting in a value share of the Fl.1,000 and Fl. 250 notes of more than 50% at end-1990. Thus, hoarding may account for the main part of the currency that cannot be traced by the micro-economic approaches. The qualitative sample design for the measurement of the demand of Fl. 1,000 notes by sector also points in this direction. Of the 60% of the Fl. 1,000 notes which could be traced, 60% to 70% were not actively used as means of payment. Moreover, the nearly 40% of notes unaccounted for can presumably be ascribed to underestimation of the hoards kept by households in particular.

As yet the money demand analysis does not provide positive evidence of a systematic influence of the tax and social security rate on the hoarding. The average tax and social security rate used in this analysis may, however, be too rough a proxy for the fiscal attractiveness of holding currency. What this analysis does, however, confirm is a relatively high income elasticity of these hoards, which may indicate that this part of the currency holdings functions as a component of the asset portfolio of the private sector and is much more dependent on financial wealth than on national income; a conclusion that also appears from the higher interest rate sensitivity as compared to the transactions balances.

4 DEMAND FOR CURRENCY IN AN INTERNATIONAL PERSPECTIVE

4.1 Introduction

As appears from Chapter 1, in the Netherlands the use of most of the alternative payments media is either of too recent origin or on too limited a scale to enable measurement of its impact on currency demand on a macro level. This conclusion also appears from the scarce currency demand studies for other countries that try to capture the effects of new payments media on a macro level 1). As yet, measurement of their impact on the basis of micro data as was performed in Chapter 2 seems the most promising alternative. An alternative way is to pool the data of countries, and thus to derive from the differences between countries and the developments per country information on the effects on the demand for currency.

The broad terms of reference of this chapter are to identify factors affecting the demand for currency in an international cross-country perspective, special attention being given to the impact of the use of alternative payments media such as credit cards, point-of-sale terminals (EFT/POS or simply POS), as well as cash dispensers and automated teller machines (ATMs). Our main aim here is to identify and to model general worldwide trends, and not to go too deeply into country-specific characteristics. Insofar as possible use has been made of results of country-specific studies performed so far, including the work of Cave and Fase (1980) and Clements (1990).

The analysis includes 15 countries: Austria, Belgium, Canada, Denmark, Finland, France, Italy, (West-)Germany, the Netherlands, Norway, Sweden,

---

1) Thus, Dombrecht (1989) finds an implausibly low income elasticity by including alternative payments media in the currency demand equation for Belgium, while Virén (1989) and Virén and Kokkola (1989) only include credit card transactions in their currency demand function for Finland (see Chapter 1, Table 1.2). Likewise, from the analysis per country by Clements (1990) on the basis of the data of this study, no consistent picture energed, the effects of alternative payments media strongly differing per country.

Switzerland and the United Kingdom, as well as the United States and Japan. In the absence of relevant data, especially regarding to the payment system, for the first 13 countries data on payments media were obtained by means of a questionnaire among central banks. The questionnaire was conceived in February 1990 by the Bank Note Printers Conference (BPC) Study Group mentioned in the Preface, of which the author was a member. The questionnaire asked for data, basically from 1970 onwards, on currency held by the banking system, denominations used in cash dispensers, denominations widely hoarded, the value and number of transactions with ATMs, POS, checks, Eurochecks and credit cards, the country's charging policy, the number of ATMs and POS terminals and manned outlets of the banking system,and the percentage of wage and salary payments in cash. The questionnaire was sent to the 17 member countries in March 1990 by the secretary of the BPC Statistics and Banknote Handling Committee. In August 1990, 14 out of the 17 member countries had returned a completed form; the information returned by Turkey was not compatible with the object of the exercise. Spain, Greece and Ireland were not able to return the questionnaire.

The information was scrutinized and supplemented by the author with figures from publications of the BIS, annual reports and other publications of the central banks, as well as with information provided to the author on request, mainly by the various central banks. Moreover, because of their importance for the underlying analysis the United States and Japan were added, using information from BIS publications and information provided to the author by the Bank of Japan. The resulting data set, which is presented in more detail by Boeschoten (1991), gives a unique quantitative overview of the state and development of the payment systems in the countries in question. As far as the economic factors such as consumption, price level and interest rates are concerned, use has mainly been made of the statistics of the OECD and the IMF. The data on the banknote circulation were derived from the yearly overview of the Bank Note Printers Conference (BPC) and from the annual reports of the central banks.

The general framework of the analysis is illustrated by Figure 4.1 2). The note circulation is the main part of the demand for currency, which stems from the use of cash as a means of payment (transactions motive) and as a store of value (hoarding). The latter may also include speculative balances. In fact there is no clear cut-off point between the transactions and hoarding demand, as the time the holder intends to hold the money is a continuum. The transactions demand is determined by economic, demographic and possibly geographic variables as well as by institutional variables and the state of the payment system. The amount of hoarding may be influenced by the same factors, albeit with a different relative intensity, and in addition by fiscal factors like the level of taxation. The possible existence of a black economy, which is generally assumed to be strongly cash-oriented, affects both the transactions and the hoarding demand.

Figure 4.1 Relationships with respect to currency circulation

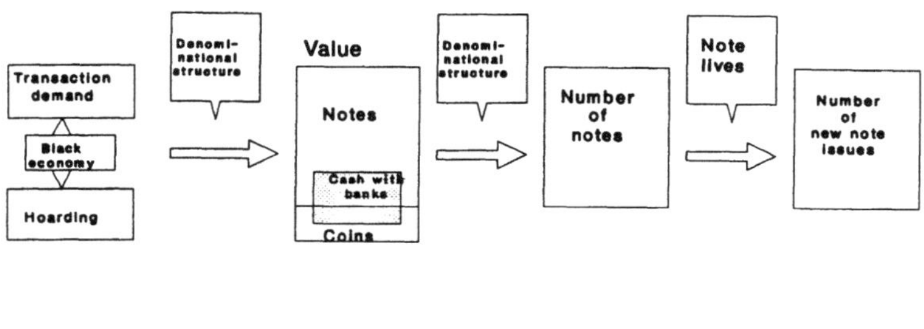

The composition of the currency circulation with respect to notes and coin is influenced by the denominational structure. Banknotes are by far the most important part of the currency circulation, in terms of value, at least. On average the share of coin is less than 6% of the circulation value in the observed countries at end-1989. In terms of number this is the other way round, coin accounting for about 92% of the total number of notes and coins in circulation.

2) For a more detailed scheme of especially the relationship between the number of notes in circulation and the number of new notes issued and their handling by the central bank, see Fase *et al.* (1979).

Within the currency circulation we distinguish demand for currency by the public (currency outside banks) from currency demand by the banks (currency inside banks). Currency outside the banks is the monetarily relevant part of the currency circulation. Currency inside banks consists of banks' till money and vault cash. The cash balances of the banking sector are only known by their total value and not by their composition. Thus neither the coin nor the banknote circulation with the public is known exactly. The size of the cash holdings of the banking system varies strongly by country, ranging from about 5% to more than 30% of the total banknote circulation and averaging 12% at end 1989.

The relationship between the value and the number of notes mainly depends on the denominational structure and the shares of the various denominations. These shares are in turn influenced by economic factors, especially the price level. In the ideal situation the number of banknotes is unaffected by inflation and determined by real economic growth alone. However, the average real value has been far from constant in the observed countries during the last 3 decades. Since 1960 it has dropped on average by some 40%, which means that the number of notes has grown more than economic activity alone.

The two main components of the note requirement are replacement notes and additional notes required for growth. In the short run the replacement notes are the dominant component for most countries, averaging about 95% of the new note requirement in 1980-1989. It can be seen that a change in quality policy could significantly affect note life and therefore the replacement requirement. In the short term this could dwarf all of the growth-related changes. However, in the long run, as growth increases the total circulation, it will, all other things remaining equal, also increase the replacement requirement proportionally.

The following sections will consider the international trends in the demand for currency within this general conceptual framework. The demand for currency outside and inside banks is analysed in sections 2 and 3 respectively, special attention being given to the effect of new developments in payment systems. Section 4 deals explicitly with the demand for banknotes as a means of hoarding and gives estimates of the importance of hoarding and its development in each country. So far we focus on total currency as there is no fundamental difference between notes and coin. Section 5 shows that in value terms the share of the coin circulation is relatively constant and of relatively little quantitative importance. Section 6 analyses the relationship between the value of the banknote circulation and the number of notes. Finally, section 7 gives the main conclusions of our multi-country analysis.

4.2 Demand for currency by the public

This section presents an empirical analysis of the demand for currency by the public, *i.e.* currency outside banks. It explicitly deals with the influence of more recent developments in payment systems. Up to now the

Figure 4.2 Currency in circulation with the public
Percentage of gross national product

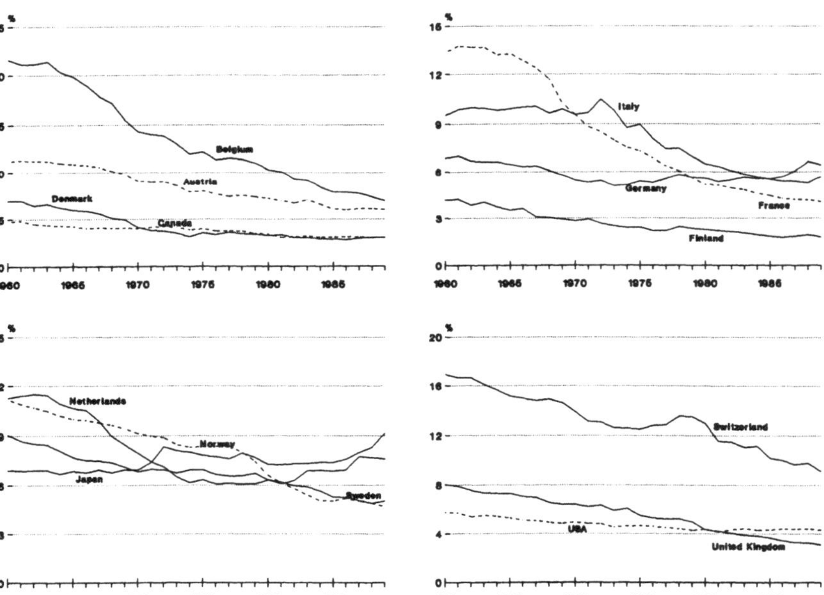

number of empirical studies that measure these effects directly is limited to a few like Dombrecht (1989) on the effect of ATMs and POS terminals in Belgium and Virén (1989) and Kokkola (1990) on the effect of credit cards and of credit cards and ATMs', respectively, on the currency demand in Finland. Other studies take account of these effects only indirectly, either by incorporating a proxy variable such as the number of bank branches (Banca d'Italia, 1988b) or the cumulative interest rate (Hall *et al.*, 1989), or - often because of a lack of relevant data - by means of a dummy (Fase and Van Nieuwkerk, 1976, 1977 and Fase, 1986b) or a trend variable (Ettlin, 1989). The present study was able to draw on a number of recent BIS publications and the data provided by the BPC questionnaire mentioned earlier. We will first briefly deal with the economic and payment system factors and then present the estimates of the effect of these factors on the demand for currency in the 15 countries, as depicted in Figure 4.2.

4.2.1 Economic factors

As in many currency demand studies, we prefer to use *private consumption* as transactions variable, although for the outcomes it makes little difference in the end whether we take consumption or income. Apart from the black economy, the demand for cash nowadays is primarily located with households or with businesses whose the production is strongly connected to consumer expenditure. As stated in Chapter 2, paying cash is not an option for a considerable part of consumer outlays, such as those on energy, housing (rent or mortgages), insurance premiums and other payments, but also for such things as medical care. This 'non-cash' part of consumption may amount to 50%, although the percentage may differ strongly by country. Nevertheless, because of data availability, we still preferred total private consumption as a proxy for the total transactions demand for cash.

The demand for currency may also be influenced by the *interest rate*, which determines the opportunity cost of holding money. According to both the transactions and the precautionary demand model, higher interest rates lead to more efficient transactions behaviour and lower cash holdings. The expected value of the interest elasticity ranges between -0.5 and zero (see Table 2.1 in Chapter 2). The *rate of inflation* reflects the opportunity costs of holding money with respect to the real sector. The higher the rate of inflation the less attractive it is to delay expenditure and hold idle cash balances. Thus, according to Banca d'Italia (1988a), the high inflation rate was one of the main factors behind the declining importance of cash in Italy in the seventies and possibly also in the UK and France. However, the validity of the effect of inflation is not undisputed and depends on the existence of direct substitutability between currency and consumer expenditures.

Apart from the transactions demand of the regular - mainly household - sector, there is a demand for cash resulting from the *irregular, black economy*. Cash is especially attractive in this sector because of its anonymous character. For instance, the average small businessman in Japan is thought to report only 60% to 70% of his true income, thanks to cash transactions which leave no records (Harrop, 1989). Likewise, Banca d'Italia (1988a) mentions the relatively large underground economy in Italy as one of the possible reasons for the still highly cash-oriented character of the Italian payments system. As a crude approximation of the attractiveness of cash for black transactions we use the average taxation rate, *i.e.* total (indirect plus direct) taxation as a percentage of GNP. For the sake of simplicity and lack of data we chose not to use a marginal tax rate, which probably would be a better measure. Clearly, the size of the black economy depends on factors that are specific to individual countries and their institutions, the existence of which may explain why countries with high tax rates may have relatively small black economies, and vice versa. Therefore, instead of the level of the tax rate we used the deviation from the tax rate in the beginning of the sample period, implicitly assuming that the 'normal' tax rate (not leading to black transactions) differs by country.

Besides the variables mentioned above, *other economic* as well as *demographic variables* may play a role, especially where specific national characteristics are concerned. For instance, in countries with a high foreign demand for their currency, like the United States, Germany and Switzerland, the actual or expected exchange rate can be important. Thus Gross (1989) finds an elasticity of banknote demand with respect to the exchange rate of -0.2 in Switzerland. In countries like Germany, the Netherlands and Switzerland, fiscal measures appear to have had a major impact on the demand for currency and especially banknotes, ranging up to 10% of the banknote circulation (*cf.* Boeschoten and Fase, 1991 and Ettlin, 1989). In the present study these factors have been ignored, either because exploratory estimates failed to reveal a general influence of such factors in the countries considered, or because of the absence of relevant data.

4.2.2 The state of the payment system

The structure of the payment system differs strongly by country, depending on historical, economic, geographical and demographic factors. As it is not feasible to incorporate all the differences, we focus on the main factors, which are at least to some degree quantified for the countries considered. These factors are the number of ATMs and POS terminals and the amount of credit card transactions per year. Table 4.1 gives a general overview of the importance of these instruments at end-1989. Not considered were the amount of personal check transactions, as the amounts reported in the BPC questionnaire of 1990 were not comparable because of differences in check definitions. The same holds for all other cashless transactions, which to a great but unknown extent are effected by businesses. They include the increased use of current account deposits for the payment of wages and salaries which has, for instance, contributed considerably to the fall in notes and coin in circulation in relation to consumption in Italy in the 1970s, although in 1985 still 44% of wages and salaries was paid in cash (Banca d'Italia, 1988a). Likewise, APACS (1989) reports for the UK a drop in the share of wages and salaries paid in cash from 58% in 1976 to 23% in 1988. On the other hand, in France the law requires that salaries be credited to a bank account. Due to the fact that hardly any country was able to answer the relevant question in our questionnaire we had to dis-

Table 4.1 Use of ATMs, credit cards and EFT/POS in 1989

	Value of transactions as % of consumption			Number of transactions *per capita*			Number of transactions per machine (thousands) c)	
	ATMs	POS	credit card	ATMs	POS	credit card	ATMs	POS
Austria	6.2	0.05	1.6	4.5	0.1	0.9	42	4.0
Belgium	4.4	1.85	1.0	5.1	4.8	0.9	56	2.1
Canada	9.8a)	0.03	11.8	12.8	0.1	31.2	37	0.6
Denmark	2.0	-	6.8	3.0	8.1	-	89	4.7
Finland	14.0	-	4.9	20.6	7.5	10.7	38	5.0
France	6.2	6.27d)	2.6c)	8.8	13.1d)	5.3d)	38	6.1
Germany	6.9a)	0.01	1.3	0.5b)	0.0	1.3	12	0.1
Italy	2.9	0.04	0.7	1.4	0.0	0.5	15	0.2
Japan a)	-	-	3.0	-	-	4.1	-	-
Netherlands	5.3a)	0.32	0.8	4.8	1.0	0.5	39	7.3
Norway	11.9	0.63	2.6	12.8	1.4	-	32	0.9
Sweden	15.9	-	4.2	20.6	-	1.9	91	-
Switzerland	5.1	-	0.7	3.9	0.1	0.5	16	0.6
United Kingdom	11.2	0.12	7.5	14.6	1.1	11.7	55	2.6
United States	10.4	0.03	12.0	22.6b)	0.6	35.5	64b)	3.2
Average	8.0	0.94	4.1	9.7	2.9	8.1	45	2.9

a) estimated; b) 1985; c) see for number of machines Annex VI; d) estimated from aggregate figures of POS and credit card transactions.

regard the effects of this development. The same holds for the development of bank branches of which only few and hardly comparable figures were available.

As argued in Chapter 2, *ATMs* have a twofold effect on the need for currency. On the one hand, these machines encourage the use of cash by facilitating withdrawals. On the other hand, easier withdrawal facilities imply lower transactions costs and therefore, according to the inventory cash model lower transactions balances, the elasticity in the simple inventory-theoretic approach being 0.5. Indeed, as appears from our findings in Chapter 2 for the Netherlands, and the results of Avery *et al.* (1986) for the United States, ATM users make more withdrawals, but of lower amounts, as compared to those who do not use ATMs. Likewise, Paroush and Ruthenberg (1986) find a positive effect of the intensity of usage of ATMs on the demand deposit holdings in Israel, from which they conclude that the effect on the currency demand is negative. The effect in question concerns, however, mainly the transactions demand for cash by households, which is only one of the components of the currency demand. The demand by business and the money in hoards will probably hardly be affected. Altogether it is not clear beforehand whether the positive effect or the negative effect of the ATMs on cash holdings will predominate. There may be also a shift over time from a positive effect in the introduction period to a negative effect, after people have adjusted their withdrawal patterns.

For reasons of availability and quality of the data we preferred the *per capita* number of ATMs to the value of transactions as an indicator of their impact on the currency demand. Moreover, from the figures on the use of ATMs (Annex VI) follows a rather stable relationship between the value of ATM transactions and the number of machines. The ratio increases only gradually, although there are significant differences in level between the various countries. The average number of transactions per ATM in 1989 in the countries mentioned in Table 4.1 amounts to nearly 45,000 per machine per year, which comes to about 4,000 transactions per month per machine. The value of the average transaction varies between about US$ 100 and US$ 200. Limits to the maximum amount provided certainly play a role here. On average, the number of ATMs amounted to 250 per million inhabitants. According to the figures in Table 4.1 the importance of ATM withdrawals in value terms is as yet limited. The total value of ATM withdrawals per year amounts on average to 8% of private consumption. As in the late 1980s on average 30% to 50% of consumer expenditures were paid for with cash (Annex I), this means that in 1989 the major part of cash - on average 70% or more - was still withdrawn in the traditional way over the counter.

In contrast to ATMs, the effect of *POS terminals* on the demand for currency is unambiguous. In the long term POS payments are likely to reduce the currency circulation in many countries. They have the clear advantage that less cash needs to be carried in the pocket. Moreover, the speed of checkout has fallen to only zero to ten seconds over cash (Harrop, 1989). However, according to experience in France, in the introductory phase POS transactions may impinge more on checks than on the note circulation (Chevalier, 1988). The impact on the currency circulation should be greatest where the use of POS terminals is growing fastest, such as France and Belgium, where the value of POS transactions in 1989 amounted to over 6% and nearly 2%, respectively, of total consumer expenditure (Table 4.1). In all other countries this percentage is still less than one, although the POS figures may be distorted downward because of statistical difficulties in distinguishing POS transactions from credit card transactions. Gas stations are probably as yet one of the main outlets where POS terminals are used. The intensity of use of POS (with a maximum of 7,300 transactions per year and on average less than 3,000) is rather low. Averaging the amount per transaction is nearly US$ 50, remarkably similar for the countries. As in the case of ATMs, the average value of transactions per terminal seems quite stable over time, be it that the information on the value of the transactions is rather limited (Annex VI).

The quantitative importance of *credit cards* as a means of payment is highest in the English-speaking countries (Table 4.1). In the United States and Canada about 12% of total consumer expenditure is paid by means of credit cards. In the United Kingdom and Denmark this is around 7%. Japan, France, Sweden, Norway and Finland, with percentages between 3% and 5%, take a mid-way position. In the other seven countries considered here, credit card transactions amount to around 1% or less. As yet the discrepancies in the use of credit cards between countries do not seem to have diminished significantly. The average amount per transaction of US$ 140 in countries with a low credit card use is more than twice as high as the average value of US$ 67 in the more credit card oriented countries, which confirms the more exclusive character of credit cards in the former.

4.2.3 The general statistical model

The impact of the variables described in the previous section on the demand for currency by the public has been estimated by means of pooled regression analysis combining the data of the 15 countries considered here over the years 1970-1989. We postulate the following semi-loglinear relationship for the currency demand in country i in year t:

$$\ln CVO_{it} = \beta_{0i} + \overset{+}{\beta}_{1i} \ln CONS_{it} + \overset{-}{\beta}_{2i} r_{it} + \overset{?}{\beta}_{3i} NATM_{it}/POP_{it}$$

$$+ \overset{-}{\beta}_{4i} NPOS_{it}/POP_{it} + \overset{-}{\beta}_{5i} VCRED_{it}/CONS_{it} + \overset{-}{\beta}_{6i} \dot{P}_{it} \qquad (4.1)$$

$$+ \overset{+}{\beta}_{7i} TAX_{it}/GNP_{it} + \epsilon_{it}$$

CVO	value of currency outside banks (average of end-year figures) in ¢ billions (¢ = currency)
CONS	consumption (in ¢ billions, current prices)
r	average of short and long-term interest rate (%)
$\dot{P}$	rate of inflation on basis of consumer price index (%)
TAX	total of direct and indirect taxes in billions
GNP	gross national product (current prices, in ¢ billions)
NATM	number of ATMs (average of end-year figures)
NPOS	number of POS terminals (average of end-year figures)
VCRED	value of credit card transactions (in ¢ billions)
POP	population (thousands)
ϵ_{it}	disturbance term

The expected signs are given above the coefficients. As in a number of earlier currency demand studies, we have finally preferred a specification in nominal terms 3). In view of the generality of the relationship with respect to the various countries the equation reads in logarithms as far as the circulation and the consumption is concerned. The other explanatory variables are not transformed but (apart from the interest rate) are scaled by either population or consumption. Due to zero values of these variables in the beginning of the observation period, taking a logarithm was no option.

3) *Cf.* Fase and Van Nieuwkerk (1977), Banca D'Italia (1988b), Galli (1980) and also Virén (1989), whose nominal and real estimates for Finland give at least qualitatively similar results (see Table 1.2 in Chapter 1). There are possibly as many currency demand studies in real terms as Lewis and Breen (1975), Ettlin (1989) and Hall *et al.* (1989), which are more appealing from the theoretical point of view. However, as Koskela and Virén (1989) point out, at least under the assumption of partial adjustment, the theory behind the real (as opposed to nominal specification) is not too compelling even though only real specifications are usually estimated.

In the most restrictive variant of pooled regression, the *constant-intercept-and-slope model*, all coefficients are the same for every time series or cross-sectional unit. The slope coefficients β_k vary only by explanatory variable. In this case, the disturbance term ϵ_{it} captures all country-specific changes in CVO_{it} and over time that are not explained by the explanatory variables. For the issues considered here, this assumption is too restrictive. Institutional factors differ between countries and, for instance, differences in the use of personal checks (which had to be omitted because of lack of comparable data) are likely to bias the coefficients in this simple model.

The obvious generalization of the constant-intercept-and-slope model is one where a *varying intercept* term is assumed to account for the effects of those omitted variables that are specific to individual countries, and where the slope coefficients are assumed to be the same for all countries ($\beta_{ki} = \beta_k$; i= 1,2,...,15). In this model $\beta_{0i} = \bar{\beta}_0 + \mu_i$ is the intercept for the ith country, where $\bar{\beta}_0$ is the 'mean intercept' and μ_i represents the difference from this mean for the ith country. The appropriate estimation procedure depends on whether the μ_i's are assumed to be random or fixed.

In the *fixed effects model* the intercepts $\beta_{0i} = \bar{\beta}_0 + \mu_i$ are assumed to be fixed parameters, which along with the slope estimators β_k (k = 1,..κ) need to be estimated. Under the assumption that $E(\epsilon_{it}) = 0$, $E(\epsilon_{it}^2) = \sigma_\epsilon^2$ and $E(\epsilon_{it}\epsilon_{jt}) = 0$ $(i \neq j)$ the least squares estimator is the best linear unbiased. The resulting estimator, which utilizes the variation of the variables within each individual country, is known as the 'within estimator'. The differences between the average level of the dependent variable per cross-sectional unit are represented by the differences between the intercept terms, and are therefore not explained explicitly. On the other hand, the error components model assumes that the μ_i are random variables with expected value $E(\mu_i) = 0$, $E(\mu_i^2) = \sigma_\mu^2$, and $E(\mu_i \mu_j) = 0$ for $i \neq j$. Moreover, μ_i and ϵ_{it} are assumed to be uncorrelated 4).

The assumption that the μ_i are random variables implies that the N countries can be regarded as a random sample from some larger population and it also implies that the μ_i and the explanatory variables are uncorrelated. As the residual is assumed to consist of a country-related component, a general component and sometimes a time-related component, this kind of model is referred to as variance-components or error-components model. Whereas in the fixed effects model μ_i is described by N parameter values, in the error components model the only parameter is σ_μ. It can be shown that the GLS (generalized least squares) estimator is a matrix-weighted average of the 'within estimator', described before and the 'between estimator' that only utilizes the variation between individuals. This between estimator follows from applying least squares to the average values of the variables per country over time. The fixed effects model can be estimated directly by means of ordinary least squares regression. The error components estimator can be obtained in a three-step estimation procedure using OLS (*cf.* Johnston, 1984).

4.2.4 Estimation results

The constant-intercept-and-slope version of specification (4.1) requires the conversion of the income and consumption figures into one unit of measurement, for instance, US$ or purchasing power parities. This might be feasible in the situation of Perlman (1970), who computes averages for liquid assets and income for 1952-1956 and 1957-1961 on the basis of an exchange rate adjusted for purchasing power parity. For the yearly figures analysed here this correction might, however, distort the estimates, as exchange rate movements often stem from financial factors and do not necessarily reflect the development of the purchasing power of a currency. Adjustment for purchasing power partity meets this

4) In the error components model the covariance matrix is identical for all countries. Disturbances in different time periods for the same country are correlated, but this correlation is constant over time and it is identical for all countries. See for an extensive discussion of the error components and the fixed effects model Judge *et al.* (1980) and Hsiao (1986).

objection to some extent, but may still leave some distortions, due to the rather rigid implicit assumptions. Alternatively, we can consider a specification in first differences or focus on the currency ratio, implicitly assuming a unity income elasticity. The latter assumption can, however, not be defended on *a priori* grounds. In all cases whether (4.1) was specified in purchasing power parities, or whether the currency ratio or its logarithm was taken as dependent variable, the constant-intercept-and-slope-model appeared to be too restrictive, the estimated μ_i's being always significantly different from zero. Thus, for the time series analysis intercept terms were allowed to vary over countries and the nominal variables were measured in the country's own currency. With respect to the pooled time series analysis the assumptions of the error components model appeared too restrictive. Especially the assumption that the μ_i and the explanatory variables are uncorrelated does not hold 5). Therefore we preferred the fixed effects model, which explains the variation over time by country, but does not explicitly take into account the inter-country differences. These differences were analysed separately by means of cross-section regressions for one or more recent years.

Basically, before estimating, the data were weighted with the square root of the total population. The underlying thought is that larger countries need a larger weight. The weighting imposes a linear relationship between the variance of the error term and the reciprocal of the population. This variance property would hold if each country-wide observation represents an average of as many independent units as there are inhabitants. On the other hand, if observations also include country-wide components in the error term, then the variance may decline less rapidly with population. A closer empirical analysis suggests that the error variance hardly decreases with population 6). Thus, the degree of heteroskedasticity is not really diminished by weighting. For this reason, we also considered estimates with unweighted data.

5) This can be tested by means of the test performed by Hausman and Taylor (1981).

6) By applying an iterative regression procedure as used by Barro and MacDonald (1979), we found an elasticity between the squared residuals and population of -0.07.

Table 4.2 summarizes the main estimation results for the fixed effects variant of specification (4.1), assuming constant slopes but varying intercept terms over the countries. According to the resulting 'within' estimates for 1970-1989 the consumption elasticity of the currency circulation is about 0.75. This roughly corresponds with the multinational findings of Perlman (1970) and Lewis and Breen (1975) and a number of more recent country-specific studies 7). For the more recent observation period 1978-1989 this elasticity comes to 0.70. Thus, over time the amount of currency is growing less than proportionally to the value of consumption. This may stem from economies of scale, as demonstrated by the inventory theory, but it may also be the result of the substitution of currency by the alternative payments not captured here, like checks and transfer payments. Thus, as appeared from Chapter 1, for the Netherlands the elasticity increases from 0.80 to 1.0 if a proxy for transfer payments is included in the currency equation. Following a number of studies in this field, we also estimated equation (4.1) by assuming a consumption elasticity of one 8). The elasticity of 1 enables us also to perform a cross-sections estimate for a specific year, like 1988 9).

According to the 'within' estimates 1-3 a one percentage point rise in the interest rate causes a decline of about 1% in the currency circulation. This (semi)elasticity corresponds with the findings of, for example, Ettlin (1989) for Switzerland, Banca d'Italia (1988b) for Italy and Virén (1989) for Finland. In the cross-section analysis for 1988 the interest rate effect becomes six times as high (estimate 6). However, including the rate of inflation (last ten-year average) the resulting interest rate effect comes much closer to the effect -0.01, which follows from the 'within' estimates (estimate 8).

---

7) Studies for Japan, Switzerland and the UK report elasticities of 0.72, 0.79 and 0.78 for nominal currency demand. Studies for Norway, Sweden, Finland and Ireland show comparable elasticities, if real and price effects are combined (see Table 2.2 in Chapter 1).

8) *Cf.* Banca d'Italia (1988b) and Hall *et al.* (1989). Moreover, for a number of countries the freely estimated elasticity is close to one.

9) An alternative approach, applied in the estimates in section 4.3 of this chapter, is to convert all values in the relevant year in terms of US$. This resulted in an elasticity of 1.

Table 4.2 Estimation results for currency outside banks

	Observation period	Estimation method	Coefficients: Consumption β_1	Interest rate β_2	ATMs β_3	POS β_4	Credit card β_5	Inflation β_6	Statistics: $\bar{R}^2$/ SE	DW/ N
1	1970-89	WLSw	0.75	-0.011	0.78	-0.18	-2.96	-	0.999	0.32
			(42.5)	(4.2)	(5.0)	(5.7)	(3.5)		0.089	172
2	1970-89	OLSw	0.73	-0.009	0.25	-0.10	-0.36	-	0.999	0.23
			(37.0)	(3.2)	(1.5)	(4.3)	(0.4)		0.083	172
3	1978-89	WLSw	0.70	-0.008	0.84	-0.11	-2.45	-	0.999	0.33
			(23.3)	(3.5)	(6.1)	(4.5)	(3.6)		0.077	141
4	1970-89	WLSw	1	-0.027	-0.25	-0.23	-4.32	-	0.900	0.45
			(-)	(8.2)	(1.2)	(5.0)	(3.4)		0.128	172
5	1978-89	WLSw	1	-0.010	-0.03	-0.14	-3.08	-	0.943	0.35
			(-)	(3.5)	(0.2)	(4.5)	(3.4)		0.093	141
6	1988	OLS	1	-0.062	0.36	-0.16	-5.92	-	0.493	-
			(-)	(-2.0)	(0.6)	(1.1)	(2.5)		0.321	15
7	1988	OLS	1	-	0.05	-0.20	-6.42	-0.069	0.511	-
			(-)		(0.1)	(1.5)	(2.8)	(2.1)	0.315	15
8	1988	OLS	1	-0.023	0.15	-0.18	-6.18	-0.048	0.463	-
			(-)	(0.3)	(0.2)	(1.2)	(2.5)	(0.7)	0.330	15
Specification in first differences										
9	1970-89	WLSw	0.70	-0.002	0.67	-0.03	-0.04	-	0.763	0.72
			(26.8)	(2.4)	(5.7)	(1.2)	(0.1)		0.030	157
10	1980-89	WLSw	0.63	-0.001	0.86	-0.03	-0.01	-	0.770	0.70
			(15.5)	(1.1)	(6.4)	(1.2)	(0.0)		0.030	119
11	1980-89	WLSb	0.98	-0.080	-0.31	-0.42	-1.67	-	0.942	-
			(8.9)	(2.5)	(0.7)	(3.7)	(0.9)		0.014	15
12	1980-89	WLSb	0.79	-0.01	0.34	-0.34	-2.13	-	0.923	
			(10.3)	(-)	(0.9)	(2.8)	(1.0)		0.017	15
Guesstimates										
13	'70-89	OLSw	0.73	-0.008	0.4	-0.05	-2.5	-	0.999	0.21
			(49.7)	(3.3)					0.085	172
14	'70-89	OLSw	0.78	-0.013	-0.2	-0.05	-2.5		0.999	0.29
			(51.4)	(4.8)					0.088	172

Explanatory notes: WLSw is weighted least squares with intercept term (not presented here) varying by country, *i.e.* 'within estimator'; OLSw is like WLSw but without weighting; WLSb is weighted least squares with one intercept term, *i.e.* 'between estimator'; t-values within parentheses; $\dot{P}$ is average inflation in foregoing ten years. For the sake of comparability the statistics are unweighted, except for the specifications in first differences. N is the number of observations.

With respect to the impact of ATMs on the circulation, the results are not unambiguous. In most specifications considered the effect is positive, indicating that one more ATM per million inhabitants is attended by a 0.02% to 0.08% rise of the currency circulation. Only in the 'within' estimates with a fixed consumption elasticity of 1 (estimates 4 and 5), and in the 'between' estimate in first differences with a free interest elasticity (estimate 11), the effect is negative. On the other hand, POS terminals and the use of credit cards cause, as assumed, in all estimations a decline in the need for currency. According to estimate 1 in Table 4.2, one more POS terminal per million inhabitants lowers the circulation by 0.018%. An increase of 1% in the ratio of credit card transactions to consumption causes a decrease of 3% in the need for currency.

The effect of the tax and social security rate as a proxy for the demand for cash by the black economy was, although positive, small and never statistically significant and is therefore not mentioned further here. For the rate of inflation in the 'within' estimates no sensible effects could be found at all. This is in line with the findings of Lewis and Breen (1975) in their cross-section study of the post-war currency demand. However, according to the cross-section estimates for 1988, the difference in currency ratio per country can to some extent be explained by the average rate of inflation during the last 10 years. A one percentage point higher inflation lowers the ratio of currency to consumption, which amounted on average to 9.3% at end-1989, by about 0.5 percentage points.

4.2.5 A closer look at the estimates

The high correlation coefficients of the 'within' estimates indicate that the model traces the development of the currency demand by country very well. For most of the estimated time series relationships the extremely low Durbin-Watson statistics point, however, at a very high degree of autocorrelation, suggesting misspecification 10). As is well known and was already stated in section 4.3 of Chapter 1, the usual tests of significance are not valid any more in this case. The high correlation coefficients may just ensue from spurious correlation, being the consequence of relating independent integrated processes (Granger and Newbold, 1986). The misspecification may stem from incorrect modelling of the dynamic structure, omission of explanatory variables, the wrong functional form or from the implicit assumption of identical slope coefficients for all countries.

With respect to the dynamic structure, various alternative specifications have been examined including lagged adjustment, an error correction mechanism, first differences (see estimates 9-12) and the assumption of first order serial autocorrelation. None of these alternatives resulted in equations acceptable from a statistical point of view. In the case of lagged adjustment and the error correction mechanism the speed of adjustment became implausibly low. However, most of the estimates did not change dramatically, be it that none of the estimated equations satisfied the Dickey Fuller (1979) test. As to the functional form, various alternatives were considered. The overall conclusion is that the results could not be improved by assuming a different type of specification.

The autocorrelation may also stem from the omission of relevant explanatory variables like the volumes of check transactions and debits, and of country-specific variables like the foreign demand for currency (Switzerland, Germany and US), the density of the retail network (Italy), and fiscal measures. If their impact is not constant over time (and thus not captured by the intercept terms), the omission of these variables distorts the estimates of the parameter values. However, the robustness of the equations when estimated over different time periods do not support this type of misspecification.

10) Estimations for a real currency demand specification show similar high correlation coefficients as the nominal specification considered here. The consumption elasticity then gets, however, an economic-theoretically implausible value of 0.15. Moreover, the estimations do not support the hypothesis of price homogeneity, which may be interpreted as an indication of misspecification (Goldfeld and Sichel, 1990).

Perhaps the main explanation of the observed autocorrelation is the assumption of equal slope coefficients for the various countries. Actually, the consumption elasticity and the impact of alternative payment systems on the currency demand may differ per country. Because for most countries not enough data were available to estimate these effects separately, this drawback and the resulting high degree of autocorrelation was yet accepted from sheer necessity, assuming that the results reflect the average relationship, from which the country-wise effects may deviate to some extent. Comparable applications of pooled regression show the same statistical shortcoming (*cf.* Lewis and Breen, 1975; and Barro and MacDonald, 1979).

A second question is the plausibility of the estimation results, especially with regard to the impact of the ATMs, POS terminals and credit cards. The positive effect of ATMs on the currency holdings, also found by Boeschoten (1990), contrasts with the negative effect concluded by Paroush and Ruthenberg (1986). On the other hand, Dombrecht (1989) reports for Belgium also a positive effect of ATMs on currency demand with an elasticity of 0.06, which is very close to the elasticity of 0.04, which follows from our estimates for Belgium. Likewise, Kokkola (1990) finds a comparable positive effect of ATMs for Finland, and Henderson (1986) reports on the displacing of checks by currency in the US under the influence of ATM programs. The positive effect found suggests that at least in the introductory phase people do not exploit the possibilities of these machines and that the stimulus of the use of cash predominates over possible savings on cash holdings. Moreover, it should be emphasized that only the transactions demand for currency, which is in some countries less than 50% of the currency circulation, is sensitive to these effects. Nevertheless, in the long term one would expect a negative effect. Thus, the at least 20% lower cash holdings of ATM users, found in the micro-analysis for the US and the Netherlands, would imply a value of β_3 of about -0.20 11).

11) Based on the assumption that, if nearly all cash is withdrawn by using ATMs, the currency holdings of the public will be 20% lower.

Table 4.3 Importance of payments media and guesstimates of coefficients

Country	Amount of currency outside banks	POS				Credit cards		
		value of payments	number of terminals	population (mlns)	coefficient β_4	value of payments	value of consumption	coefficient β_5
Austria	100	0.44	229	7.6	-0.015	14.5	927	-0.93
Belgium	422	70.9	22399	10.0	-0.007	36.6	3833	-0.91
Canada	20	0.12	4278	26.2	-0.004	44.3	376	-1.92
Denmark	23	-	8825	5.1	-	27.3	404	1.77
Finland	9	-	7420	5.0	-	13.7	257	-2.93
France	246	230	120000	56.0	-0.044	94.0	3667	-1.49
Germany	146	0.14	10928	61.6	-0.001	15.8	1213	-0.83
Italy	67481	300	10018	57.4	-0.003	5400.0	722902	-1.07
Japan	35727	-	642	123.0	-	6590.0	220473	-0.62
Netherlands	36	0.9	2047	14.9	-0.018	2.2	281	-0.78
Norway	29	2	6656	4.3	-0.004	8.3	315	-1.08
Sweden	61	-	3420	8.5	-	26.7	634	-1.03
Switzerland	26	0.07	640	6.5	-0.003	1.2	166	-0.63
United Kingdom	16	0.4	24300	57.0	-0.006	24.0	322	-2.04
United States	225	1	44000	248.0	-0.003	414.0	3455	-1.53
Average					-0.010			-1.30

Explanatory note: Amounts in billions of the country's own currency.

The value of -0.18 for the POS coefficient β_4 in estimate 1 implies that on average one extra POS terminal lowers the circulation by about US$ 200 thousand, which is even more than the average yearly turnover per machine and only US$ 120 less than the maximum turnover of US$ 320 in France. This comes to a transactions velocity of about 1.5 at most, compared to an actual velocity of about 10 12). Thus the coefficient seems to overestimate the effect of the use of POS. Possibly it picks up some of the effects of alternative payments media not included in the equations. At a transactions velocity of 10, a reasonable guesstimate for the POS coefficient β_4 lies between -0.01 and -0.05 depending on whether the average or the maximum turnover per terminal is taken as the point of departure (Table 4.3).

12) This velocity has been computed by relating the available cash turnover figures to the currency circulation, exluding idle currency not used for transactions (see Table I.1 in Annex I).

Figure 4.3 Currency outside banks as percentage of consumption in 1988

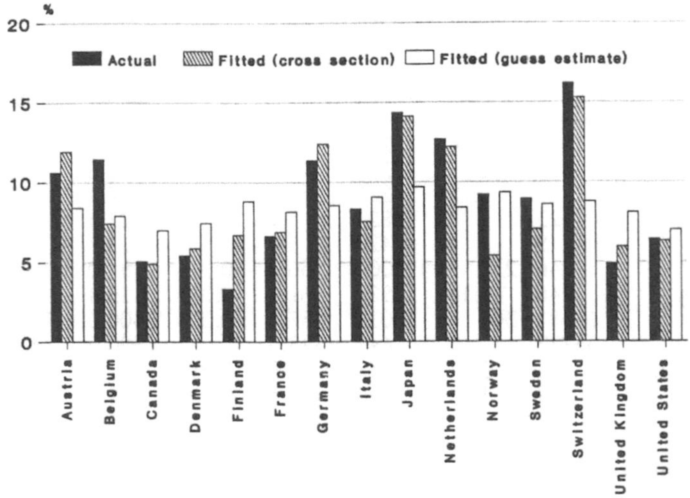

According to the value of β_5 of -3.0 in estimate 1, a one percentage point rise in the ratio of credit card transactions to consumption causes a decrease of about 3% in the currency demand. This is of the same order of magnitude as the average value of 2.5%, which Virén (1989) reports for the nominal currency demand functions for Finland, and corresponds to the coefficient value of 2.9 which can be computed for Finland directly by assuming a transactions velocity of 10 (Table 4.3). On average, a somewhat lower coefficient of 2.5 at most seems more appropriate. The general conclusion of this evaluation is that as yet the coefficients of the alternative payments media probably overestimate their effect on the currency demand. This especially holds for the cross-section estimates, where the number of POS terminals as well as the amount of credit card transactions are probably also proxies for the degree of forwardness of the payments system in a certain country. Therefore the relevant guesstimates in the bottom lines of Table 4.2 are considerably lower than the coefficients that follow if they are freely estimated by means of regression analysis.

Table 4.4 Calculated contributions to average annual percentage growth of currency outside banks 1981-1989

Country	Actual annual growth	Computed annual growth	Contribution						Residual
			consumption		interest rate	ATMs	POS terminals	credit card	
			volume	price					
Austria	3.8	4.2	1.6	2.2	0.3	0.4	-0.0	-0.4	-0.4
Belgium	1.6	3.4	1.1	2.8	0.6	0.2	-1.2	-0.2	-1.8
Canada	7.2	6.0	2.5	3.4	0.1	1.2	-0.1	-1.2	1.2
Denmark	7.0	2.7	1.0	3.8	0.8	0.2	-1.0	-1.9	4.1
Finland	8.2	6.9	2.7	4.1	-0.0	2.1	-0.6	-1.4	1.3
France	5.9	5.3	1.9	3.9	0.3	0.8	-1.1	-0.6	0.6
Germany	6.4	3.1	1.2	1.5	0.3	0.6	-0.1	-0.4	3.3
Italy	10.9	8.7	2.0	6.1	0.5	0.3	-0.1	-0.2	2.2
Japan	7.6	5.2	2.5	1.1	0.6	2.0	-0.0	-1.0	2.4
Netherlands	6.2	2.8	0.9	1.3	0.4	0.4	-0.1	-0.1	3.4
Norway	5.1	6.5	1.4	4.9	-0.0	1.4	-0.8	-0.3	-1.4
Sweden	6.5	6.9	1.3	4.9	0.2	0.5	-0.2	0.2	-0.4
Switzerland	2.1	3.7	1.2	2.0	-0.2	0.9	-0.0	-0.2	-1.6
Unit.Kingdom	4.9	5.9	2.8	3.7	0.3	1.0	-0.4	-1.5	-1.0
Unit.States	7.4	5.9	2.4	3.0	0.4	1.1	-0.1	-0.9	1.5
Average	6.0	5.2	1.8	3.2	0.3	0.9	-0.4	-0.7	0.8

Explanatory notes: Computed with coefficients of guesstimate 13 from Table 4.2. The standard deviation of residual is 1.9.

According to the cross-section estimate 7 for 1988, the model explains about 50% of the variation between countries. In the case of the same model with the more plausible guesstimate coefficients this is 40%. The remaining 50% to 60% has to be explained from factors not considered here. Thus the model only partly explains the very low currency ratio in Finland (Figure 4.3). This may illustrate Finland's except-ionally advanced payment system (Lilja and Lempinen, 1988).

An intriguing question is to what extent the estimated relationships are able to describe the average annual growth of the currency circulation by country. Apart from the quality of the model, this exercise can afford insight into deviant developments in certain countries. The results are computed with the guesstimate 13 from Table 4.2. In general the annual growth is described rather well, with a tendency towards some underestimation of on average 0.8 percentage point per year (see Table 4.4). This underestimation may partly stem from a more than proportional growth of hoarding in countries like Germany and the Netherlands, where the currency growth is underestimated by more than 3 percentage points per year. The reason for the higher-than-expected growth in Japan and Denmark is less clear. On the other hand, the overestimate of the currency growth in Switzerland may reflect the dishoarding in the mid-eighties after the termination of measures against foreign money (*cf.* Ettlin, 1989).

Of the other contributory factors, the increase of nominal consumption, of which two-thirds are due to inflation, predominates. The negative effects of credit card and POS transactions are, on average, less than 1 percentage point growth per year, but in a number of countries had a major impact. Finally, as yet the results suggest a rather large positive influence for the number of ATMs on the currency circulation. Only if *a priori* a consumption elasticity of 1 is assumed, as for the estimates 4, 5 and the guesstimate 14 in Table 4.2, the ATMs get the more or less expected negative effect. As yet this assumption is not supported by the estimates.

4.3 Cash holdings of banks

The cash holdings of the banks are in the nature of things closely linked with currency with the public 13). Nevertheless, the relative amount of cash needed by banks to meet the public's demand for currency differs strongly by country (Table 4.5). Moreover, as Figure 4.4 shows, it changes over time. On average, banks' cash balances in the fifteen countries considered here amounted at end-1989 to about 15% of currency with the public, following a slight increase of, on average, 0.8 percentage point (excluding Finland) in the 1980s. The inter-country discrepancies stem from economic and institutional differences. The latter include differences in the density of the central bank branch network and of the branch network of the banking or (more broadly)

---

13) The relationship with deposits considered by Banca d'Italia (1988b) is, at least statistically, less clear. Moreover, the international comparison of the importance of this variable is strongly hampered by diverging definitions.

Table 4.5 Cash holdings of banks and relevant characteristics in 1989

Country	Cash holdings of banks as % of		Number of ATMs per million inhabitants	Density of branch network (branches per mln inhabit.)		Deductibility of cash from reserve requirements b)
	currency outside banks	deposits		banking system	central bank	
Austria	15.2	1.1	108	1049	1.05	+(1990)
Belgium	8.4	1.5	90	1392a)	2.51a)	-
Canada	22.2	1.0	343	503a)	0.34a)	+
Denmark	8.7	0.9	34	932	0.59	-
Finland	49.4	1.7	536	1293a)	2.42	+(1980)
France	7.9	1.5	233	832	4.18	-
Germany	10.5	1.1	151	997	3.43	+(1978)
Italy	5.8	0.3	93	514a)	1.69	-
Japan	10.5	0.6	628	540	0.28	-
Netherlands	7.4	0.7	124	556a)	0.88	-
Norway	7.7	0.7	405	1074	4.65	-(1988)
Sweden	10.6	1.3	226	642	2.70	+
Switzerland	18.0	1.5	253	1447a)	1.54	-(1988)
United Kingdom	23.4	0.8	266	1121	0.12	-
United States	15.6	2.1	351	450	0.15	+
Average	14.7	1.1	256	889	1.77	

a) 1988; b) the year indicates the starting of the regulation; based on Kneeshaw and Van den Bergh (1989), Banque de France (1989), Deutsche Bundesbank (1990) and on direct information from central banks.

financial sector as a whole 14). The density of the central bank branch network determines the cash requirements of the banks. The higher this density, the easier banks can replenish or reduce their cash holdings and the lower their average cash balances will be. On the other hand, the larger number of branches of banks and other deposit-taking financial institutions will require a higher total of cash balances. With a multiplicity of branches (each facing uncertain fluctuations in demand) the aggregate of their stores will be greater than if stores and demand were pooled. Other institutional factors determining cash facilities, like tariffs and the opening hours of central bank branches, are difficult to quantify and have as yet been left out of the analysis, although they may be of considerable importance. Thus, the transition

14) The figures mostly also contain the cash holdings of other money creating institutions, including the central government. The share of the latter is, however, very limited.

Figure 4.4 Cash with banks as percentage of currency outside banks

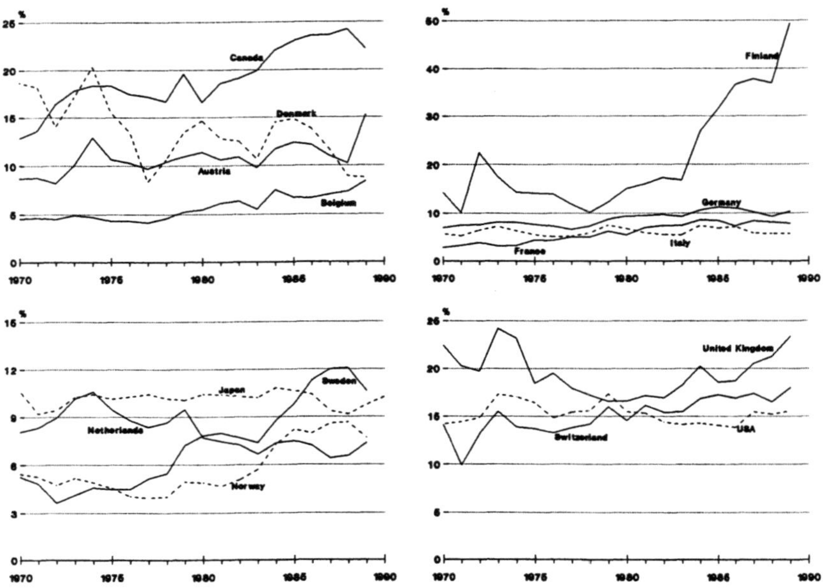

from a six-day to a five-day workweek in Japan in February 1989 was attended by a one percentage point rise in the share of the banks' cash holdings (Bank of Japan, 1990).

An important economic factor affecting banks' cash holdings is the opportunity cost, *i.e.* the interest forgone by holding cash balances. In a number of countries such as Canada and Finland, no such opportunity costs are involved as long as cash balances do not exceed the level set by reserve requirements. The ceilings on cash balances then depend on storage and insurance costs only, which may be relatively low as storing cash in ATMs is as yet relatively cheap and incurs only low insurance costs. This may explain the relatively high cash holdings of the banking system in countries like Finland (Virén, 1989), where banks can deduct their cash balances from the reserve requirements.

Changes in the payments system influence the cash balances of the banking system basically through the currency demanded by the public. Thus an increasing use of POS terminals may lower the public's need for currency and consequently the cash holdings of the banking system. ATMs form an exception, since they affect banks' cash holdings by requiring considerable amounts of till money. It is generally assumed that an increase in the number of ATMs, if not offset by a decrease of the number of branches, will raise the amount of cash held by the banks.

As in the case of currency with the public, banks' cash holding behaviour has been quantified by means of pooled regression analysis. In equation (4.2) the cash holdings of the banks depend on the amount of currency with the public, opportunity costs, the number of ATMs *per capita* and the density of the branch networks of the banking system and the central bank, respectively, measured by the number of their branches *per capita* 15). The expected signs are given above the coefficients.

$$\ln CVI_{it} = \beta_{0i} + \overset{+}{\beta}_1 \ln CVO_{it} + \overset{-}{\beta}_2 \, dum_{it} \, r_{it} + \overset{+}{\beta}_3 \, NATM_{it}/POP_{it} + \overset{+}{\beta}_4 \, NBB_{it}/POP_{it} + \overset{-}{\beta}_5 \, NBCB_{it}/POP_{it} + \overset{+}{\beta}_6 \ln(CVI)_{it-} \qquad (4.2)$$

CVI	currency inside banks, (value in ¢ billions, end of year)
CVO	currency outside banks (value in ¢ billions, end of year)
dum	dummy interest costs of banks' cash holdings (dum = 0 if interest costs for banking system are zero, otherwise dum = 1)
r	short term interest rate (%)
NATM	number of ATMs
NBB	number of branches of banking system
NBCB	number of branches of central bank
POP	population (in thousands)

The coefficient β_1 gives the elasticity of the currency inside banks with respect to currency outside banks. Lag in the adjustment is accounted for by including the last-year's cash holdings of the banks as

15) Another density measure, the number of branches per square kilometre, is probably distorted by the fact that even in large countries the population is mostly concentrated in a limited number of regions. With respect to the density of the central bank branch network, the number of central bank branches per branch of the banking system has also been considered. Although the estimation results are quite similar, we have preferred the number *per capita* because of lower cross-correlation.

explanatory variable. The fixed effects model of (4.2) has been estimated with intercept terms β_{0i} varying per country, for the period 1970-1989 as well as by means of cross-section analysis for the years 1985 and 1988. The density of the branch network was, at least for the central banks, practically constant in most countries during the observation period. For this reason its effect has only been estimated by means of cross-section analysis. As the dependent variable is mainly explained by specific institutional factors, no weighting by population was applied here.

The various estimation results in Table 4.6 show a remarkable uniformity with comparable, mostly statistically significant effects of the explanatory variables. This suggests a rather high degree of robustness, although the estimates for individual countries, not shown here, are less robust as far as the impact of the ATMs is concerned. The elasticity β_1 of about 0.95 for the whole estimation period indicates that the cash balances of the banks grow slightly less than proportional to the public's demand for currency. By shortening the estimation period the elasticity drops to a value of about 0.8, suggesting some increase in economies of scale over time. This is supported by the cross-section estimates for 1985 and 1988. In those countries where the banks' vault cash is not included in the reserve requirements, the banks' cash holdings appear to be rather sensitive to interest changes. A 1-percentage point higher interest rate causes a drop in the banks' vault cash by about 3.5%. On average, in the relevant countries this implies an elasticity of 0.4, which is almost equal to the elasticity of 0.5 reported by Virén (1989) for Finland. The effect on the total circulation is, however, limited to 0.3%, which comes to an elasticity of about 0.04.

The use of ATMs clearly enlarges the banks' cash holdings. According to estimate 2 for the more recent period 1978-1989, one additional ATM increases the circulation on average by US$ 0.13 million. This amount should be approximately the equivalent of the average inventories in the machines and the additional inventories kept at bank branches for

Table 4.6 Estimation results for cash holdings of banks

	Observation period	Coefficients					Statistics	
		currency outside banks	interest rate	number of ATMs	branch network		$\bar{R}^2$/ SE	DW/ N
					banks	central bank		
		β_1	β_2	β_3	β_4	β_5		
1	1970-89	0.94	-0.034	0.44	-	-	0.998	2.06
		(3.8)	(2.3)	(0.8)			0.12	256
2	1978-89	0.77	-0.035	0.97	-	-	0.998	1.92
		(2.7)	(1.8)	(1.4)			0.11	184
3	1985	0.90	-0.031	1.74	0.63	-207	0.959	-
		(11.6)	(2.0)	(1.9)	(2.2)	(3.7)	0.29	15
4	1988	0.87	-0.050	1.85	0.42	-136	0.943	-
		(11.1)	(2.4)	(3.1)	(1.3)	(2.1)	0.34	15

Explanatory notes: Estimation method is OLSw. t-values within brackets. N is the number of observations. In the case of the pooled time series results the long term effects are presented. The Durbin's-h statistic for the estimates 1 and 2 is -0.53 and 0.74, respectively. The cross-section results are based on values converted into US$.

filling the machines. The relevant elasticity of 0.18 for Finland is somewhat higher than the elasticity of about 0.1 resulting from Virén (1989).

As appears from the cross-section estimates for 1985 and 1988 in Table 4.6, the coefficients of in particular the interest rate strongly correspond with those found earlier, while on the other hand statistically significant, though small, effects were found for the branch networks of the banks and the central banks. An extension of the banks' branch network by one branch per thousand inhabitants raises the banks' currency holdings by on average 5%. On the other hand, an extension of the central bank branch network by one branch per million inhabitants results in 2% lower currency holdings. The effect of one more bank branch nearly equals the effect of an extra ATM following from the estimates 1 and 2.

Figure 4.5 Currency inside banks as percentage of currency outside banks in 1988

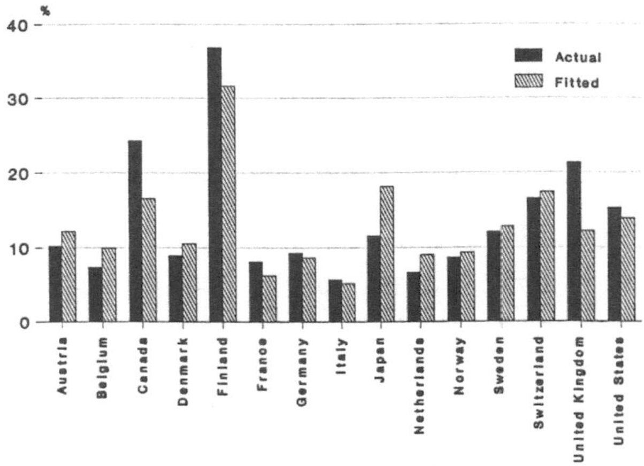

Figure 4.5 illustrates that the model explains the inter-country differences in the cash holdings of banks reasonably well, apart from the rather large discrepancies for Canada, Japan and the UK. To investigate the performance of the model over time, as in the case of the currency outside banks, we compared in Table 4.7 the computed growth of the currency inside banks with its actual growth during 1981-1989. It appears that the average annual growth of the banks' cash holdings in 1981-1989 for most of the reported countries is rather satisfactorily explained by the model.

However, Finland and Sweden show a considerably higher growth of the banks' cash holdings than follows from the model. This is probably due to the inclusion of these holdings in the cash reserve requirements. On the other hand, in Japan, the Netherlands and Denmark, the growth was considerably less than computed. Economies of scale and increasing efficiency in cash management may be factors of importance. In the case of the Netherlands, the strong rise of hoarding (see next section), which increases the currency circulation outside but not necessarily inside banks, may also be responsible for the overestimation of the banks' cash holdings. A great deal of the countries show, however, a parallel development in the currency inside banks, growing at 8% per

Table 4.7 Computed contributions to average annual growth currency inside banks, 1981-1989

Country	Actual annual growth (%)	Computed annual growth a) (%)	Contribution currency outside	Contribution interest rate	Contribution ATMs	Residual	Contribution bank branches
Austria	5.4	4.9	3.1	0.7	1.1	0.5	(0.3)
Belgium	5.9	3.7	1.3	1.8	0.6	2.1	(2.1)
Canada	10.0	8.8	5.7	0	3.0	1.2	(-0.1)
Denmark	1.8	8.5	5.6	2.5	0.4	-6.7	-
Finland	20.9	11.7	6.6	0	5.1	9.3	(-0.5)
France	9.4	7.7	4.7	0.9	2.1	1.7	(-0.8)
Germany	7.3	6.6	5.1	0	1.5	0.7	(0.3)
Italy	8.5	10.7	8.7	1.1	0.8	-2.2	(0.3)
Japan	7.6	12.4	6.1	1.3	5.0	-4.8	(0.4)
Netherlands	3.9	7.5	4.9	1.5	1.1	-3.5	(-0.3)
Norway	10.7	9.0	4.1	1.4	3.6	1.7	-
Sweden	11.0	6.5	5.2	0	1.3	4.6	(-0.5)
Switzerland	3.4	4.0	1.7	0	2.3	-0.6	(0.3)
United Kingdom	8.2	7.7	3.9	1.2	2.5	0.6	(-0.4)
United States	6.8	8.8	5.9	0	2.8	-2.0	(-0.3)
Average	8.0	7.9	4.8	0.8	2.2	0.2 c)	(0.1)

Explanatory notes: Computed with estimate 2 from Table 4.6. The reserve requirement change in Switzerland in 1988 has been ignored because of lag in adjustment; standard deviation: 3.85. The figures for Japan are based on annual averages. Because of limited data quality and inter-country comparibility the results are rather tentative, and mentioned only additionally (on basis of $\beta_4 = 0.42$).

year, of which more than 2 percentage points was the consequence of the instalment of ATMs.

4.4 The importance of hoarding

Not only for the Netherlands but for other countries as well, there are strong indications that a substantial part of the currency and especially note circulation is kept (hoarded) as a store of value. Some of the empirical evidence for the United States was already mentioned in Chapter 3. But also in other countries hoarding is a well-known phenomenon. Thus in Switzerland, hoarding because of measures taken against foreign money in 1972-1980 has been estimated at 10% of the banknote circulation in 1980, followed by dishoarding which ended in the mid-1980s (Ettlin, 1987). Moreover, the effect of the Swiss taxation system with a two-year cycle results in a nearly 3% higher circulation

Table 4.8 Estimation results for relationship between average life and real value of small notes

Country	Denominations hoarded	Denominations used for estimation	Estimation results				
			a_0		a_1		$\overline{R}^2$
Austria	1000	500,100,50,20,10	2.39	(6.6)	0.16	(1.7)	0.02
Belgium	5000,1000	500,100	2.09	(32.7)	-		-
Canada	1000,100,50	20,10,5,2,1	1.34	(20.4)	0.43	(7.6)	0.51
Denmark	1000,500	100,50,20,10	0.61	(6.3)	0.22	(5.3)	0.33
Finland	1000,500	100,50,10,5	0.28	(3.6)	0.32	(9.2)	0.55
France	500	200,100,50,20,10	0.43	(1.7)	0.55	(5.9)	0.34
Germany	1000,500,100	50,20,10	0.15	(1.1)	0.42	(11.8)	0.70
Italy	100000,50000	5000,2000	2.06	(26.7)	-		-
Netherlands	1000,250,100	50,25,10,5	1.17	(28.8)	-		-
Norway	1000,500	100,50,10,5	0.03	(0.1)	0.53	(5.4)	0.34
Sweden	10000,1000	500,100,50,10,5	0.91	(6.4)	0.21	(3.8)	0.15
Switzerland	1000,500,100	50,20,10	2.42	(45.7)	-		-
United King.	-	50,20,10,5,1,0.5	1.39	(22.3)	0.50	(9.5)	0.61
United States		100,5020,10,5,1	1.74	(19.1)	0.48	(7.5)	0.46

Explanatory notes: The denominations hoarded are selected on basis of the deviation of the actual lifefrom the expected normal life. A few small denominations have been excluded from the estimation due to strong fluctuations in their computed average life. In the case of Germany a linear time trend has been included in the equation to correct for the increase of the average lives of the denominations over time. t-values within parentheses.

at the end of each even year, located in the higher denominations (Ettlin and Fluri, 1986). Likewise, in Germany the announcement of a 10% withholding tax on interest payments at end-1987 caused a rise in the banknote circulation of about 10 percent, mainly in the highest denominations.

In order to quantitify the importance of currency hoarding in the countries considered we have estimated the amount of hoarding in the years 1970-1989 on the basis of note life figures, as described in section 3.1 of Chapter 3. Table 4.8 summarizes the estimation results for the relationship $AL = a_0 + a_1 \ln RD_t$, with AL the average note life and RD the real value of a denomination, which is used to compute the normal average note life. The results indicate that (depending on the country considered) a 100% increase in the real value of a note causes an increment in its average life of 0 to 0.55 years. For Switzerland, Italy, Belgium and the Netherlands an insignificant negative relationship was found between average life and real value of the smaller denominations, and the relevant coefficient was therefore put at zero 16). For these countries the normal average life equals the mean of the average lives of the smaller denominations.

Figure 4.6 shows by denomination the resulting 'normal' average life following from the estimated relationships as well as the actual average life and its trend, for the period 1970-1989. For most countries the actual average life of the higher denominations exceeds the normal average life. The resulting amounts of hoarding (as percentages of GNP) that follow from the difference between the actual and normal computed average life of the highest denominations, after correcting the actual average life for short-run fluctuations by imposing a linear trend, are given by country in Table 4.9 and in Figure 4.7.

The importance and development of hoarding differ strongly between the countries observed. Apart from Sweden, with its hardly used 10,000 Krone note, hoarding is especially important in countries with upper-range denominations of relatively high values, such as Germany, Switzerland and the Netherlands, where hoarding percentages were around 50% at end-1989. For the United Kingdom, which has a relatively low highest denomination, no hoarding was found at all. This agrees with the questionnaire response that no notes are hoarded in these countries. On the other hand, for Denmark and Italy hoarding is estimated at 17% and 34% of the circulation value at end-1989, against zero according to the questionnaire. In general the denominations that are estimated as being used for hoarding correspond remarkably well with those reported in the questionnaire.

16) The estimation results for the Netherlands differ from those in Chapter 3 due to the shorter estimation period considered here in view of the consistency with the estimates for the other countries.

Figure 4.6 Average note life by denomination, 1970-1989

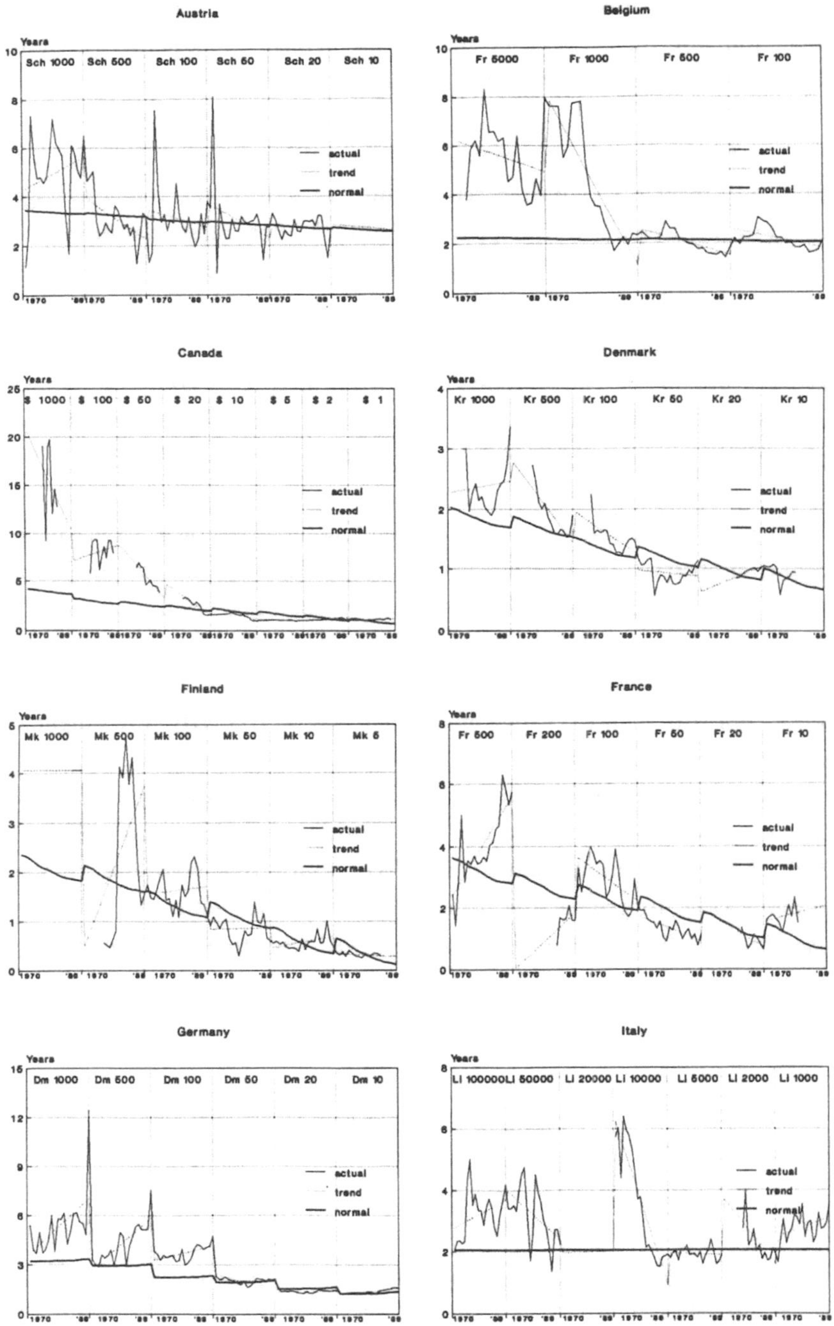

Figure 4.6 Average note life by denomination, 1970-1989 (continued)

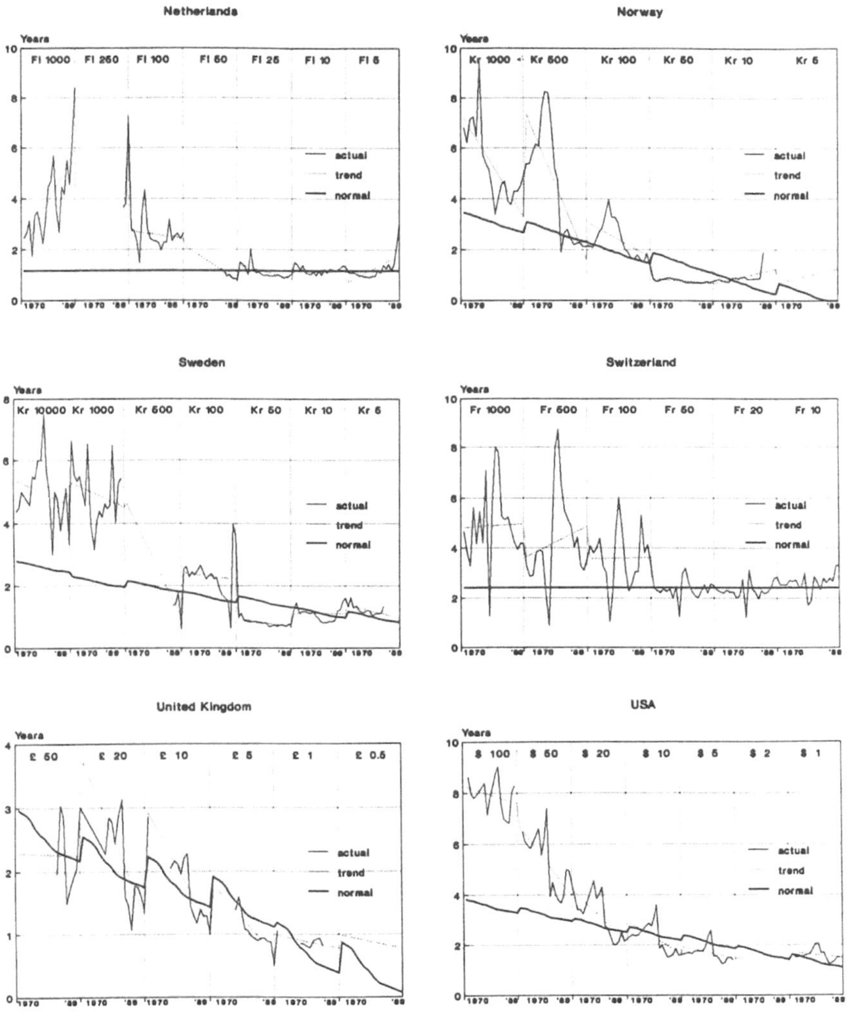

Figure 4.7 Banknote circulation, total and excluding hoarding as percentage of GNP

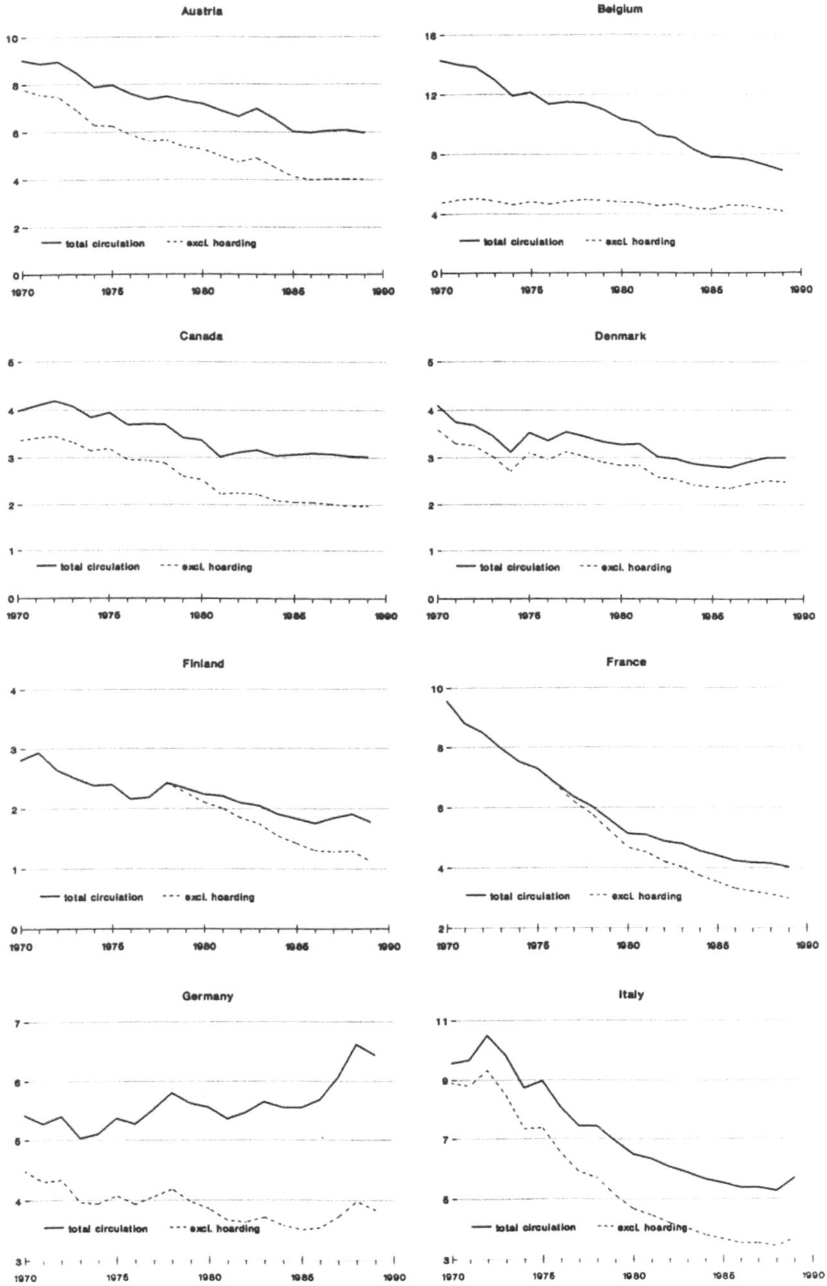

Figure 4.7 Banknote circulation, total and excluding hoarding as percentage of GNP (continued)

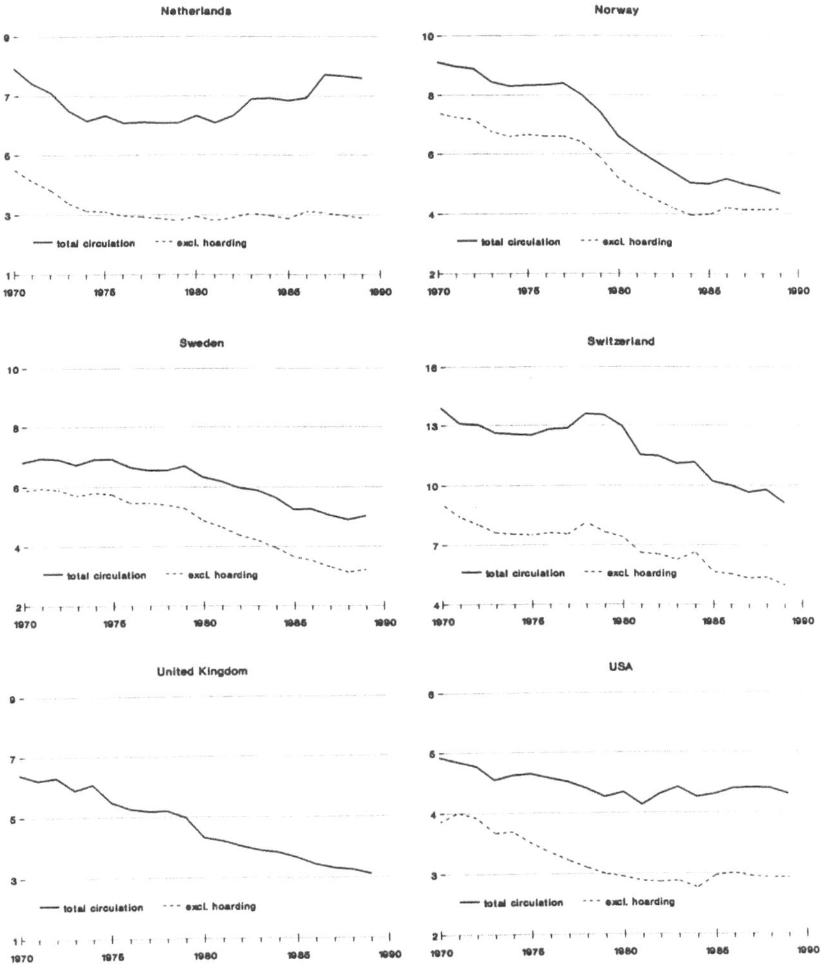

Table 4.9 Estimated importance of hoarding in various countries

Country	Hoarding as % of currency outside banks		Currency outside banks as % of GNP				Contribution of hoarding to annual growth of currency	
			unadjusted		adjusted			
	1970	1989	1970	1989	1970	1989	1970-89	1980-89
Austria	14	32	9.0	6.0	7.8	4.0	1.4	1.0
Belgium	67	40	14.3	6.9	4.8	4.2	-3.3	-3.1
Canada	16	34	4.0	3.0	3.4	2.0	1.4	1.6
Denmark	12	17	4.1	3.0	3.6	2.5	0.3	0.5
Finland	0	37	2.8	1.8	2.8	1.1	2.6	4.7
France	0	26	9.6	4.0	9.6	3.0	1.7	2.5
Germany	17	40	5.4	6.4	4.5	3.8	1.8	1.8
Italy	7	35	9.6	5.7	8.9	3.7	2.1	1.2
Netherlands	43	62	7.9	7.6	4.5	2.9	2.3	2.4
Norway	19	11	9.1	4.7	7.4	4.1	-0.5	-1.4
Sweden	14	36	6.8	5.0	5.9	3.2	1.7	2.1
Switzerland	35	45	13.9	9.1	9.1	5.0	1.0	0.5
United Kingdom	0	0	6.4	3.1	6.4	3.1	0.0	0.0
United States	18	39	4.9	4.3	4.0	2.6	1.7	1.0
Average	19	33	7.7	5.0	5.9	3.2	1.0	1.1

Our estimate of a hoarding percentage of about 40% of outstanding currency for the US in 1975 is considerably lower than the nearly 70%computed by Anderson (1977) taking the life of the one dollar note as the normal average life. This difference mainly stems from the fact that Anderson does not take into account a positive relationship between the real value of a denomination and its average life and that he assumes that every denomination, except the one dollar note, can be hoarded. In both studies the importance of hoarding is, however, strongly rising over time. Whitehead (1982) also finds that the importance of hoarding is increasing over time, with almost 70% of currency in hoards in 1980. Kimball (1981) comes to a similar conclusion by estimating currency demand functions grouped by denomination for the period 1960-1980, with a wealth variable as a proxy for hoarding. Moreover, as in this study, mainly US$ 50 and US$ 100 notes appear to be kept in hoards. According to Kimball 58% of currency was kept in hoards in 1980. Generally speaking, the importance of hoarding seems to be increasing, with the exception of Norway and especially Belgium, where a remarkable decline of the number of 1,000 Franc notes was attended by a strong drop in the

Figure 4.8 Currency outside banks as percentage of GNP, 1989

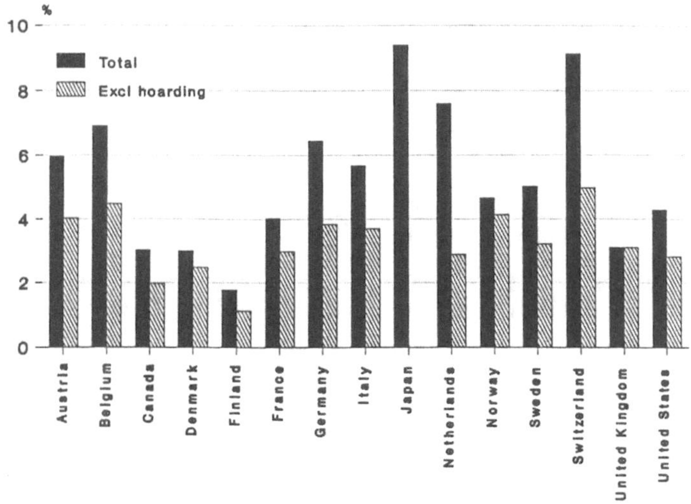

life of this note, probably caused by the introduction of the 1,000 and 5,000 Franc notes at end-1980 and in 1982, respectively. Besides these countries, Switzerland shows a small decline in hoarding as a percentage of GNP. As mentioned before, estimation based on the note lives only provides overall information on the probable importance and trend of hoarding. It is too crude a method to detect short-term fluctuations in the amount of hoarding, as for instance in Switzerland in the late 1970s. Thus, considerable distortions may result from changes in policy: for example, when there is a change in withdrawal policy, when new types or denominations of notes are issued and/or old ones withdrawn. There are further, although probably minor, distortions when circulation figures do not allow for lost or destroyed notes (BPC, 1966). Finally, the estimated amount of hoarding also includes currency kept abroad that is not regularly returning to the home country. This may be an additional explanation for the relatively high hoarding estimates for Switzerland, Germany and the United States.

According to regression estimates for 1970-1989 and for 1989, there is no statistically significant relationship between the importance of hoarding and the average tax and social security rate, which, however, is probably too crude a measure of fiscal motives. The relationship

Table 4.10 Estimation results for currency outside banks excluding hoarding

Obser-vation period	Estima-tion method	Coefficients					Statistics	
		con-sump-tion	interest rate	ATMs	POS	credit card	$\bar{R}^2$/ SE	DW/ N
		a_1	a_2	a_3	a_4	a_5		
1970-89	WLSw	0.63	-0.007	0.46	-0.13	-1.1	0.998	0.20
		(38.6)	(2.8)	(3.1)	(4.8)	(1.4)	0.097	166
1978-89	WLSw	0.61	-0.006	0.51	-0.09	-1.3	0.999	0.34
		(23.3)	(2.8)	(4.1)	(4.5)	(2.2)	0.071	135
1988	OLS	1.04	-0.016	0.03	-0.06	-5.0	0.922	-
		(11.1)	(0.4)	(0.0)	(0.4)	(1.6)	0.35	14

Explanatory notes: WLSw is weighted least squares, with intercept terms (not presented here) varying by country. t-values within parentheses. In the cross-section estimate for 1988 values are converted into US$.

between hoarding and the value in US $ of the highest denomination appears to be nearly statistically significant with, in the cross-section regression for 1989, a t-value of 1.9. Increasing the value of the highest denomination by US$ 100 is attended by an increase in hoarding of roughly 3%. This result may, however, be distorted to a certain extent by the way hoarding has been estimated. Apart from fiscal and denominational influences, there are of course many other important factors like, for example, demographic and geographical factors, foreign use of a country's currency (as in the case of the US, Switzerland and Germany, but also Austria) and illegal transactions. Most of these factors are, however, hard to quantify and have so far been left out of the analysis.

As figure 4.8 shows, a good deal of the inter-country discrepancies in the currency ratio can be explained from hoarding. After correction for hoarding the currency ratios are much more similar over the countries, most of them ranging between 2% and 4% of gross national product. The regression results in Table 4.10 for the currency outside banks, after correction for hoarding show some support to this result. As expected, the estimated consumption elasticity and the interest elasticity are lower for these currency transactions balances than for the currency including hoarding while the rate of inflation completely loses its statistical significance. Finally, the size of the estimated effect of the use of alternative payments media is more in accordance with the expected values than in the case of currency including hoards.

Thus, the estimation results to date indicate that in some countries the hoarding of banknotes is a quite significant phenomenon, accounting perhaps for 50% or more of value of banknotes in circulation. Moreover, in most countries the importance of these hoards seems to be rising.

4.5 Share of coin in currency circulation

In value terms banknotes form the main part of the currency circulation. On average the coin share amounts to about 5% and it hardly exceeds 10% (Table 4.11). In the long run this share appears to be rather constant, despite the fact that in most countries the value of the highest coin has not kept pace with inflation in the last twenty years. The level of the coin share differs, however, strongly by country and, as Figure 4.9 shows, there can be considerable fluctuations in the short run 17).

The share of coin in the currency circulation is to a great extent determined by the denominational structure, especially by the level of the note-coin boundary. According to Table 4.11, in 1989 eight out of the fifteen countries observed have both a coin and a note at this boundary, the coin generally being by far the most important of the two. The average value of the highest coin in the fifteen countries observed equals US$ 1.7. From the statistical, economic and logistic points of view no unequivocal objective criterion for the optimal level of the note-coin boundary exists (Mori, 1983). Thus Payne and Morgan (1981) suggest a mainly heuristic criterion involving the average day's pay D in a country. They ascertain that the note-coin boundary is usually found between D/50 and D/60. However, the average net day's pay proves

17) The figures on the coin circulation may be distorted to some extent due to coins lost or destroyed and to the impossibility to exclude (all) commemorative coins.

Figure 4.9 Share of coin in total amount of currency circulation

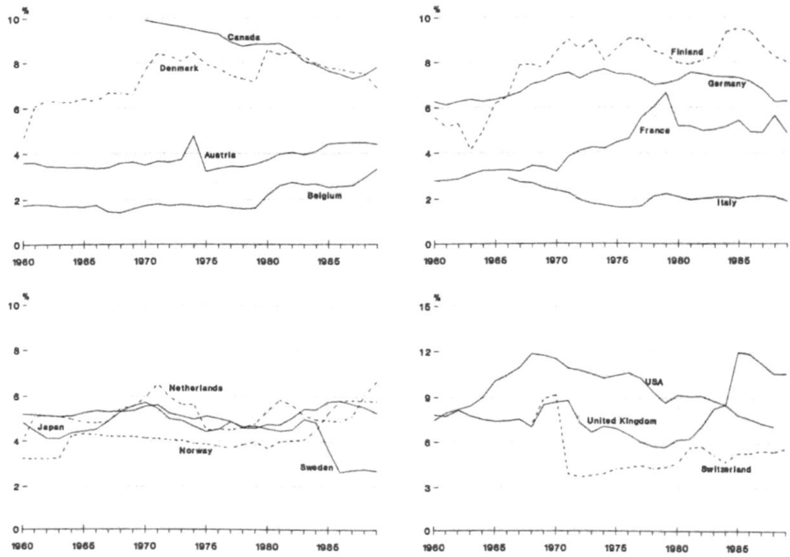

to be rather difficult to evaluate and, moreover, no other payments means like checks and credit cards, that undoubtedly do affect the use of notes are taken into account (Van Droogenbroeck, 1988).

Business economic reasons play an important role. Generally speaking, the life of notes decreases with their real value. Thus, when real value decreases, more banknotes have to be withdrawn from circulation per year and thus costs increase. Moreover, if the actual average life of the lowest note becomes lower than the mean time between issue and return at the central bank, the quality of circulation will worsen, making replacement of the lowest note by a coin desirable at a certain point. For this reason Koeze (1988) proposes the ratio of the observed average life to the mean time between issue and return of banknotes as an

Table 4.11 Share of coin in currency circulation and value of highest coin and lowest note

Country	Share of coin in total currency circulation (%)				Value highest coin (US$) 1989	Value lowest note (US$) 1989	Real value highest coin (1970 = 100)	
	1960	1970	1980	1989			1980	1989
Austria	3.6	3.5	3.7	4.4	1.6	1.6	109	79
Belgium	1.7	1.7	2.2	3.3	1.4	2.7	101	167
Canada	-	9.9	8.8	7.8	0.8	0.8	49	30
Denmark	4.6	7.7	8.6	6.9	1.5	1.5	75	43
Finland	5.6	8.5	8.0	8.0	1.2	2.3	33	19
France	2.8	3.2	5.2	4.9	1.7	1.7	39	22
Germany	6.3	7.4	7.2	6.3	2.8	2.8	61	48
Italy	-	2.4	2.1	1.9	0.4	0.8	51	53
Japan	4.8	5.6	4.8	5.3	3.7	7.3	44	189
Netherlands	4.0	6.0	5.4	6.7	2.5	2.5	48	79
Norway	3.2	4.1	3.7	5.8	1.5	7.6	45	46
Sweden	5.2	5.7	4.6	2.7	0.8	1.6	39	20
Switzerland	-	9.2	4.6	5.6	3.3	6.7	60	45
United Kingdom	7.8	8.7	6.2	10.6	1.7	1.7	29	34
United States	7.5	11.5	9.2	7.1	1	1	49	33
Average	4.8	6.3	5.6	5.9	1.7	2.8	56	61

Explanatory note: Notes and coins no longer issued and commemorative coins have been excluded as far as possible.

objective technical criterion for the note-coin boundary. When this ratio tends to 1, the banknotes of the denomination concerned should be replaced by coins. The result of all these considerations is a lower limit for the note-coin boundary, equalling about US$ 1 in the fifteen observed countries. Below this point, the currency is often used to give change and the notes cannot withstand such wear. The upper limit, equalling about US$ 3, is determined by, among others factors, the profitability of counterfeiting. The counterfeiting of coins is relatively easier, but more expensive than the counterfeiting of banknotes. Thus a high-value coin involves the risk of large-scale counterfeiting (*cf.* Voigtlaender, 1976). Finally, there is the general need for a balanced spread of the denominational mix over notes and coins.

In the ideal situation the value of the highest coin keeps pace with the price level (Payne and Morgan, 1981). However, for practical and political reasons, the frequency with which the level of the note-coin boundary can be raised, is limited. Moreover, the consistency of the denominational structure allows only discrete and relatively large shifts, by a factor 2, 2.5 or even 5. As a consequence the value of the highest coin decreased, on average, by more than 40% in the inflationary 1970s, but has remained practically constant since (Table 4.11).

One of the other factors influencing the share of coin in the currency circulation is inflation. A rise in the price level may cause a shift from coins to notes, as far as this price rise is not compensated by an increase in the note-coin boundary. Moreover, the use of ATMs and POS terminals could be of some importance, the ATMs increasing the use of notes. POS terminals, on the contrary, may diminish the use of cash for higher amounts in particular, thus causing a rise of the relative importance of coin. The number of coin-operated machines, also a relevant variable, had to be disregarded because of lack of data. The use of vending machines may, however, be of considerable importance. Thus, in the UK and Germany in 1988 4% and 5%, respectively, of the number of coins in circulation were located in coin operated machines (Harrop, 1990). As mainly coins with a higher face value are used in these machines, the value share is considerably higher. In Germany the value share was 13% in 1988. Besides, some other factors, like the interest rate, may be of importance in explaining the share of coins, as far as they influence the demand for coin in a different way from the demand for notes. Moreover, as said before, hoarding may play an important role. On the basis of the foregoing the following relationship has been estimated for the fifteen countries observed, with the expected sign above the coefficients 18):

18) The demand for coin is considered as part of total demand for currency. This approach basically follows that of Fase (1981b), who assumes, however, a constant ratio between the two types of currency. Separate explanation of the coin circulation, using multivariate analysis, as applied by Fase (1985b) and Van der Knoop and Hooijmans (1989), seems less appropriate for explaining long-term development.

$$\ln CVC_{it}/CV_{it} = \beta_{0i} + \overset{+}{\beta}_1 \ln HCV_{it} + \overset{-}{\beta}_2 \ln P_{it} + \overset{+}{\beta}_3 r_{it}$$

$$+ \overset{-}{\beta}_4 NATM_{it}/POP_{it} + \overset{+}{\beta}_5 NPOS_{it}/POP_{it} + \overset{?}{\beta}_6 trend_t \qquad (4.3)$$

CVC	value of coin circulation (end-of-year figure)
CV	value of total circulation (end-of-year figure)
r	rate of interest (average of short and long-term rate)
HCV	value of highest coin (¢, current prices)
P	price level (consumer price index)
NATM	number of ATMs (average end-of-year figures)
NPOS	number of POS-terminals (average end-of-year figures)
POP	population (in millions)
trend	trend variable (trend = 1, 2, 3 .....20)

The OLS regression estimates are summarized in Table 4.12. The coefficient of the trend term was not significantly different from zero. This implies that, if there are no changes in the other determinants, the share of coin in the total value of the currency circulation is constant and the coin circulation growths proportionally to the banknote circulation. According to the estimation results, a 10 percent higher value of the highest coin increases the coin share by about 2.5 percent, or 0.5 percentage points. The estimates are nearly the same if in equation (4.3) the value of the lowest note is used instead of the value of the highest coin, and are therefore not mentioned here. The size of this effect appears to be the same for countries that have notes as well as coins at the note-coin boundary. The effect of a higher nominal coin value is significantly greater than the negative effect of the price level, thus indicating a kind of 'coin illusion'. A rise in the interest rate increases the coin share. This is so because the higher denominations, which are partly used as a store of value, are more interest elastic than coin, which is mainly used as a means of transaction. The ATMs have only a (small) negative effect when the equation is estimated over the whole sample period. The impact of POS terminals on the share of coins is positive, indicating that the use of coins is less strongly affected by this alternative payments medium.

Table 4.12 Estimates for share of coin in circulation value

Estimation period	Coefficients					Statistics	
	Value highest coin β_1	Price level β_2	Interest rate β_3	ATMs β_4	POS β_5	$\bar{R}^2$/ SR	DW/ N
1970-89	0.21 (7.7)	-0.09 (2.9)	0.005 (1.4)	-0.21 (1.7)	0.10 (3.6)	0.995 0.128	0.43 261
1978-89	0.24 (6.8)	-0.17 (2.8)	0.010 (2.4)	0.10 (0.6)	0.06 (2.0)	0.995 0.122	0.53 170
1988	0.38 (0.3)	-	0.25 (1.0)	-7.6 (2.3)	0.13 (0.2)	0.233 1.61	- 15
1988	-0.41 (0.6)	-	-	-5.4 (1.7)	0.42 (0.9)	0.223 1.63	- 15

Explanatory notes: The estimation method is OLSw. t-values within parentheses; ATMs and POS terminals per thousand inhabitants.

The estimated equations are rather successful in explaining the development of the coin share over time by country. As appears from the cross-section estimates for 1988, the inter-country differences can, however, hardly be explained by a comparable relationship. The interest elasticity becomes implausibly high, and if the interest rate is excluded, the coefficient of the value of the highest coins (in terms of US$) gets the wrong, negative sign. Apparently, with respect to these differences other factors play a role, like tradition, the size and weight of coins 19) or the spread of vending machines which we were not able to take into account owing to lack of data.

4.6 Number of notes and denominational structure

A final interesting question is how many notes are required to meet the currency demand. We concentrate here on banknotes which, as seen before amount on average to nearly 95% of the total currency circulation. The average number of notes *per capita* in the countries considered shows a

19) *Cf.* Kohli (1988), who explains the distribution of the Swiss banknote circulation partly from the physical size of the various denominations.

Table 4.13 Number of notes and some relevant characteristics in 1989

Country	Number of notes *per capita* 1960	1970	1980	1989	Notes value *per capita* in US$	Size of note range	Value highest note in US$	Value lowest note in US$	Average note value in US$	Real average note value 1960=100
Austria	13	18	31	40	1,157	6	400	1.6	29	50
Belgium	22	29	34	33	1,200	4	135	2.7	36	52
Canada	13	19	36	45	650	8	769	0.8	14	48
Denmark	17	19	21	27	664	6	147	1.5	25	55
Finland	11	9	18	26	566	5	233	2.3	22	72
France	18	22	23	24	751	6	83	1.7	32	59
Germany	10	12	19	29	1,358	7	556	2.8	47	82
Italy	9	16	25	38	938	7	77	0.8	24	5
Japan	26	32	50	67	2,232	3	73	7.3	33	27
Netherlands	15	15	23	24	1,222	7	500	2.5	51	91
Norway	19	23	40	27	1,044	4	152	7.6	39	71
Sweden	19	25	49	45	1,250	6	1613	1.6	28	51
Switzerland	-	22	30	37	2,987	7	667	6.7	81	58
United Kingd.	31	28	35	24	469	5	83	1.7	19	97
United States	18	23	36	50	931	7	100	1.0	19	53
Average	17	21	31	36	1,161	5.9	373	2.8	33	58

Explanatory note: Real average note value of Switzerland on basis 1970=100.

considerable increase from, less than 20 in the 1960s to over 35 in 1989 (Table 4.13). The growth as well as the level differ strongly by country. Thus, the United Kingdom managed to lower the number of notes *per capita* from 31 to 24, due to the relatively low *per capita* value of the note circulation and the introduction of the £ 1 coin in 1982. On the other hand, in the United States the number more than doubled to 50 notes *per capita* in 1988, mainly due to a considerably higher circulation value and the intensive use of the US$ 1 note, with a relatively low face value. Besides the value of the lowest note, other denominational features are of importance. Thus, in Japan the number of notes *per capita* amounts to 67, despite of the high face value of its lowest note, being equivalent to US$ 7. Apart from the high circulation value *per capita*, this may be the consequence of the limited number of denominations of only 3.

Table 4.14 Elasticities of number of notes *per capita* in 1989

Dependent variable	Circulation value of notes *per capita*	Value lowest note	Value highest note	Number of denominations	$\bar{R}^2$
Number of notes *per capita*	0.68 (4.0)	-0.51 (3.5)	0.05 (0.6)	-0.90 (2.5)	0.51 0.22
Number of notes *per capita*	0.70 (4.3)	-0.49 (3.5)	-	-0.78 (2.7)	0.54 0.21

Explanatory note: all values were converted in US $.

As appears from the cross-section estimations in Table 4.14, more than 50% of the variation in the number of notes *per capita* in the fifteen countries observed can be explained from the factors mentioned (see also Figure 4.10). A 10% higher circulation value is attended by a 7% higher number of notes. A 10% higher value of the lowest note allows a 5% lower number of notes. On the other hand, the value of the highest note has only a small, statistically insignificant, positive influence. Apparently, in general the value at the top of the note range is not a significant bottleneck. A higher variety of denominations clearly decreases the number of notes by enabling a more efficient payment pattern. A one-denomination smaller note range is attended on average by a 15% higher number of notes.

The analysis shows that the denominational structure is of major importance for the number of notes needed. No unequivocal criterion for the structure of the banknote range exists. As explained in section 5, with respect to the lowest note denomination technical and economic factors play a role as well as counterfeiting aspects. This results at present in a value of the lowest note of, on average, about US$ 3. The value of the highest note, which on average equals nearly US$ 375 in the countries considered, is mainly based on tradition, although the development of the payment system is of some importance. Thus, credit card oriented countries like the United States, the United Kingdom and France, have relatively low highest notes equivalent to US$ 80 to US$ 100. On the other hand, the highest note in Japan of less than US$ 75 does not reflect its still heavily cash-oriented payment system.

Figure 4.10 Actual and computed number of notes *per capita*, 1989

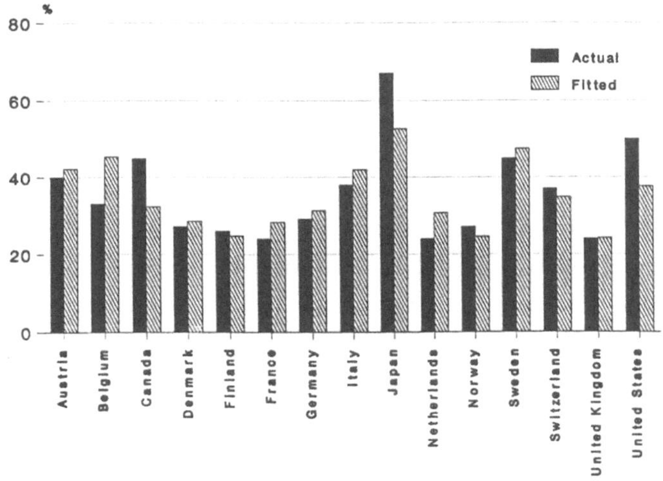

With respect to the banknote series it is generally assumed that the denominations should approach as much as possible a geometric distribution, with equal multiplicative distances 20). The series 1-2-5-10-50, used in nearly all the countries, basically meets this restriction. However, in a number of countries the series shows one or more gaps or relatively large distances as in Japan with its series 100-1000-10000. Given the ideal (geometrically) equidistant denominational structure, inflation can, in principle, be absorbed by simultaneously raising the lowest and highest note after a period when the price level has gone up by 200% (replacement face value 1 by 2) or 250% (replacement face value 2 by 5). The more denominations are available, the smaller the mutual distances and the smaller the gaps, and the more gradually inflation can be absorbed. However, practical factors, like clarity, put

20) *Cf.* Hentsch (1973). On the basis of the observed correlations Hentsch (1983, 1985) defines the normalized circulation of a denomination as its circulation divided by the square root of its face value. Deviations from the 'circulation corrigée' indicate an unbalanced banknote structure. Van Droogenbroeck (1988) and Temmerman (1990) apply this approach to evaluate the denominational structure of Belgium and the BPC countries, respectively. The method helps to spot anomalies. As with the method of Payne and Morgan (1981) it has only empirical foundation and the effect of alternative payments media are not taken into account. This last objection also holds for the the theoretically much more fundamental approach of Cramer (1983a and 1986a), who computes the average frequency of notes and coins, assuming efficient payment, involving a minimum number of coins and notes (see also Chapter 2).

limits to the number of denominations. On average, the series in the countries observed consists of six different notes, with a minimum of three and a maximum of eight (Table 4.13).

The idea of inflationary invariance assumes that notes with the same real value are basically equivalent, regardless of face value. That means that a note of 10 takes over the function of a note of 5 after a period of 100% inflation, *i.e.* a doubling of the price level. Actually this is not always the case, as can be seen from the development of the composition of the note circulation in the various countries. In particular the denominations that are a multiple of 10 seem to be preferred by the public, probably because of their computational ease. For a proper evaluation of this phenomenon, however, the position of the relevant notes in the note range has to be reckoned with. Thus, in a (1-5-10-50) range, the relative distance to the next higher note is 2.5 times higher for the notes whose face values are powers of ten than those whose face values are five times powers of ten. According to Manski and Goldin (1987) the 2.25 times higher demand which they find for the former denominations in Israel corresponds to this fact.

On average, over the last twenty years neither the bottom nor the top of the banknote range has kept pace with inflation in the countries observed. The value of the lowest note has dropped, on average, by 50% since 1970. The highest note, which has been kept unchanged by ten out of the fifteen countries, has dropped, on average, by 37% in value since 1970. The average real average, *i.e.* deflated, note value has, on average, fallen by 40% since 1970 in the observed countries 21). This may reflect the diminishing use of banknotes for higher-value payments. Apart from possible rigidities within the banknote range, this phenomenon reflects the substitution of banknotes as a means of payment for high amounts by alternative payments media. But the drop in the real average note value also results from the fact that the adjustment of the

21) The huge increase in the real average note value in Finland in 1966 is because all Finnish notes were changed (so that 100 'old' FIM equalled 1 'new' FIM). The old notes were, and are, in fact, still valid.

Figure 4.11 Real average note value

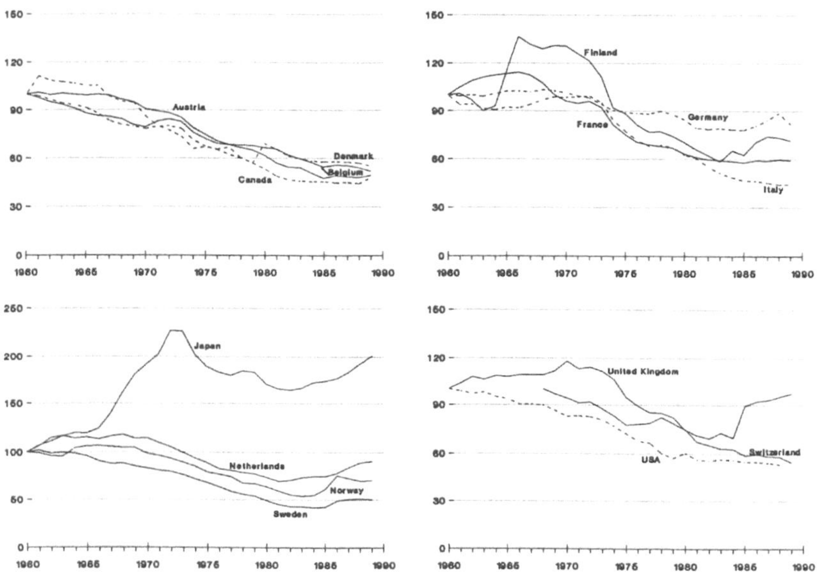

note boundaries has lagged behind inflation. This is illustrated by the United Kingdom, which, due to appropriate denominational adjustment, shows a stable real average note value over the last 30 years, despite major innovations in the payments system. A relative constant real average note value may also reflect an increase in hoarding, which raises the circulation of the highest denominations in particular. This is probably the case in countries like Germany and the Netherlands.

To quantify the relationship between the number and the value of notes and the degree of inflation invariance of the circulation over time, we start with the identity

$$BN = (BN/BV) * BV = BV/BAV \qquad (4.4)$$

BN number of notes
BV value of notes
BAV average value of notes

which says that the number of notes grows proportionally to their nominal value if the average note value BAV is constant. Actually, this average value in all countries shows a significant upward trend, mainly as a result of inflation. Given the value of notes, analysed in the earlier chapters, explaining the number of notes boils down to explaining the average note value BAV. The further analysis in this section thus mainly concentrates on the latter variable, for which the following loglinear specification has been estimated with the expected signs shown above the coefficients.

$$\ln BAV = \beta_{0i} + \overset{+}{\beta}_1 \ln P_{it} + \overset{+}{\beta}_2 \ln VLN_{it} + \overset{+}{\beta}_3 \ln VHN_{it} + \overset{+}{\beta}_4 \, cons_{it} + \overset{+}{\beta}_5 \ln BAV_{it-1} \quad (4.5)$$

P price level (consumption)
cons real consumption
VLN value lowest note
VHN value highest note
i country index (i = 1,2,...15)

A higher price level P leads to a higher average note value BAV. If $\beta_1 = 1$ then, *ceteris paribus*, the real average note value BAV/P remains constant. The growth of the number of notes then mainly depends on the real economic development. As mentioned before, in most countries the average note value does not keep pace with inflation, so that β_1 is expected to lie between 0 and 1. The expected impact of real consumption, if any, is positive, assuming an increasing average value of purchases with increasing consumption.

The variables VHN and VLN relate to the value of the highest and lowest note, respectively. The higher these values, the higher the expected average note value. The impact of the number of denominations, which can also influence the degree of inflation invariance, fluctuates too little in time to make its influence statistically measurable. Besides the specification with direct adjustment ($\beta_5 = 0$), an equation has also been presented under the assumption of lagged adjustment of the average value to changes in the price level and denominational structure. The

Table 4.15 Long-run elasticities for average note value

	Type of Adjust-ment	Price level β_1	Value lowest note β_2	Value highest note β_3	R^2/SE	DW/N
1970-89	without lag	0.61 (47.4)	0.18 (8.2)	0.007 (0.5)	0.998 0.088	0.31 298
1970-89	lagged	0.56 (12.2)	0.25 (28.5)	0.090 (1.8)	1.000 0.043	1.77 282
1978-89	without lag	0.69 (20.8)	0.17 (6.9)	-0.007 (0.4)	0.998 0.082	0.42 180
1978-89	lagged	0.60 (5.8)	0.26 (3.2)	0.042 (0.7)	0.999 0.047	1.69 180

Explanatory notes: t-values within parentheses. The Durbin-H statistics for the lagged specification are 2.26 and 2.62, respectively.

coefficients, or elasticities, found for the above equation are shown in Table 4.15. It was found that the long-term elasticity with respect to the price level is fairly robust, lying between about 0.6 and 0.7. This means that 60% to 70% of the price increase is absorbed by a higher average note value, which corresponds with the earlier findings of the cross-section analysis. The elasticity with respect to real consumption appeared to be statistically insignificant and very small. Consumption was therefore deleted as explanatory variable in the regression.

The elasticities for the denominational structure indicate that the average value is especially sensitive to changes in the level of the note-coin boundary. An increase of the value of the lowest note by 10% raises the average note value by 2.5% at most, which is half the effect that follows from the cross-section results in Table 4.14. As in the case of the cross-section analysis, the impact of the highest note is considerably less and statistically insignificant.

As yet no significant influence on the average note value could be found for the state of the payments system as reflected by the number of ATMs and POS terminals and the value of credit card transactions. So far the results show that only 60% to 70% of inflation is absorbed by a rise in the average note value. The remaining part leads to a further increase of the number of notes. Moreover, changes in the denominational structure appear to be an adequate instrument to advance the inflation invariancy of the banknote circulation and to lower the number of notes.

4.7 Conclusions

Our cross-country analysis supports the validity of the inventory model for the transactions demand for currency, indicating economies of scale and some interest sensitiveness, though less strong than predicted by the original inventory model. The rate of inflation only plays a role insofar as the inter-country differences in currency holdings are concerned. Other economic variables like the tax rate do not have any quantitative influence on the currency demand in the fifteen industrial countries observed. According to the findings, the effect of plastic money on the demand for currency as a whole is still limited. On average, the use of credit cards and POS terminals has diminished the average currency growth by about one percentage point per year. Moreover, this negative effect was to a considerable extent compensated by the positive effect of the use of ATMs. Apparently the stimulus of the use of cash by the public and the extra inventories needed by these machines have exceeded the negative effect of a more efficient cash management expected on the basis of micro-economic studies. Only if we assume a transactions elasticity of one (which is not confirmed by the data) the ATMs have a negative influence on demand.

One reason for the rather slow movement in the direction of a cashless society is that the degree of dispersion and the intensity of use of these alternative means of payment are as yet by far too low for a substantial reduction in the use of cash. The limited importance of plastic money and especially EFTS/POS is not only due to cost and charging problems (see Ravensloot, 1990, for calculations for the Netherlands) but also to problems regarding malfunctions, fraud, privacy and standardisation (Morelli, 1985; Moore, 1986; OECD, 1989). The other reason for the relatively slow decline of the importance of cash is that currency is also extensively used as a store of value. This part of the currency demand, which runs in a number of countries to as much as 50% and explains a good deal of the inter-country differences in the currency ratio, is rather insensitive to changes in the payment system. Thus, even if, as a result of significant changes in charging policies, plastic money will crowd out currency as a means of payment to a more significant extent, currency will in a great number of countries still be used on a significant scale as a store of value.

The currency inside banks, *i.e.* the till money and vault cash of the banking system, which amounts on average to as much as 15% of the currency outside banks, follows generally speaking the demand for currency by the public, be it that especially the last ten years have shown an increasing degree of economies of scale. Moreover, these cash holdings appear to be rather sensitive to the level of the opportunity costs, as they are reflected by the interest rate (as far as these balances are not included in the cash reserve requirements). Also the density of the branch networks, both of the banks themselves and of the central bank, influence the banks need for currency, the former inducing an increase, the latter allowing some reduction.

Where the components of the currency circulation are concerned, it appears that, in the long run, the share of coin in the currency circulation is rather stable, depending on inflation and the denominational structure, in particular the level of the note-coin boundary. The number of notes that are required for the note circulation, on average accounting for nearly 95% of the currency circulation, increases, on average, more than the real value of the currency circulation. Partly due to insufficient adjustments of the banknote ranges, only about 60% to 70% of inflation is actually absorbed by a shift in the average banknote value. The inter-country comparison clearly shows a statistically significant influence of the efficiency of the denominational structure on the number of notes needed.

In general, the analysis is rather successful in explaining the development of the various variables by country over time. The differences between the countries are in general more difficult to explain, and have partly to be attributed to other, economic, historical, sociological and institutional factors not included in our analysis. Nevertheless, in most cases we were able to explain 50% or more of the inter-country variation by our analysis.

5 EPILOGUE

5.1 Summary

For those economists who regard currency primarily as a means of payment, things looked rather sunny in the 1950s. The inventory theory approach as proposed by Baumol in 1952 provided an elegant underpinning of the way in which the demand for transactions balances would depend on income, interest rates and transfer cost. In particular, the model predicted that households and firms could considerably economize on cash balances relative to income, as income rose. In the subsequent twenty-five years, however, a battery of arguments was elaborated to show why Baumol's 'suggestive oversimplification' would not hold for the real world. By taking into account the real value of time effects, mutual interdependencies and the presence of uncertainty, the original theoretical values of the relevant elasticities were replaced by wide ranges for the various effects. The income elasticity might even range from economies to diseconomies of scale, as is shown by the overview of the literature in the first chapter of this study. Consequently, the answer regarding the actual relationship is to be found in empirical evidence, which is, however, complicated by the impossibility of distinguishing the transactions motive from other motives for holding currency.

Since then, the currency circulation in most countries has decreased considerably relative to income. Consequently a number of studies for currency and broader money concepts, including demand deposits, show substantial economies of scale and interest rate sensitivity, though mostly less than predicted by the inventory model. The declining importance of narrow money may, however, equally well ensue from financial innovation, through both more efficient payments systems and wider availability of high interest-earning near moneys. Likewise, the effects of the interest rate may be overestimated, insofar as higher interest rates have speeded up financial innovation. Studies which explicitly model the technological change indeed find that this factor has a considerable effect on the demand for money. Cross-sectional studies, not distorted by these kinds of problems common to the time series approach, do, at least for firms, not show any substantial economies of scale. A number of factors, such as the easier availability of credit to larger firms as well as limits on overdrafts and minimum deposit requirements may, however, conceal the actual presence of economies of scale. For households, as far as we know, hardly any systematic testing of the transactions theory has been performed, neither with respect to currency demand nor with respect to payment patterns.

In this study we shed some light on these so far unanswered questions regarding the money demand along four lines, realizing that this is only possible by taking into account the influences of alternative payments media. Thus we implicitly provide insight into the use of various kinds of plastic money. The analysis of the *aggregate currency demand in the Netherlands* since 1955 shows that the demand for currency is slightly dependent on the interest rate and inflation, but does not indicate any economies of scale, if allowance is made for the large-scale introduction of debitable accounts and guaranteed checks since 1965. These two dominant alternative payments media - credit card and point-of-scale transactions amount as yet to less than 1% of consumer expenditure - are fully responsible for the 40% fall in the currency ratio between 1965 and 1975, reducing the nominal currency circulation growth by, on average, 5 percentage points per year.

But this is not where the story ends. Since 1975 the currency ratio in the Netherlands has increased by nearly one percentage point to 7.2% of gross national product in 1990. This increase, which is mainly located in the highest two denominations of Fl. 1,000 and Fl. 250, has been due to the use of currency, and especially banknotes, as a *store of value*. On the basis of the decreasing average life of banknotes, which reflects a decline in the intensity of their use, we estimate that in 1990 50% to 60% of the currency circulation, or Fl. 20 billion, was hoarded. This result is supported by an abundance of independent empirical evidence, varying from a sample survey on the money demand by sector in 1971 to a non-conventional qualitative survey on the use of Fl. 1,000 notes in 1986, and from an analysis of movements in the banknote circulation after fiscal rumours and withdrawals of old types of notes to the implications of a micro-econometric analysis of the payments and cash management behaviour of households. Presumably the interest forgone, the storage costs and the costs of possible loss or theft are outweighed by its liquidity, the risk perception of bank deposits and the protection of anonymity. It can indeed be shown theoretically, as we did, that it may well be worthwhile to keep currency in hoards out of fiscal motives. In any case, the share of hoarded balances in the broad money concept M3, including savings deposits, is remarkably stable, suggesting that they function as one of the possible portfolio assets. After excluding the hoarded balances, the currency demand function shows clear economies of scale. This means that the transactions elasticity of unity of Dutch currency demand ensues from economies of scale in the transactions balances and diseconomies of scale in the store of value balances, hoards being a luxury. Moreover, the corrected currency figures show a much stronger effect of guaranteed check payments, confirming the hypothesis that currency hoards may be rather insensitive to the use of alternative payments media. However, in this respect the results are somewhat ambiguous.

Generally speaking, this picture is supported by the *findings for the total of fifteen industrial countries* considered in this study, indicating economies of scale in the currency holdings and a statistically significant, negative effect of the interest rate. The size of both effects is, however, smaller than predicted by the original inventory model and the economies of scale may be overrated due to the incomplete modelling of financial innovations, especially the substitution effects of checks. Additionally, hoarding currency appears to be a worldwide phenomenon. Nearly all of the fifteen countries show a substantial degree of hoarding, especially the low-inflation countries Germany and Switzerland. Together with the Netherlands and Sweden, these two are also the countries where the highest banknote denomination has by far the highest value. Considering the relatively low hoarding percentage in Sweden it would, however, be going too far to put these two observations together. According to the analysis of the use of Fl. 1,000 notes in the Netherlands, these notes are notably used in illegal or grey sectors and hoarded by households. For countries like Switzerland, Germany and the United States, the storage in foreign countries may also be significant. There is, however, no fundamental reason why these uses would be strongly diminished by the withdrawal of the highest denomination. Apart from some marginal decline due to greater inconvenience, it would simply be replaced by the next lower denomination and this would lead to a larger note production.

As a consequence of hoarding, the *transactions velocity* of currency is rather low. According to our estimates the currency circulation in the Netherlands turned over less than 5 times in 1990, accounting for a total amount of payments of about Fl. 170 billion. This is the outcome of about 55% of the circulation being kept in hoards and hardly moving at all, and 45% turning over about 11 times a year. The overall currency velocity, which showed a remarkable decline in the 1980s due to the increase of hoarding, is considerably lower than is mostly assumed. However, none of the currency turnover figures we could distil from international publications suggest a velocity of more than 10 times a year. Thus, despite its high degree of moneyness, currency is substantially less intensively used than demand deposits, which turned over in the Netherlands in the late-1980s about 40 times a year. As was already suggested by Keynes in 1930, the intensity of use is much more connected with the type of balances than with the type of money. Thus currency kept in transactions balances has a much higher rate of turnover than currency kept in hoards. Likewise, the demand deposits of households have a much lower turnover rate than the demand deposits of firms. This is the major reason why the transactions velocity of both currency and demand deposits declined, when in the years 1965-1975 households were induced to shift part of their active currency balances to demand deposits. The velocity of currency and demand deposits together remained, however, nearly unchanged.

Assuming that the substitution of checks for currency payments has largely come to an end, the *future of currency* strongly depends on the impact of *plastic money*. This concerns primarily the use of credit and prepayment cards and point-of-sale terminals. Our multi-country analysis points at the expected negative effect of these alternative payments media on currency demand, be it that their effect in general is somewhat overrated, possibly also reflecting some of the substitution effects of the perforce not considered check payments. We estimate that the credit card and point-of-sale transactions reduced the nominal growth of the currency circulation of 6.0% in 1981-1989 in the countries considered by, on average, 1.1 percentage points per year. The effects were the strongest in Denmark, the United Kingdom and France, where they came to a total annual growth reduction of 2.9, 1.9 and 1.6 percentage points, respectively. The substitution effects are in general supported by the results of our cross-section analysis of the payment patterns of Dutch households in 1990 based on survey data.

Our findings are, however, mixed where it comes to the effect of the use of *cash dispensers and automated teller machines* (ATMs). It is theoretically not clear beforehand to what degree economizing on average transactions balances due to lower disbursement costs is offset by the increased use of currency induced by its lower overall costs and wider availability. The results of our multi-country analysis suggest that the latter effect predominates. Thus, the introduction of these machines has raised the nominal currency growth, on average, by 0.9 percentage point per year. This positive effect also follows from the two available country studies for Belgium and Finland and from our exploratory estimates for the Netherlands, but is contradicted by the findings for Israel. The positive effect we found is, however, not very robust. For instance, ATMs have a negative impact on currency demand as soon as we assume unit elasticity with respect to consumer expenditure. This ambiguity may also reflect that households slowly adjust when economizing on their balances.

According to our microeconometric analysis of the *cash management* of Dutch households in 1990, the use of ATMs induces households to economize on their transactions balances by more than 15%. In fact ATM users economize by nearly 35% on these balances, withdrawing Fl. 200 as compared to Fl. 300 in the case of non-users. Part of this discrepancy is, however, due to the different characteristics of ATM users, being younger, more check-oriented and so forth. The second effect of ATMs, *i.e.* to stimulate people to pay by currency, is not clearly supported by the data. The reduced amount per disbursement is for the greater part compensated by the increased frequency of disbursement. Neither do we find an equivocal positive effect of the use of ATMs on cash payments.

Consequently, our estimates do not show a statistically significant effect of the use of ATMs on total cash turnover, thus not firmly supporting our macro-economic findings. The pure transactions balances of households account, however, for only about 6% of the total amount of currency in circulation. This means that even substantial economizing on households' cash balances may be hardly observable in the total circulation figures. Of the remaining circulation 6% has to be found in savings balances of households, 15% with the business sector and 1% offshore. The remaining 70% or so, which probably consists mainly of banknotes of Fl. 250 and Fl. 1,000, is to be found notably in grey sectors, like the drugs trade, the gambling sector and the car trade, as well as in hoards of households.

The micro-econometric approach provides us with the opportunity to test the *validity of the inventory model* with respect to the cash management and the transactions balances of households. This issue has not been dealt with in the empirical literature thus far. In general, our regression results suggest the predicted economies of scale on the individual level, the transactions elasticity being 0.4 or even less. Moreover, our results confirm the validity of a number of the refinements, in particular of the value of time hypotheses. Thus a higher value of time, resulting in higher opportunity costs of withdrawing money, may be the main reason for individuals with jobs, with higher incomes, and with larger families, to withdraw cash less often, but in larger amounts. On the other hand, lower transactions costs due to smaller distances to the bank (reflected by the degree of urbanization) and the availability of ATMs and less effort (as reflected by age) result in relatively higher frequencies of withdrawal, with lower amounts per disbursement. What the outcomes, however, also suggest is that the opportunity costs as represented by the brokerage fee are probably low relative to the costs involved in loss or theft and storage costs. Without these costs it would be much more rational to withdraw all the money needed each month at once.

When it comes to *payment patterns* and currency as a means of payment, we have to distinguish between total payments and household payments. The share of currency payments in total payments declined between 1965 and 1975 from more than 12% to 6.5%, mainly due to the large-scale introduction of salary accounts. Since then this share has remained fairly constant. The total amount of currency payments in 1990 may be estimated at Fl. 170 billion. Things look, however, quite different where the payments by households are concerned, which we estimate at Fl. 100 billion in 1990. In 1986 nearly 40% of the total amount of household expenditure was still paid cash, as compared to 14% by means of checks and 47% by means of giro transfers. Since then the picture seems to have hardly changed, credit card and POS payments still being of minor importance and check payments having shown a remarkable stagnation due to the fees charged by part of the banking system since 1988. In terms of numbers, currency accounts for nearly 80% of all household payments. As payments by households predominate in terms of numbers, payments in the business sector involving much larger amounts but being much less numerous, currency is still the most widely used means of payment.

As predicted by elaborations of the inventory model, the way purchases are paid for depends primarily on the size of the amount involved. In addition, the type of the good or service and the spending place are important, as well as a number of personal characteristics. If we concentrate on the behaviour of individuals, it appears that employed people with higher incomes, and people with larger families pay significantly less in cash. This confirms the validity of the value of time hypothesis, which tells us that the higher the opportunity costs, the more people will economize on the time spent going to the bank. Moreover, better educated people experience a lower barrier to paying with alternative payments media. Furthermore, the degree of urbanization, reflecting the wider availability of alternative payments media, seems to reduce the amount paid in cash. This result is, however, not unambiguous, probably due to the fact that in urbanized regions cash is also relatively easier to obtain.

So far we considered currency in circulation as an aggregate, not distinguishing between notes and coin. Moreover, we ignored the currency holdings of the banking sector, which are not included in the monetary-theoretic currency concept, but which are of equal importance as far as the total currency needs and the size of seigniorage are concerned. In the Netherlands the *till money of the banking sector* accounts for about 7% of the total currency circulation, as compared to nearly 13% in the fifteen countries considered. Generally speaking the banks' till money moves in parallel with the currency demand by the public, showing some, especially in the last ten years increasing, economies of scale. High interest rates induce banks to economize on their till money. In countries where till money is included in the cash reserve requirements, and thus interest costs are not relevant, the till money holdings are significantly higher. Moreover, the branch network is also of significance, more bank branches requiring additional till money. Alternatively, a denser central bank branch network will lead to a reduction of the need of banks for vault cash. Finally, the installation of cash dispensers and ATMs *ceteris paribus* significantly increases the banking system's need for currency. The restriction is that the installation of ATMs is not compensated by the closing of branches. Consequently, even if, in the long run, the use of ATMs reduces the currency balances of the public, this effect may be largely compensated for by the increase in the vault cash needs of the banking sector as a whole.

The share of *coin* in the currency circulation is fairly stable in the long run, amounting to about 7% in the Netherlands in 1990. The same is true for the fifteen countries considered here, where the average amounts to 6%. The constancy of the coin share is to a great extent the result of the absorption of price level changes by an upward shift of the note-coin boundary. At least in the 1970s the level of this boundary did not, on average, keep pace with the rise in the price level. The use of POS terminals appears to reduce the note circulation more than the need for coin, as the relevant payments tend to involve higher amounts.

Where *the demand for banknotes* is concerned, there are large differences between the numbers of notes *per capita*, ranging from around 25 in the United Kingdom, France and the Netherlands, to 50 in the United States and 67 in Japan. Half the inter-country variation can be explained from the nominal demand *per capita* as well as from the value of the lowest note and the efficiency of the banknote range, as reflected by the number of denominations. The more denominations, the fewer notes are needed. Contrary to what has been suggested in the literature, a more efficient denominational structure, however, does not necessarily imply lower nominal balances. These outcomes are confirmed by our simulations on the basis of the frequency distribution of payments of Dutch households. The simulations also suggest that the efficiency of the Dutch banknote range can hardly be improved by changes in the composition.

5.2 Conclusions

Thus, the main conclusions of our study may be summarized as follows. First, our findings support to some extent the *applicability of the inventory theory* to the demand for currency. On a cross-sectional basis we find clear economies of scale in the neighbourhood of the values predicted by the inventory model. The less strong economies of scale resulting from the time series analysis may reflect the real value of time effect and the presence of other motives for holding money. Our micro-analysis suggests very high opportunity costs of holding money, not so much because of the interest forgone, but more because of the perceived costs of loss and theft. The effect of the interest rate *per se* as observed in the time series analysis is therefore considerably lower than predicted by the original inventory model. We can explain about half the differences in the currency ratio between countries, mainly from the interest rate, the inflationary performance and the use of alternative payments media. By taking into account the size of the currency hoards in the various countries we may explain more than 90% of inter-country discrepancies. Moreover, the resulting transactions balances then show higher a degree of economies of scale over time.

Secondly, the presence of a substantial degree of hoarding means that, even in a basically cashless society *there may still remain a considerable amount of currency in circulation*, being sensitive to interest rates, alternative investment opportunities and fiscal changes, much more than to the use of plastic money. Consequently, the currency circulation may shift in the direction of a composition consisting mainly of low-value coins used as change and high-value notes used for hoarding. Due to the high face value of notes used for hoarding purposes, large amounts may be involved, but only a limited number of notes are needed. Thus in 1990 in the Netherlands, although accounting for more than 50% of the amount of banknotes in circulation, their number amounted to 30 million, or 9% of the total number of notes.

Thirdly, for the time being, the *effects of the use of plastic money* on the demand for currency should not be overrated. Despite the introduction and promotion of credit cards, POS and checks, the amount of currency in circulation in the fifteen industrial countries observed has grown in the 1980s by, on average, 6.5% per year. In real terms this growth was more than 3%. Even in France, the country which has made most advances in the use of plastic money, real balances still increased by more than 1% per year. One reason for these modest effects is that part of the currency is used as a store of value and is thus insensitive to changes in the payment system. The other reason is that the proliferation of plastic money is still limited. Only in the United States and Canada did plastic money transactions account for as much as 12% of consumer expenditure in 1989. In all the other countries this was less than 10%, averaging at 5%. The limited importance of plastic money and especially EFTS/POS is partly due to problems regarding malfunctions and fraud, privacy and standardisation. The other crucial problem to be solved is that of costs and the charging policy. As shown by our micro-analysis, individuals are very sensitive not only to loss and theft, but also to changes in transfer costs. This implies that the large-scale acceptance of plastic money first of all depends on whether the charging problems are solved in a way which is acceptable to consumers and retailers. If so, we may indeed expect a more dramatic decline in the transactions balances of currency. This effect may range from a reduction of some 25% as expected by the consumer according to our findings, to a reduction of about 40% as also resulted from the introduction of salary accounts and guaranteed checks since 1965.

Fourth and finally, as far as the consequences for *monetary policy* are concerned, a shift from currency to demand deposit balances ensuing from an increased use of credit card, POS, or prepayment card facilities *ceteris paribus* has no essential implications for the assessment of the monetary aggregates M1, M2 or M3. One may assume that the use of the relevant transactions balances as well as their velocity will remain basically unchanged. Thus, contrary to the premise of the 'motion' theory, *viz.* that the velocity of circulation is a property of money, as a kind of energy inherent in it, it is much more a property of a certain type of balances, depending on the purpose for which they are used.

ANNEX

ANNEX I TOTAL PAYMENTS, CASH PAYMENTS, VELOCITY OF CURRENCY CIRCULATION AND ECONOMIC KEY VARIABLES IN A NUMBER OF COUNTRIES

Table I.1 Total payments, cash payments and transactions velocity of currency

Country	Year	Total payments: value (blns) (1)	Total payments: number (blns) (2)	Cash payments: value (blns) (3)	Cash payments: as % of total (4)	Cash payments: number (mlns) (5)	Cash payments: as % of total (6)	Cash payments: average US $ value (7)	Number of payments per cap per day (8)	Cash payments as % cons. (9)	Currency outside banks (blns): total (10)	Currency outside banks (blns): excluding hoarding (11)	Transactions velocity of currency: total (12)	Transactions velocity of currency: excluding hoarding (13)	Total payments as % of GNP (14)	Gross national product (blns) (15)	Private consumption (blns) (16)	Population (mlns) (17)	Source of figures
Belgium a)	1989	274064 b)	0.8 b)						0.23 b)		422.4	254.2			44.8	6117	3833	10.0	BIS (1989)
Canada	1989	20100 b)	3.2 b)						0.33 b)		19.6	12.9			31.0	649	376	26.2	BIS (1989)
Finland	1985						70 ?				6.1	4.8				494	182	5.0	Lilja/Lempinen (1985)
France	1987	51961 c)	33.7 c)	1039 c)	2.0	26.8 c)	80	6.5	1.66	32	222.0	171.5	4.7	6.1	9.8	5321	3246	55.6	BIS (1987)
Germany	1985		40.5			35	86.4		1.81		102.3	64.7				1844	1038	61.2	Schimmelmann (1985)
	1989	24504	46.9	1000	4.1	40	85.3	13.9	2.09	82	145.6	86.8	6.9	11.5	10.8	2260	1213	61.6	BIS (1990)
Italy	1989	14568135 b)	1.6 b)								67481.0	43959.0			12.3	1187992	1213	57.4	BIS (1990)
Japan	1988	5328000	11.7	70000 d)	1.3	10.5 d)	90	24.4 d)	0.26	33	30547.0		2.3		14.5	367380	209529	122.8	Bank of Japan (1990)
Nether-	1982	2136 e)		118	5.5					53	23.3	14.3	5.1	8.3	5.8	369	213	14.3	this study
lands	1986	207 f)	4.9 f)	81 f)	39.0	3.8	78	10.6	0.90	31	29.8	15.5	2.7	5.2	0.5	429	256	14.9	Boeschoten/Fase(1989)
	1989	16599 b)	1.7 b)						0.31 b)		36.0	16.3			35.0	474	281	14.9	BIS (1990)
Sweden	1989	11861 b)	0.8 b)				95 g		0.26 b)		61.3	39.3			9.7	1221	634	8.5	BIS (1990)
Switzerland	1989	61134 h)	0.4 h)						0.16 b)		26.2	14.3			212.9	287	166	6.5	BIS (1990)
United	1972	428 i)	63.5 j)	100 k)	23.4	61.5	97		3.12	248	4.1	4.1	24.5	24.5	6.6	65	40	55.8	Evans and Hailey (1974)
Kingdom	1981	154	50.0	100	65.0	46.5	93		2.43	50	10.7	10.7	9.3	9.3	0.6	254	154	56.4	Trundle/Temperton (1982)
	1976						93 l)				6.6	6.6				125	76	55.9	APACs; Kirkman (1987)
	1981						88 m)				10.0	10.0				254	154	56.4	APACS (1989)
	1984						86 m)				12.4	12.4				324	198	56.5	APACS (1989)
	1987	20101	68.9			62	90		3.32		13.8	13.8			48.0	419	262	56.9	BIS (1989)
	1989	26850 b)	6.0 b)		75.0 f)		78 m)		0.29 b)		15.8	15.8			52.8	509	322	57.0	APACS (1989)
United	1975		233.0			200	86		2.99		74.3	59.4				1598	1009	213.9	Little (1975)
States	1983	181600	159.1	2800	1.5	112	70	25.0	1.84	126	150.6	97.8	18.6	28.6	53.3	3406	2224	237.0	Berger/Humphrey (1986)
		39600n)	159.0n)	2800	7.1	112	70	25.0	1.84	126	150.6	97.8	18.6	28.6	11.6	3406	2224	237.0	Berger/Humphrey (1986)
	1984	2464		887 l)	36.0 l)					37	160.8	104.2	5.5	8.5	0.7	3772	2420	237.0	Avery *et al.* (1986)
	1985										173.1	119.3				4015	2616		Chorafras (1988)
	1987	342523	59.3b)	2190 o)	0.6				0.66	73	199.3	133.2	11.0	16.4	75.7	4524	2998	248.0	BIS (1989)
	1987	342240	334.0	1400	0.4	278.6	83	5.0	3.69	47	199.3	133.2	7.0	10.5	75.6	4524	2998	248.0	Humphrey/Berger (1990)
		61200 n)	333.9 n)	1400	2.3	278.6	83	5.0	3.69	47	199.3	133.2	7.0	10.5	13.5	4524	2998	248.0	Humphrey/Berger (1990)

Explanatory notes: where relevant, the known figures of the total value and/of number of cashless payments have been increased by the estimated cash payments.

a) including (inevitable) double counting.
b) cashless payments only.
c) as far as cash transactions are involved, retail transactions only.
d) figures for banknotes calculated on assumption that notes issued by Bank of Japan in 1988 have been used only once during the year.
e) excluding money market payments.
f) payments by households only.
g) payments at retail outlets only.
h) total giro transfers including interbank payments; excluding cash payments.
i) including Town clearing: 1663; 12% cash; Turnover/GNP - 25.7.
j) excluding cash withdrawals.
k) 1/2 times total turnover of cash over bank counters and with the general public.
l) payments of £ 0.50 and higher.
m) consumer payments of £1 or more.
n) excluding wire transfers.

ANNEX II MONEY, PAYMENTS, TRANSACTIONS AND ECONOMIC KEY VARIABLES IN THE NETHERLANDS 1955-1990

II.1 Elucidation of transactions estimates

The series of current transactions, income transfers and capital transactions for 1965-1990 in Table II.1, are revised actualisations of the estimates by Boeschoten and Fase (1984) 1). The figures for the years 1955-1960 are derived from Cramer (1981), adjusting for the discrepancies in 1965, which are mainly due to different definitions used. By this approach of the total turnover basically purely financial transactions can be excluded. On the other hand, in constructing the series from the national accounts and other sources, it is hardly possible to include all those transactions where money is involved and to avoid double counting. According to Figure I.1, the resulting current transactions, which are connected to output, have slightly declined over time, possibly due to an ongoing vertical and horizontal integration and the increase of the share of services in total output. The other two components, income transfers and especially capital transactions, which are the most closely related to purely financial transactions, increased significantly in relation to the national income.

Figure II.1 Transactions as percentage of gross national product

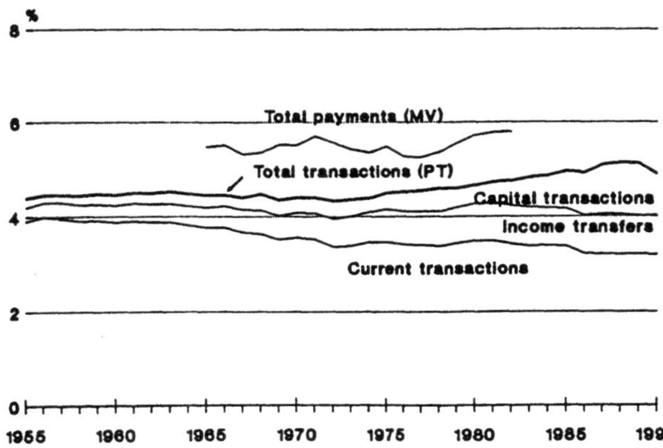

1) See for earlier estimates for the Netherlands Jonker (1973), Cramer (1978) and Cramer (1981).

Table II.1 Money, payments, transactions and economic key variables in the Netherlands
Amounts in billions of guilders

Year	Currency outside banks		Currency in hoards (year average)	Demand deposits (end of year)	M3	Cash withdrawals				Currency payments on basis of			Payments from demand deposits						Total of payments (on note life basis)
	end of year	year average				amount		number (mlns)	average amount (guilders)	note life	note return	cash withdrawals	total	credit card	point of sale	guranteed checks b)			
						total	with ATMs									amount (blns)	number (mlns)	average amount	
1955	4.0	3.7	0.7	5.5	18.6					27.3									
1956	4.2	4.0	0.8	5.1	18.9					28.0	23.0								
1957	4.3	4.1	0.8	4.7	19.7					28.7	23.5								
1958	4.5	4.2	0.8	5.6	22.5					29.8	24.1								
1959	4.6	4.3	0.9	5.9	24.3					30.4	25.5								
1960	5.0	4.6	0.9	6.2	26.5					32.7	27.4								
1961	5.4	5.0	1.0	6.7	28.6					35.0	28.9								
1962	5.8	5.3	1.2	7.1	31.3					37.7	30.5								
1963	6.3	5.8	1.3	7.9	34.9					40.2	32.8								
1964	7.0	6.5	1.5	8.3	38.4					44.1	36.3								
1965	7.7	7.1	1.8	9.2	42.0					48.2	38.4		351						399
1966	8.3	7.7	2.0	9.8	45.2					51.1	41.1		385						436
1967	8.5	8.1	2.1	10.7	50.8					52.5	41.8		410						463
1968	8.6	8.2	2.2	12.8	57.3					53.7	40.9		460			0.3	10.2	30.3	514
1969	9.1	8.7	2.4	13.9	63.7					56.8	39.6		544			0.8	22.6	34.0	601
1970	9.6	9.1	2.6	16.1	70.9					59.6	42.2		612			1.7	40.4	40.9	672
1971	10.1	9.6	2.8	19.5	79.9					62.3	45.6		719			2.8	65.9	42.7	781
1972	11.0	10.3	3.1	24.0	90.4					67.0	51.3		796			3.8	84.7	44.7	863
1973	11.4	11.0	3.5	23.6	104.5					69.4	60.5		893			5.2	104.1	50.2	962
1974	12.3	11.7	3.9	27.0	119.3					73.7	68.9		1007			6.6	118.9	55.4	1081
1975	13.9	12.8	4.4	33.3	133.9	84.5				80.3	79.0	88.7	1127			8.1	142.7	57.0	1207
1976	15.3	14.6	5.3	35.0	155.0	88.0				86.0	90.7	92.4	1242			10.5	167.5	62.5	1328
1977	16.8	15.9	5.9	41.6	174.4	90.4				92.3	99.9	94.9	1357			12.6	184.0	68.7	1449
1978	18.1	17.2	6.6	43.3	192.9	92.2	0.03			98.1	106.1	96.8	1494			16.0	203.9	78.3	1592
1979	19.2	18.4	7.3	43.7	213.0	98.0	0.06			103.7	111.0	102.9	1647			18.5	220.5	84.1	1751
1980	21.3	20.2	8.1	45.6	226.1	102.7	0.07			111.5	117.6	107.8	1810			21.5	242.9	88.4	1922
1981	21.7	21.1	8.6	43.8	243.5	104.6	0.08			112.0	122.6	109.8	1924			23.6	260.0	90.7	2036
1982	23.3	21.8	9.0	49.4	259.7	108.3	0.10			118.3	125.8	113.7	2018			25.8	279.7	92.3	2136
1983	26.3	24.6	10.5	53.8	272.2	113.7	0.11	212	537	128.7	127.4	119.4		1.0		26.8	285.9	93.6	
1984	27.7	26.3	11.7	57.8	287.8	119.5	0.17	227	526	133.6	127.4	125.5		1.0		28.0	287.8	97.5	
1985	28.6	27.8	12.8	62.8	307.1	124.7	0.30	238	524	135.7	131.6	130.9		1.1		30.1	302.3	99.7	
1986	29.8	28.6	13.6	68.1	322.3	130.9	0.64	257	509	135.8	135.9	137.4		1.1		30.7	307.2	100.0	
1987	33.3	30.5	15.1	71.6	331.8	137.2	1.30	277	495	144.1	144.1	144.1		1.6	0.1	32.4	308.4	105.0	
1988	34.6	33.3	17.0	76.7	358.0	148.5	3.61	303	490	147.7	151.3	155.9		1.6	0.3	28.9	263.2	109.9	
1989	36.0	34.5	17.9	83.0	391.8	161.2	7.80	336	480	154.3	157.6	169.3		2.2	0.9	28.6	252.7	113.2	
1990	36.4	35.2	18.5	89.2	421.5		22.90			157.3	175.9			3.1		30.6	250.3	122.2	

Explanatory notes: The series are corrected for breaks. The series of the currency hoards are estimated according to the note life method as described in Chapter 3. The figures on cash withdrawals and payments from demand deposits are estimated from figures published or provided by the banking system. The guaranteed check payments are excluding off shore payments and cashing of checks. The estimates of the cash payments are based on a cash loop of 1,05 in 1987 (see Chapter 1).

Table II.1 Money, payments, transactions and economic key variables in the Netherlands (continued)
Amounts in billions of guilders

Year	Velocity of circulation			Transactions (value)				Gross national product (value)	Private consump-tion (value)	Price level (1980 = 100)	Number of salary accounts (mlns)	Population		Interest rate		Number of ATMs	Number of POS termi-nals
	currency (with note life)	demand depo-sits	total	current trans-actions	income trans-actions	capital trans-actions	total					total	16 years and older	long term	short term		
1955	7.3			124.4	9.5	6.0	139.9	31.9	19.1	28.5	0.8	10.8	7.4	3.2	1.0		
1956	7.0			137.0	10.2	5.5	152.7	34.3	21.0	31.1	0.8	10.9	7.5	3.4	2.4		
1957	7.0			147.2	12.4	5.8	165.4	37.2	22.2	30.9	0.9	11.0	7.5	4.2	4.1		
1958	7.1			147.5	13.0	7.2	167.7	37.8	22.6	31.3	0.9	11.2	7.6	4.2	3.0		
1959	7.0			158.2	13.7	9.2	181.1	40.4	23.9	31.7	0.9	11.3	7.7	4.3	1.9		
1960	7.1			174.3	15.8	9.9	200.0	44.9	26.0	32.5	1.0	11.5	7.8	4.5	2.2		
1961	7.1			185.8	17.8	10.5	214.1	47.6	28.0	33.3	1.1	11.6	8.0	4.2	1.1		
1962	7.1			198.0	18.7	12.0	228.7	51.0	30.5	34.2	1.1	11.8	8.1	4.2	1.9		
1963	6.9			215.6	21.4	14.3	251.3	55.5	33.8	35.5	1.1	12.0	8.3	4.3	2.0		
1964	6.8			249.8	25.6	16.6	292.0	65.3	38.3	37.9	1.2	12.1	8.4	5.1	3.4		
1965	6.7	40.2	25.1	275.1	30.6	18.4	324.1	72.8	42.8	39.4	1.3	12.3	8.6	5.5	4.0		
1966	6.6	40.5	25.3	298.2	35.5	17.9	351.6	79.0	46.5	41.5	1.5	12.5	8.7	6.6	4.9		
1967	6.5	40.1	25.3	319.1	41.0	22.4	382.5	86.9	50.5	42.7	1.9	12.6	8.9	6.4	4.7		
1968	6.5	39.3	25.8	349.7	47.1	33.0	429.8	96.0	55.2	43.8	2.4	12.7	9.0	6.5	4.5		
1969	6.6	40.8	27.3	384.0	54.5	35.4	473.9	108.8	63.2	46.5	3.2	12.9	9.1	7.5	5.7		
1970	6.5	40.7	27.8	434.1	63.5	39.1	536.7	121.7	70.8	48.5	4.1	13.0	9.3	8	6.1		
1971	6.5	40.4	28.5	483.2	75.5	43.8	602.5	136.9	78.9	52.3	5.0	13.2	9.4	7.6	4.5		
1972	6.5	36.6	26.9	522.9	90.3	58.6	671.8	155.0	88.5	56.7	5.8	13.3	9.5	7.4	2.2		
1973	6.3	37.5	27.6	603.5	109.5	62.2	775.2	177.3	99.8	61.5	6.4	13.4	9.7	7.9	4.2		
1974	6.3	39.8	29.2	700.3	126.2	56.9	883.4	201.5	113.4	67.4	7.1	13.5	9.8	9.8	7.2		
1975	6.3	37.4	28.1	763.9	151.0	74.6	989.5	219.9	129.0	74.2	7.6	13.7	10.0	8.8	4.6		
1976	5.9	36.4	27.2	862.3	175.5	101.1	1138.9	252.1	148.0	80.8	8.1	13.8	10.1	9	6.0		
1977	5.8	35.4	26.7	939.5	192.8	119.1	1251.4	275.4	164.3	85.8	8.5	13.9	10.3	8.1	3.9		
1978	5.7	35.2	26.7	1003.6	215.8	143.8	1363.2	296.3	179.2	89.7	8.9	13.9	10.4	7.7	5.5	15	
1979	5.6	37.8	28.3	1086.2	236.4	124.9	1447.5	315.2	192.4	93.5	9.4	14.0	10.6	8.8	8.5	17	
1980	5.5	40.5	29.6	1174.8	261.9	130.1	1566.8	336.1	205.8	100.0	9.8	14.1	10.7	10.2	10.1	20	
1981	5.3	43.0	30.9	1229.6	277.2	155.8	1662.6	351.9	213.2	106.3	10.2	14.3	10.9	11.5	10.7	24	
1982	5.4	43.3	31.2	1266.5	294.4	192.1	1753.0	368.5	221.8	111.9	10.5	14.3	11.0	9.9	7.9	28	
1983	5.2			1292.2	309.1	240.7	1842.0	381.6	229.9	114.9	10.9	14.4	11.1	8.2	5.5	32	
1984	5.1			1359.1	315.6	271.4	1946.1	399.8	236.8	117.2	11.4	14.4	11.3	8.1	6.0	57	
1985	4.9			1419.3	326.6	330.9	2076.8	418.9	247.7	119.7	11.8	14.5	11.4	7.3	6.2	102	20
1986	4.8			1380.7	339.8	385.5	2106.0	427.6	256.2	120.5	12.2	14.6	11.6	6.4	5.5	238	277
1987	4.7			1379.6	361.6	448.0	2189.2	429.4	263.9	120.0	12.6	14.7	11.7	6.4	5.2	450	385
1988	4.4			1437.7	378.2	484.2	2300.1	447.4	268.9	120.7	13.0	14.8	11.8	6.1	4.3	1017	1495
1989	4.5			1533.2	378.1	530.3	2441.6	476.0	281.4	122.5	13.4	14.9	12.0	7.2	6.8	1839	2047
1990	4.5			1629.0	420.7	446.3	2496.0	509.0	298.8	125.5	13.9	14.9	11.7	8.93	8.6	2480	2223

Explanatory notes: Series are corrected for breaks. The computation of the transactions value is described in the introduction of this Annex.

ANNEX III COMPOSITION OF CONSUMER EXPENDITURES IN THE NETHERLANDS

Table III.1 Household expenditures by type of goods and services 1987

Category	Amount per household (guilders)		Share (%) in total expenditure	Share (%) in expenditure potentially in cash	
Food	23.8		10.4	17.3	
- groceries		3.3			2.4
- dairy products		5.2			3.8
- bread		2.5			1.8
- greengrocer		5.2			3.8
- meat		6.9			5.0
- fish		0.6			0.5
Luxury	10.6		4.6	7.7	
- almond pastry, chocolate, ice cream	4.2			3.0	
- smoking materials		2.1			1.5
- spirits		4.4			3.2
Durables	36.1		15.7	26.3	
- textile and clothing		12.7			9.3
- Shoes and leather goods		3.3			2.4
- household articles		5.2			3.8
- furniture		6.7			4.9
- cars and accessories a)		8.1			5.9
- other durables		0.0			
Fuel	6.7		2.9	4.9	
Hotels, restaurants *etc.*	6.3		2.7	4.6	
Amusement	21.3		9.3	15.5	
Transport	5.8		2.5	4.2	
Postal services	0.0				
Other goods and services b)	26.9		11.7	19.6	
Sub-total (potentially cash)	137.3		60.0	100	
Electricity, water *etc.*	10.6		4.6		
Dwelling (rents and nominal rent income)	42.5		18.5		
Medical care	23.1		10.1		
Cars (new)	7.9		3.5		
Various payments c)	7.6		3.3		
Sub-total (mainly non-cash)	91.7		40.0		
Total	229.0		100		

a) Including gross expenditure on second-hand cars; excluding new cars.
b) Including expenditure on rebuilding and maintenance of houses.
c) Including payments on road tax and contributions to life insurance (savings part).
Source: CBS, Budget survey 1987.

ANNEX IV AVERAGE NOTE LIFE AND RETURN RATE BY DENOMINATION IN THE NETHERLANDS 1955-1990

Table IV.1 Average note life and average return rate

	Average note life (in years)								Average return rate (times per year)							
Year	Fl. 1000	Fl. 250	Fl. 100	Fl. 50	Fl. 25	Fl. 10	Fl. 5	Total	Fl. 1000	Fl. 250	Fl. 100	Fl. 50	Fl. 25	Fl. 10	Fl. 5	Total
1955	5.11		3.39		2.68	1.85		2.39								
1956	5.48		3.01		2.53	1.62		2.24	3.56		1.64	0.88	2.23	2.08		2.07
1957	6.36		3.24		2.83	2.35		3.03	3.70		1.65	0.74	2.13	2.12		2.07
1958	1.04		3.31		2.61	2.23		3.00	3.79		1.63	0.99	2.14	2.12		2.08
1959	2.33		3.29		3.20	1.97		2.66	3.90		1.66	0.52	2.23	2.28		2.13
1960	1.70		2.77		2.08	1.61		2.07	4.27		1.65	2.43	2.22	2.23		2.12
1961	2.39		3.16		2.22	1.55		2.04	3.79		1.65	0.73	2.22	2.17		2.09
1962	2.36		2.87		1.96	1.56		1.98	3.62		1.66	0.28	2.18	2.15		2.07
1963	2.17		2.83		1.95	1.45		1.85	3.45		1.64	0.16	2.15	2.09		2.02
1964	2.17		2.57		1.78	1.46		1.85	3.49		1.67	0.12	2.08	1.99		1.95
1965	2.24		2.77		1.95	1.59		2.02	3.27		1.63	0.08	2.00	1.85		1.85
1966	2.29		3.17		1.93	1.57		2.03	3.03		1.67	0.07	2.00	1.77		1.82
1967	2.63		3.37		1.98	1.64	1.40	2.15	2.79		1.66	0.04	1.98	1.72	0.58	1.71
1968	2.34		2.89		1.70	1.53	1.68	1.86	2.56		1.58	0.02	1.94	1.62	0.88	1.64
1969	2.62		2.82		1.55	1.53	1.22	1.81	2.22		1.45	0.01	1.87	1.50	0.92	1.53
1970	2.33		2.65		1.43	1.44	1.07	1.65	2.10		1.50	0.01	1.97	1.49	0.89	1.55
1971	2.52		2.67		1.40	1.40	1.07	1.59	2.01		1.57		2.10	1.46	0.92	1.60
1972	3.02		2.28		1.25	1.19	1.08	1.47	2.00		1.66		2.34	1.44	0.92	1.68
1973	1.67		1.44		1.01	1.39	1.02	1.26	2.09		1.84		2.55	1.48	0.97	1.81
1974	3.24		3.44		2.02	1.09	1.00	1.71	2.06		2.02		2.69	1.48	0.99	1.91
1975	3.46		4.20		1.27	1.04	0.95	1.57	1.93		2.19		2.98	1.51	1.01	2.05
1976	2.96		2.81		1.09	1.02	0.94	1.41	2.07		2.15		3.14	1.48	1.04	2.08
1977	2.21		2.41		1.13	1.13	0.92	1.42	2.16		2.14		3.27	1.46	1.07	2.11
1978	3.10		2.32		1.03	0.97	0.90	1.32	1.94		2.16		3.34	1.40	1.07	2.12
1979	4.32		2.32		0.98	1.17	0.95	1.37	1.79		2.15		3.38	1.36	1.06	2.11
1980	4.67		2.27		1.00	1.00	0.95	1.34	1.60		2.14		3.52	1.33	1.03	2.12
1981	5.68		3.42		1.06	1.20	1.31	1.59	1.55		2.23		3.52	1.32	1.01	2.16
1982	2.80		2.12	0.50	0.97	1.11	1.08	1.30	1.43		2.27	3.87	3.70	1.38	1.06	2.24
1983	2.78		2.34	1.46	0.97	1.24	1.62	1.57	1.14		2.10	4.11	3.54	1.34	1.08	2.15
1984	4.19		2.98	1.14	0.98	1.15	1.11	1.50	0.99		2.00	4.11	3.57	1.34	1.10	2.11
1985	4.25		2.49	1.00	0.97	1.14	1.55	1.50	0.92		2.02	4.06	3.55	1.32	1.11	2.10
1986	6.22	1.21	2.19	0.92	0.83	1.19	1.13	1.29	0.88	1.36	2.15	4.13	3.64	1.35	1.19	2.18
1987	4.35	3.44	2.78	0.93	0.95	1.33	1.47	1.58	0.90	1.14	2.20	4.34	3.79	1.35	1.22	2.23
1988	7.81	4.88	2.52	0.90	0.98	1.36	2.49	1.61	0.79	0.16	2.28	4.55	4.02	1.36	1.09	2.32
1989	7.90	6.00	2.45	0.87	1.03	1.27	2.97	1.62	0.75	0.39	2.36	4.61	4.16	1.32	0.76	2.42
1990	5.87	5.59	2.13	0.74	1.15	1.24	0.66	1.38	0.78	0.96	2.71	4.99	3.91	1.32	0.57	2.57

Explanatory note: The figures for the Fl. note are influenced by its replacement by a coin since 1986.

ANNEX V TABULAR SUMMARY OF SURVEY-ESTIMATION OF SECTOR DEMAND FOR FL. 1,000 NOTES

Table V.1 Key data on survey-estimation of holdings of Fl. 1,000 notes

Sector	Number of units (Thousands)	Turnover (billion guilders per year)	Survey results: Number of respondents			Share of cash in turnover(%)			Share Fl.1,000 in cash turnover(%)			Number of days notes are kept			Notes stored per unit			Number of Fl.1,000 notes per unit			Composition (%) of circulation Fl.1,000		
Phase:			1	2	3	1	2	(s)	1	2	(s)	1	2	(s)	1	2	(s)	1	2	3	1	2	3
Agriculture/fisheries	136.6	42.4	16			40.2			77.6			12.5			8.5			14.3	14.3	4	16.2	4.6	4.6
- farmers				19			16.7	(20.9)		24.1	(17.4)		14.9	(10.1)		2.1	(2.7)						
- casual work				12			2.6	(6.2)		5.0	(5.4)		1.2	(1.3)		0.3	(0.6)						
- cattle-breeding				12			31.7	(27.1)		32.6	(16.9)		5.4	(8.1)		1.4	(1.8)						
- nursery-gardens				11			15.6	(19.7)		10.0	(10.0)		1.4	(3.5)		0.3	(0.7)						
Industry	46.5	551.0	16	15		0.8			37.7			4			3			3.7	3.7	3.7	1.7	1.7	1.7
Construction	41.8	48.2	15	18		11.8	11.4	(17.6)	58.4	27.7	(21.1)	5.5	4.8	(3.8)	14	3.8	(4.3)	16.8	5.7	5.7	5.8	2.0	2.0
Motor trade	9.4	22.0	11	19	2	48.5	48.0	(34.8)	30.0	37.1	(20.2)	7.5	5.9	(15.3)	14	2.1	(2.1)	38.1	10.0	88	4.9	0.7	6.7
Retail trade	131.4	103.0	15		1	32.4			1.9			5			5			5.1	2.6	2.6	5.6	2.8	2.8
- butchers' shops				7			37.1	(21.1)		13.0	(6.2)		4.8	(2.1)		1.6	(1.8)						
- super markets				5			22.3	(3.8)		4.2	(3.7)		1.9	(0.7)		-	(0.0)						
- clothes shops				6			22.0	(19.7)		4.8	(2.8)		3.4	(3.4)		2.3	(2.3)						
- furniture shops				11			19.1	(13.5)		14.6	(14.2)		1.8	(1.4)		4.5	(10.3)						
- radio, tv and hifi				7			19.1	(19.3)		2.4	(0.9)		3.5	(3.6)		0.4	(0.9)						
- antique trade				11			41.5	(25.2)		16.1	(11.0)		6.3	(3.0)		1.9	(2.4)						
Wholesale/distr.trade	62.3	246.0	10	13		2.7	3.3	(9.4)	70.6	17.7	(20.2)	5	2.3	(2.2)	10	2.1	(1.6)	10.8	2.3	2.3	5.6	1.2	1.2
Licensed trade	43.0	13.6	10	18		14.4	23.9	(21.2)	4.7	11.8	(3.8)	10	4.1	(4.4)	4.7	0.5	(1.3)	5.9	0.6	0.6	2.2	0.2	0.2
Real estate	29.0	36.5	10	15		5.4	5.5	(5.3)	77.3	46.9	(10.3)	9			15	4.4	(5.9)	18.4	7.4	7.4	4.5	1.8	1.8
Other services	29.1	6.8	10									5			5			5.8	5.8	5.8	1.4	1.4	1.4
Households	5558.0	283.0	20	2000											0.1			0.2	0.2	0.2	9.2	9.2	9.3
Cash banks	8.3		2																		6.4	6.4	6.4
Foreigners	140.0				2															2.4			2.7
Caravan dwellers	7.1				2															50			2.9
Drug trade	-	4.5	1																		10.1	10.1	10.1
Gambling community	-	1.5	1																		3.7	3.7	3.7
Unknown holdings																					29.1	54.2	42.5
Total		1373.6	138	190	7																100	100	100

Explanatory notes: The symbol s denotes standard deviation. In phase 2 a number of turnover figures were slightly adapted; moreover the trade in new and second hand cars were combined. Changes in phase 3 are based on 7 expert-interviews, apart from the omnibus survey for the households sector. The figures on the motor trade in phase 3 include approximately 1,000 car-breaking yards.

ANNEX VI IMPORTANCE OF ATMs, POS AND CREDIT CARDS IN FIFTEEN COUNTRIES 1978-1989

Table VI.1 Importance of ATMs

Country	1978	1979	1980	1981	1982	1983	1984	1985	1986	1987	1988	1989
Number of ATMs per million inhabitants												
Austria				12	15	20	29	43	56	68	81	108
Belgium	14	28	41	46	52	57	66	71	73	81	85	90
Canada	11	14	19	25	41	79	122	143	176	205	238	342
Denmark							2	7	27	29	34	34
Finland		6	26	45	62	80	119	144	196	316	421	531
France	19	26	36	49	68	93	120	164	175	201	205	233
Germany					19	26	31	72	96	123	123	151
Italy	4	9	13	18	22	26	31	35	48	60	81	93
Japan	111	137	169	209	258	320	382	445	480	508	597	628
Netherlands	1	1	1	2	2	2	4	7	16	31	69	124
Norway					80	84	93	113	192	305	392	405
Sweden	58	87	116	109	121	135	144	147	158	196	206	226
Switzerland			33	37	39	42	44	76	126	160	225	253
United Kingdom	18	21	31	51	72	100	121	162	186	220	243	266
United States	45	77	110	142	174	204	231	256	265	310	331	351
Value of transactions per ATM per year (US$ million)												
Austria				2.5	5.0	5.7	5.7	5.1	5.2	5.4	5.8	5.6
Belgium		0.7	1.6	2.2	2.8	3.7	3.8	4.4	5.1	5.6	6.4	5.0
Canada												
Denmark							1.4	1.7	2.2	4.4	5.5	6.9
Finland								2.3	2.5	2.6	3.0	3.2
France						1.4	1.4	1.8	2.7	2.8	2.9	2.9
Germany						1.0		0.4				
Italy						0.2		2.5		2.7	2.6	3.1
Japan												
Netherlands										1.4	1.8	2.1
Norway											2.6	3.3
Sweden			5.7	6.9	6.9	6.8	6.9	7.3	7.9	8.0	8.1	8.5
Switzerland			2.5	3.4	4.2	5.1	6.2	4.0	3.7	3.8	3.3	3.4
United Kingdom			1.0	1.2	1.7	2.1	2.5	3.0	2.9	3.3	3.5	4.0
United States								0.1				

Explanatory note: Value in US $ on basis of average exchange rate 1987-1988.
Source: Questionnaire among central banks, held in spring 1990 by the Bank Note Printers Conference on behalf of the Study Group on Trends in National Economies and in Payment Systems and their Effect on Note Circulation and Demand; supplemented by information from BIS publication Payment Systems, in Eleven Developed Countries, issues 1985, 1988 and the supplement 1989, as well as by information obtained from central banks on our own request.

Table VI.2 Importance of POS

Country	1978	1979	1980	1981	1982	1983	1984	1985	1986	1987	1988	1989
Number of POS terminals per million inhabitants												
Austria											15	30
Belgium		4	6	14	36	89	221	479	973	1551	1925	2247
Canada								2	3	34	163	
Denmark							98	235	676	1221	1704	1724
Finland											402	1499
France							183	455	725	992	1258	2147
Germany									3	109	142	177
Italy									2	7	76	174
Japan								1	3	5	5	
Netherlands								1	19	26	101	138
Norway									450	895	1445	1548
Sweden										13	161	402
Switzerland											20	98
United Kingdom							2	4	6	228	426	1053
United States					1	3	13	50	113	177	178	
Value of transactions per POS terminal per year (US$ thousand)												
Austria											86	154
Belgium							184	125	95	84	97	86
Canada										56	16	22
Denmark												
Finland												
France												
Germany										8	6	5
Italy										41	23	23
Japan												
Netherlands										130	100	220
Norway											22	46
Sweden												
Switzerland											26	46
United Kingdom											28	
United States												

Explanatory note: Value in US $ on basis of average exchange rate 1987-1988.
Source: See Table VI.1.

Table VI.3 Importance of credit cards

Country	1978	1979	1980	1981	1982	1983	1984	1985	1986	1987	1988	1989
Number of credit card transactions per inhabitant												
Austria					0.1	0.1	0.2	0.3	0.4	0.5	0.6	0.9
Belgium							0.3	0.4	0.5	0.7	0.9	0.9
Canada			13.7	15.4	16.7	17.9	19.4	22.0	24.4	26.4	28.4	31.2
Denmark												
Finland									5.1	9.7	8.7	10.6
France	0.5			1.1	1.4	1.8	2.6	3.5	6.0	9.5	14.9	18.4
Germany						0.1		0.3	0.0	0.6	0.8	1.3
Italy						0.1	0.1	0.0	0.2	0.3	0.5	
Japan								0.6	0.0	1.7	4.1	
Netherlands	0.4								0.2	0.4	0.4	0.5
Norway												
Sweden					1.6	1.6	1.8	1.8	1.9	2.0	1.8	1.9
Switzerland							0.1	0.1	0.2	0.3	0.3	0.5
United Kingdom	1.9	2.1	2.7	3.1	3.9	4.7	5.7	6.9	7.9	9.2	10.6	11.7
United States	11.4					12.3		21.4		37.1	35.7	
Value of credit card transactions as percentage of private consumption												
Austria					0.2	0.3	0.3	0.5	0.8	1.0	1.2	1.6
Belgium		0.1	0.1	0.2	0.3	0.4	0.5	0.7	0.8	0.9	1.1	1.0
Canada			7.6	8.2	7.8	9.5	10.2	9.0	11.8	12.0	12.8	11.8
Denmark								0.1	0.3	1.4	3.9	6.8
Finland							3.5	4.2	4.1	4.3	4.2	4.9
France	0.1	0.4	0.6	0.7	1.0	1.1	1.6	2.1	3.3	5.0	7.4	8.8
Germany						0.2	0.4	0.6	0.7	0.7	1.0	1.3
Italy			0.1	0.1	0.1	0.2	0.2	0.2	0.3	0.4	0.5	0.7
Japan								1.8	2.1	2.3	3.1	
Netherlands	0.5	0.5	0.5	0.5	0.4	0.4	0.4	0.4	0.4	0.6	0.6	0.8
Norway						2.1	2.2	2.1	2.1	2.2	2.5	2.6
Sweden			4.8	4.9	4.9	4.9	4.9	4.8	4.7	4.4	4.2	4.2
Switzerland							0.2	0.3	0.3	0.4	0.5	0.7
United Kingdom	1.5	1.7	2.2	2.6	3.0	3.2	4.0	4.6	5.5	6.5	6.8	7.5
United States	10.7	10.3	9.9	9.6	9.6	9.4	10.8	12.1	12.4	12.5	12.9	

Source: See Table VI.1.

REFERENCES

Ahmad, S., 1977, Transactions demand for money and the quantity theory, *Quarterly Journal of Economics* 91, no 2 (May), 327-335.

Aitchison, J. and J.A.C. Brown, 1957, *The Lognormal Distribution*, Cambridge University Press, Cambridge.

Akerlof, G.A. and R.D. Milbourne, 1978, New calculations of income and interest elasticities in Tobin's model of the transactions demand for money, *Review of Economics and Statistics* 60, no 4 (November) 541-546.

Alessie, R., R. Gradus and B. Melenberg, 1990, The problem of not observing small expenditures in a consumer expenditure survey, *Journal of Applied Econometrics* 5, 151-166.

Anderson, P.S., 1977, Currency in use and in hoards, *New England Economic Review*, Federal Reserve Bank of Boston, (March/April), 21-30.

APACS, 1989, Consumer payments and financial behaviour, *APACS Research Brief*, (December), Association for Payment Clearing Services, London.

Avery, R.B., G.E. Elliehausen, A.B. Kennickell and P.A. Spindt, 1985, A microanalytic view of the payments mechanism: some preliminary results from the survey of currency and transaction account usage, *Paper presented at the annual meeting of the Financial Management Association*, (October 9-11).

Avery, R.B., G.E. Elliehausen, A.B. Kennickell and P.A. Spindt, 1986, The use of cash and transaction accounts by American families, *Federal Reserve Bulletin* 72, no 2 (February), 87-108.

Avery, R.B., G.E. Elliehausen, A.B. Kennickell and P.A. Spindt, 1987, Changes in the use of transaction accounts and cash from 1984 to 1986, *Federal Reserve Bulletin* 73, no 3 (March), 179-196.

Banca d'Italia, 1988a, *White Paper on the Payment System in Italy*, Banca d'Italia, (April).

Banca d'Italia, 1988b, Principal features of the Italian payment system, with reference to the role of banknotes, *Paper presented at the Stockholm Meeting of the Banknote Printers Conference Statistics and Banknote Handling Committee* (April), 12-14.

Bank of Japan, 1990, The Japanese cash payment system: synopsis, *Working paper*, (March), Research and Statistics Department, Bank of Japan.

Banque de France, 1989, Instruments de politique monetaire, *Dossiers Économiques et Monétaires sur l'Étranger*, no 1 (February).

Banque de France, 1989, *Les moyens de Paiement et Circuits de Recouvrement*, Annuaire Statistique.

Barnett, W.A., 1978, The user cost of money, *Economics Letters* 1, no 2, 145-149.

Barro, R.J., 1976, Integral constraints and aggregation in an inventory model of money demand, *Journal of Finance* 31, no 1 (March), 77-87.

Barro, R.J. and G.M. MacDonald, 1979, Social security and consumer spending in an international cross section, *Journal of Public Economics* 11, no 3 (June), 275-289.

Barro, R.J. and A.J. Santomero, 1972, Household money holdings and the demand deposit rate, *Journal of Money, Credit and Banking* 4, no 2 (May), 397-413.

Baumol, W.J., 1952, The transactions demand for cash: an inventory theoretic approach, *Quarterly Journal of Economics 66*, (November), 545-556.

Berger A.N. and D.B. Humphrey, 1986, The role of interstate banking in the diffusion of electronic payments technology; in: C. Lawrence and R.P. Shay (eds), *Technological Innovation, Regulation, and Monetary Economy*, Ballinger Publishing Company, Cambridge, Mass., 13-52.

BIS (Bank for International Settlements), 1987, *Payments Systems in Eleven Developed Countries*; Update of Tables B, C and D of the Red Book (March), Basle.

BIS, 1989, *Payment Systems in Eleven Developed Countries*, (April), Basle.

BIS, 1990, *Statistics on Payment Systems in Eleven Developed Countries, Figures for end-1989* (December), Basle.

Boeschoten, W.C., 1984, Purchasing power of money and the underground economy, *Research Memorandum WO&E*, no 8409 (August), De Nederlandsche Bank, presented at the European Meeting of the Econometric Society, Madrid (September 3-7).

Boeschoten, W.C., 1986, The withdrawal from circulation of the Fl. 100 'De Ruyter' bank note, *De Nederlandsche Bank Quarterly Bulletin*, no 1 (June), 27-33.

Boeschoten, W.C., 1990, The use of means of payments, *Research Memorandum WO&E*, no 9005 (April), De Nederlandsche Bank, presented at Eurobanking 1990, Rome (May 22-25).

Boeschoten, W.C., 1991, National trends in payment systems and the demand for currency and banknotes, *Research Memorandum WO&E*, no 9108 (March), presented at the meeting of Statics and Handling Committee of the Bank Note Printers Conference in Frankfurt (April).

Boeschoten, W.C., 1991, De bankbiljettencirculatie in de jaren negentig (The banknote circulation in the 1990s), *Research Memorandum WO&E*, no 9112 (May), De Nederlandsche Bank.

Boeschoten, W.C. and M.M.G. Fase, 1984, *The Volume of Payments and the Informal Economy in the Netherlands 1965-1982*, Martinus Nijhoff Publishers, Dordrecht.

Boeschoten, W.C. and M.M.G. Fase, 1987, Betaalgedrag in Nederland (Manner of payment in the Netherlands), *Economisch Statistische Berichten* 72, (August 26), 780-786 and 794.

Boeschoten, W.C. and M.M.G. Fase, 1988, Het Bankbiljet van f 1.000 (The Banknote of Fl 1,000), *Economisch Statistische Berichten 73*, (June 1), 523-527.

Boeschoten, W.C. and M.M.G. Fase, 1989, The way we pay with money, *Journal of Business & Economic Statistics* 7, no 3 (July), 319-326.

Boeschoten, W.C. and M.M.G. Fase, 1991, The demand for large banknotes, *Research Memorandum WO&E*, no 9106 (March), De Nederlandsche Bank, to appear in *Journal of Money, Credit and Banking* 24, no 3 (August 1992).

Boorman, J.T., 1980, The evidence on the demand for money: theoretical foundations and empirical results, in J.T. Boorman and T.H. Havrilesky (eds), *Current Issues in Monetary Theory and Policy, AHM Publishing Corporation, Arlington Heights*, 315-360.

Bordo, M. D. and L. Jonung, 1987, *The Long-run Behaviour of the Velocity of Circulation: The International Evidence*, Cambridge University Press, Cambridge.

Boughton J.M. and G.S. Tavlas, 1991, What have we learned about estimating the demand for money?; A multicountry evaluation of some new approaches, *IMF Working Paper* WP/91/16.

BPC (Bank Note Printers Conference), 1966, *Statistics*, (September).

Broesterhuizen, G.A.A.M, 1983, The unobserved sector and the national accounts in the Netherlands, *CBS-note* 395-83-PS.E8, Central Bureau for Statistics.

Braak, L. ter, 1991, Cross boarder movements of Netherlands banknotes, to appear in *De Nederlandsche Bank, Quarterly Bulletin*, no. 3 (December).

Browne, F.X., 1981, Forecasting the demand for currency and its denominational mix, *Technical paper*, (June), Bank of Ireland.

Brunner, K. and A.H. Meltzer, 1967, Economies of scale in cash balances reconsidered, *Quarterly Journal of Economics* 81, no 3 (August), 422-436.

Buiter, W.H. and C.A. Armstrong, 1978, A didactic note on the transactions demand for money and behavior towards risk, *Journal of Money, Credit and Banking* 10, no 4 (November), 529-538.

Butter, F.A.G. den, 1985, Opinion surveys on bank notes, *De Nederlandsche Bank Quarterly Bulletin*, no 1 (June), 31-39.

Butter, F.A.G. den and R.L. Coenen, 1981, Het bankbiljet als produkt (The banknote as product), *Economisch Statistische Berichten* 66, (February 18), 302-328.

Butter, F.A.G. den and R.L. Coenen, 1982, The process of soiling and the life of banknotes in the Netherlands, *The Journal of the Royal Statistical Society, Series C (Applied Statistics)* 31, no 3, 226-237.

Cagan, P., 1958, The Demand for Currency Relative to Total Money Supply, *Journal of Political Economy* 66, no 4 (August), 303-328.

Cameron, A.C. and P.K. Trivedi, 1986, Econometric models based on count data: comparisons and applications of some estimators and tests, *Journal of Applied Econometrics* 1, 29-53.

Cave, C.J. and M.M.G. Fase, 1980, General reflections on forecasting the note issue, *Paper presented at the Rome-meeting of the Bank Note Printers Conference Statistics and Banknote Handling Committee.*

CEC, 1990, *Developing Europe's Payment Systems (Draft of Green Paper)*, Commission of the European Communities, (June), Brussels.

Chen, C., 1976, Currency denominations and the price level, *Journal of Political Economy* 84, no 1 (February), 179-183.

Chevalier, M., 1988, New payment systems and their effect on note circulation in France, Banque de France, *Paper presented at the Stockholm - meeting of the Bank Note Printers Conference Statistics and Banknote Handling Committee*, (April), Bank of France.

Clements, I.M., 1990, The demand for banknotes in individual countries, *Working paper* (November), Bank of England.

Cloutier, P., 1986, A banknote model with agency and denomination dimensions (update), *Working paper*, (October), Bank of Canada.

Coates, C.R., 1976, *The Demand for Money by Firms*, M. Dekker, New York/Basel.

Coenen, R.L., M. van Nieuwkerk and J.J. van der Weyden, 1978, Determinanten van de levensduur van bankbiljetten in Nederland 1900-1975 (Determinants of the use life of banknotes in the Netherlands 1900-1975), *Research Memorandum WO&E*, no 7815 (November), De Nederlandsche Bank.

COTOB (Study Group on Future Development on Banknote Circulation), 1976, *Final Reports I, II and III*, (April), De Nederlandsche Bank.

Cox, D.R., 1962, Further results on tests of separate families of hypotheses, *Journal of the Royal Statistical Society* (series B) 24, no 1, 406-424.

Cramer, J.S., 1964, Efficient grouping, regression and correlation in Engel curve analysis, *Journal of the American Statistical Association* 59, (March), 233-250.

Cramer, J.S., 1979, De omvang van het betalingsverkeer en de omloopsnelheid van het geld: enige ramingen voor 1974-1977 (the volume of payments and the velocity of circulation of money: some estimates for 1974-1977), in: J.J. Klant, W. Driehuis and H.J. Bierens (eds), *Samenleving en Onderzoek*, Stenfert Kroese, Leiden, 209-223.

Cramer, J.S., 1981, The work money does: the transaction velocity of circulation of money in the Netherlands, 1950-1978, *European Economic Review* 15, no 3 (March), 307-326.

Cramer J.S., 1983a, Currency by denomination, *Economics Letters* 12, no 3-4, 299-303.

Cramer, J.S., 1983b, Contanten: wit, zwart, onzichtbaar (Cash: white, black, unobservable, *Kwantitatieve Methoden* 4, no 9 (February), 2-28.

Cramer, J.S., 1986a, De optimale coupure-opbouw (The optimal denominational structure), in: M.M.G. Fase, J.R. Steinhauser and Joh. de Vries (eds), *Het Nederlandse Bankbiljet in zijn Verscheidenheid*, Kluwer, Deventer, 175-194.

Cramer, J.S., 1986b, The volume of transactions and the circulation of money in the United States, *Journal of Business & Economic Statistics* 4, no 2 (April), 225-232.

Cramer, J.S., 1987, Betaalgedrag in een warenhuis (Payment pattern in a department store), *Working paper* (April), Stichting voor Economisch Onderzoek der Universiteit van Amsterdam, Amsterdam.

Cramer, J.S., 1988, Cash payments of households and their suppliers, *De Nederlandsche Bank Quarterly Bulletin*, no 1 (June), 45-53.

Cramer, J.S., 1991, *The Logit Model*, Edward Arnold, London.

Cramer, J.S. and G.M. Reekers, 1972, *Het Houderschap van Liquiditeiten in Nederland* (The Demand for Liquid Assets in the Netherlands), NIBE, Amsterdam.

Cramer, J.S. and G.M. Reekers, 1976, Money demand by sector, *Journal of Monetary Economics* 2, no 1 (January), 99-112.

Davidson, J.E.H., D.F. Hendry, F. Srba and S. Yeo, 1978, Econometric modelling of the aggregate time-series relationship between consumers expenditure and income in the United Kingdom, *Economic Journal* 88, 661-692.

Deutsche Bundesbank, 1990, Mindestreserveregelungen im Ausland, *Monatsberichte der Deutschen Bundesbank* 42, no 3 (March), 22-29.

Dickey, D.A. and W.A. Fuller, 1979, Distribution of estimates for autoregressive time series with unit root, *Journal of the American Statistical Association* 74, no 366 (June), 427-431.

Dombrecht, M., 1989, Determinanten van de vraag naar bankbiljetten (Determinants of the demand for banknotes), *Working paper*, (April), National Bank of Belgium .

Droogenbroeck, J. van, 1988, Considerations about the denominational distribution in the Belgian banknote circulation, *Working paper*, National Bank of Belgium.

Dutton, D.S. and Gramm, W.P., 1973, Transactions costs, the wage rate, and the demand for money, *American Economic Review* 63, no 4 (September), 652-665.

Engle, R.F. and B.S. Yoo, 1987, Forecasting and testing in cointegrated systems, *Journal of Econometrics* 35, 143-159.

Engle, R.F. and C.W.J. Granger, 1987, Co-integration and error correction: representation, estimation and testing, *Econometrica* 55, no 2 (March), 251-276.

Ettlin, F. and R. Fluri, 1986, Der Einfluss der Steuerveranlagung auf den Notenumlauf - Identifikation und Quantificierung, *Geld, Währung und Konjunktur* 4, no 3 (September), National Bank of Switzerland, 194-199.

Ettlin, F., 1989, Der Schweizerische Notenumlauf 1962-1988, *Geld, Währung und Konjunktur* 7, no 3 (September), National Bank of Switzerland, 257-268.

Evans, S.A. and M.J. Hailey, 1974, A cashless society, *Transactions of the Manchester Statistical Society, Session 1973-1974*, London, Manchester Statistical Society, 1-28.

Falls, G.A. and P.A. Natke, 1988, The demand for liquid assets: a firm level analysis, *Southern Economic Journal* 54, no 3 (January), 630-642.

Fase, M.M.G., 1981a, Forecasting the demand for banknotes; some empirical results for the Netherlands, *European Journal of Operation Research* 6, no 3 (March), 269-278.

Fase, M.M.G., 1981b, Forecasting the need for coins: a case study for the Netherlands, *Technological Forecasting and Social Change* 19, no 2 (March), 147-159.

Fase, M.M.G., 1984, Informele economie en geldomloop (Informal economy and money circulation), in: *De Informele Economie*, Preadviezen van de Vereniging voor de Staathuishoudkunde, Stenfert Kroese, Leiden/Antwerpen 59-95.

Fase, M.M.G., 1985a, The Fl 1,000 bank note: means of payment or means of hoarding?, *De Nederlandsche Bank Quarterly Bulletin*, no 4 (March), 31-38.

Fase, M.M.G., 1985b, Multivariate tijdreeksen en marktonderzoek (Multivariate time series and marketing research), *Jaarboek van de Nederlandse Vereniging van Marktonderzoekers*, 155-172.

Fase, M.M.G., 1986a, *Geldtheorie en Monetaire Normen* (Theory of money and monetary norms), Inaugural address at University of Amsterdam (October 14), Stenfert Kroese, Leiden/Antwerpen.

Fase, M.M.G., 1986b, De toekomst van het Nederlandse bankbiljet (The future of the Dutch banknote), in: Fase, M.M.G., J.R. Steinhauser and Joh. de Vries (eds), *Het Nederlandsche Bankbiljet in zijn Verscheidenheid*, Kluwer, Deventer, 195-218.

Fase, M.M.G. and W.C. Boeschoten, 1985, The distribution of payments and the use of bank notes, *De Nederlandsche Bank Quarterly Bulletin*, no 3 (December), 43-53.

Fase, M.M.G. and J.B. Kuné, 1974, De vraag naar liquiditeiten in Nederland, 1952-1971 (The demand for liquid assets in the Netherlands, 1952-1971), *De Economist* 122, no 4, 326-356.

Fase, M.M.G. and J.B. Kuné, 1975, The demand for money in thirteen European and non-European countries: a tabular survey, *Kredit und Kapital* 8, no 3, 410-419.

Fase M.M.G. and M. van Nieuwkerk, 1976, The bank note circulation in the Netherlands since 1900; prospect and retrospect, *De Nederlandsche Bank Quarterly Bulletin*, no 1 (June), 12-22.

Fase, M.M.G. and M. van Nieuwkerk, 1977, The demand for bank notes in four countries, *De Nederlandsche Bank Quarterly Bulletin*, no 1 (June), 84-98.

Fase M.M.G. and C.C.A. Winder, 1990, The demand for money revisited, *De Economist* 138, no 3, 276-301.

Fase, M.M.G., D. van der Hoeven and M. van Nieuwkerk, 1979, A numerical planning model for a central bank's bank notes operations, *Statistica Neerlandica* 33, no 1, 7-25.

Fayyad, S.K., 1986, A microeconomic system-wide approach of the estimation of the demand for money, *Review*, Federal Reserve Bank of St Louis 68, no 7 (August/September), 22-31.

Feige, E.L., 1979, How big is the irregular economy?, *Challenge* 22 (November/December), 5-13.

Feige E.L., 1987, The theory and measurement of cash payments: a case study of the Netherlands, in R.D.H. Heijmans and H. Neudecker (eds), *The Practice of Econometrics*, Martinus Nijhoff Publishers, Dordrecht, 67-98.

Feige E.L. and M. Parkin, 1971, The optimal quantity of money, bonds, commodity inventories, and capital, *American Economic Review* 61, (June), 335-349.

Feige E.L. and D.K.Pearce, 1977, The susbstitutability of money and near-monies: a survey of time-series evidence, *Journal of Economic Literature* 15, no 2 (June), 439-469.

Fisher, I., 1909, A practical method of estimating the velocity of circulation of money, *Journal of the Royal Statistical Society* 72, no 2 (September), 604-618.

Fisher, I., 1911, *The Purchasing Power of Money,* (second revised edition in 1922), MacMillan, New York.

Flikweert, J.D., 1985, De Muntreeks: opbouw en begrenzing (The coin range: composition and boundaries), *Working paper* (May), Ministry of Finance, The Hague.

Frenkel, J.A. and B. Jovanovic, 1980, On transactions and precautionary demand for money, *Quarterly Journal of Economics* 95, no 1 (August), 25-43.

Friedman, M., 1956, The quantity theory of money, a restatement, in: M. Friedman (ed), *Studies in the Quantity Theory of Money,* University of Chicago Press, Chicago, 3-21.

Friedman, M., and A.J. Schwartz, 1963, *A Monetary History of the United States: 1867-1960*, Princeton University Press, Princeton.

Galli, A., 1980, Die Nachfrage nach Bargeld in der Schweiz, *Beilage zum Monatsbericht der Schweizerischen Nationalbank*, no 3 (March), 2-10.

Garvy, G. and M.R. Blyn, 1969, *The Velocity of Money*, Federal Reserve Bank of New York, New York.

Gathon, H-J. and S. Perelman, 1990, Measuring technical efficiency in European railways, a panel data approach, Université de Liège, *Paper presented at Econometric World Congress* (August 22-28), Barcelona.

Goldfeld, S.M. and D.E. Sichel, 1990, The Demand for Money, in B.M. Friedman and F.H. Hahn (eds) *Handbook of Monetary Economics, Volume I,* Elsevier Science Publishers, Amsterdam, 300-356.

Goldin, E., 1985, Statistical analysis of coins lost in circulation, *Journal of Business and Economic Statistics* 3, no 1 (January), 36-42.

Goodman, L.A., and W.H. Kruskal, 1979, *Measures of Association for Cross Classifications*, Springer Verlag, New York.

Granger, C.W.J. and P. Newbold, 1986, *Forecasting Economic Time Series* (second edition), Academic Press Inc., San Diego.

Gross, D.M., 1989, Une analyse économétrique des sorties de billets de la Banque nationale Suisse, *Monnaie et Conjoncture* 7, no 1 (March), National Bank of Switzerland, 67-75.

Gurley, J.G. and E.S. Shaw, 1960, *Money in a Theory of Finance*, The Brookings Institution, Washington D.C.

Gutmann, P.M., 1977, The subterranean economy, *Financial Analysts Journal* 33, (November/December), 26-28.

Hafer, R.W. and S.E. Hein, 1984, Financial innovations and the interest elasticity of money demand: some historical evidence, *Journal of Money, Credit and Banking* 16, no 21 (May), 247-252.

Hall, S.G., S.G.B. Henry and J.B. Wilcox, 1989, The long-run determination of the UK monetary aggregates, *Bank of England Discussion Papers*, no 41 (August).

Hamburger, M.J., 1966, The demand for money by households, money substitutes and monetary policy, *Journal of Political Economy* 74, no 6 (December), 600-623.

Hamilton, J.D., 1989, The long-run behavior of the velocity of circulation: a review essay, *Journal of Monetary Economics* 23, no 2 (March), 335-344.

Harrop, P., 1989, *The Future of Payment Media, Plastic Money, Banknotes, Coins and Cheques*, Financial Times Business Information, London.

Hausman, J.A. and W.E. Taylor, 1981, Panel data and unobservable individual effects, *Econometrica* 49, no 6 (November), 1377-1398.

Henderson, P.B., 1986, Modern Money, in: E.H. Solomon, *Electronic Funds Transfers and Payments: The Public Policy Issues*, Kluwer-Nijhoff Publishing, Boston/Dordrecht/ Lancaster, 17-37.

Hentsch, J.C., 1973, La circulation des coupures qui constituent une monnaie, *Journal de la Société de Statistique de Paris 114*, no 4, 279-293.

Hentsch, J.C., 1983, Distribution de la monnaie fiduciaire entre les coupures qui la représentent, *Journal de la Société de Statistique de Paris* 124, no 4, 263-272.

Hentsch, J.C., 1985, Distribution de la monnaie fiduciaire entre les coupures, *Journal de la Société de Statistique de Paris* 126, no 4, 139-144.

Holtrop, M.W., 1928, *De Omloopssnelheid van het Geld* (The Velocity of Circulation of Money), Paris, Amsterdam.

Holtrop, M.W., 1929, Theories of the velocity of circulation of money in earlier economic literature, *Economic Journal History Supplement*, no 4 (January), 504-524.

Hsiao, C., 1986, *Analysis of Panel Data*, Cambridge University Press, Cambridge.

Humphrey, D.B. and A.N. Berger, 1990, Market failure and resource use: economic incentives to use different payment instruments; in: D.B. Humphrey (ed.), *US Payment System; Efficiency, Risk and the Role of the Federal Reserve*, Kluwer Academic Publishers, Boston.

Isachsen, A.J., J.T. Klovland and S. Strøm, 1982, The hidden economy in Norway, in: V. Tanzi (ed.), *The Underground Economy in the United States and Abroad*, Lexington Books, Lexington, Mass., 209-232.

Jevons, W.S., 1875, *Money and the Mechanism of Exchange*, Routledge and Kegan Paul, London.

Johnston, J., 1984, *Econometric Methods* (third edition), McGraw-Hill, Singapore.

Jonker R., 1973, Raming van de transacties in Nederland (Estimation of the transactions in the Netherlands), *Economisch Statistische Berichten* 58, (July 25), 675-676.

Judd, J.P. and J.L. Scadding, 1982, The search for a stable money demand function: a survey of the post-1973 literature, *Journal of Economic Literature*, 20, no 3 (September), 993-1023.

Judge, G.G., W.E. Griffiths, R. Carter Hill and Tsoung-Chao Lee, 1980, *The Theory and Practice of Econometrics*, John Wiley & Sons, New York.

Kalton, G., 1983, *Compensating for missing data*, Survey Research Center, University of Michigan.

Karni, E., 1973, The transactions demand for cash: incorporation of the value of time into the inventory approach, *Journal of Political Economy* 81, no 5 (September/October), 1216-1225.

Karni, E., 1974, The value of time and the demand for money, *Journal of Money, Credit and Banking* 6, no 1 (February), 45-64.

Kerr, P.M., 1985, Turnover statistics and federal government balances in money supply targets, *Southern Economic Journal* 52, no 2 (October), 344-350.

Keynes, J.M., 1930, *A Treatise on Money*, Macmillan, London.

Keynes, J.M., 1936, *The General Theory of Employment, Interest and Money*, Macmillan, London.

Kimball, R.C., 1981, Trends in the use of currency, *New England Economic Review*, (September/October), Federal Reserve Bank of Boston, 43-53.

Kirkman, P., 1987, *Electronic Funds Transfer Systems*, Blackwell, Oxford.

Klovland, J.T., 1980, In search of the hidden economy: tax evasion and the demand for currency in Norway and Sweden, *Discussion paper* 18/80, Norwegian School of Economics and Business Administration, Bergen.

Klovland, J.T., 1983, The demand for money in secular perspective: the case of Norway 1867-1980, *European Economic Review* 22, no 2 (July), 193-218.

Kneeshaw, J.T. and P. van den Bergh, 1989, Changes in central bank money market operating procedures in the 1980s, *BIS Economic Papers,* no 23 (January).

Knoop, H.S. van der and F.C. Hooijmans, 1989, A multivariate intervention model for the Dutch Mint circulation: estimation and Monte Carlo simulation, *Journal of Business & Economic Statistics* 7, no 2 (April), 179-189.

Koeze, P., 1988, A new technical criterion for the note-coin boundary, De Nederlandsche Bank, *Paper presented at BPC General Meeting, Istanbul.*

Kohli, U., 1984, La demande de monnaie en Suisse, *Monnaie et Conjoncture* no 4 (December), National Bank of Switzerland, 64-70.

Kohli, U., 1988, A note on banknote characteristics and the demand for currency by denomination, *Journal of Banking and Finance* 12, no 3 (September), 389-399.

Kokkola, T., 1990, Kontantpenningefterfrågan, betalningsmedel och teknisk utveckling (The demand for currency, means of payment and technological development), *Bank of Finland Discussion Papers* 10/90 (June).

Koopmans, J.G., 1933, Zum Problem des neutralen Geldes, in: F.A. Hayek (ed.), *Beiträge zur Geldtheorie,* Vienna, 211-359.

Koskela, E. and M. Virén, 1990, Dynamics of the demand for money and uncertainty: the US demand for money revisited, in: Artus, P. and Y. Barroux (eds), *Monetary Policy: A Theoretical and Econometric Approach,* Kluwer Academic Publishers, Dordrecht/Boston/London, 99-116.

Laidler, D.E.W., 1985, *The Demand for Money: Theories, Evidence and Problems* (Third Edition), Harper & Row Publishers, New York.

Laurent, R.D., 1970, *Currency Transfer by Denomination, Ph.D.thesis,* University of Chicago.

Laurent, R.D., 1974, Currency in circulation and the real value of notes, *Journal of Money, Credit and Banking* 6, no 2 (May), 213-226.

Leeuw, D.H. de, 1989, Betalingsverkeer in beweging: elektronisch betalen (The payment system in motion: electronic payments), *Bank en Effectenbedrijf* 38, no 1/2 (January/February), 30-34.

Lewis, K.A. and F.F. Breen, 1975, Empirical issues in the demand for currency: a multinational study, *The Journal of Finance* 30, no 4 (September), 1065-1079.

Lieberman, C., 1977, The transaction demand for money and technological change, *Review of Economics and Statistics* 59, no 3 (August), 307-317.

Lilja, R. and U. Lempinen, 1988, The Finnish payment system: an international comparison, *Bank of Finland.*

Little, A.D., 1975, *The Consequences of Electronic Funds Transfer*, National Science Foundation, Cambridge, Mass.

Lucas, R.E. Jr. and N.L. Stokey, 1987, Money and interest in a cash-in-advance economy, *Econometrica* 55, no 3 (May), 491-513.

Madalla, G.S., 1983, *Limited-dependent and Qualitative Variables in Econometrics*, Cambridge University Press, Cambridge.

Mandell, L., 1972, *Credit card use in the United States*, Institute for Social Research, University of Michigan, Ann Arbor, Michigan.

Manski, C.F. and E. Goldin, 1987, The denomination-specific demand for currency in a high-inflation setting: the Israeli experience, in: R.D.H. Heijmans and H. Neudecker (eds), *The Practice of Econometrics*, Martinus Nijhoff Publishers, Dordrecht, 99-120.

Markowitz, H., 1952, Portfolio selection, *Journal of Finance* 7, no 1 (March), 77-91.

Meltzer, A.H., 1963, The demand for money: a cross-section study of business firms, *Quarterly Journal of Economics* 77, no 3 (August), 405-422.

Miller, M.H. and D. Orr, 1966, A model of the demand for money by firms, *Quarterly Journal of Economics* 80, no 3 (August), 413-435.

Miller, M. H. and D. Orr, 1968, The demand for money by firms: extensions of analytic results, *Journal of Finance* 23, no 5 (December), 735-759.

Mitchell, G.W., 1985, Similarities and contrasts in payment systems, *The World of Banking*, (November/December), 24-26.

Moore, K.S., 1986, Payments and the economic transactions chain, in: E.H. Solomon, *Electronic Funds Transfers and Payments: The Public Policy Issues*, Kluwer-Nijhoff Publishing, Boston/Dordrecht/Lancaster, 39-62.

Morelli, G., 1985, Some observations on payment systems, *The World of Banking*, (November/December), 22-26.

Mori, R., 1983, The boundary between banknotes and coin and the new Lit. 1,000 note, Bank of Italy Rome, *Paper presented at BPC-Statistics Committee Meeting in Vienna*, (May 9-11).

Mot, E.S. and J.S. Cramer, 1990, Mode of payment in household expenditures, *SEO-working paper*, SEO, Foundation for Economic Research of the University of Amsterdam, Amsterdam (to appear in *De Economist*).

Mot, E.S., J.S. Cramer and E.M. van der Gullik, 1989, *De Keuze van een Betaalmiddel; het Betaalgedrag van Nederlandse Gezinnen in 1987*, (The choice of a means of payment; the payment pattern of Dutch households in 1987), SEO, Foundation for Economic Research of the University of Amsterdam (February), Amsterdam.

Nieuwenburg, C.F.K., 1969, Het liquiditeitsbezit van gezinshuishoudingen in Nederland (The demand for liquid assets by households in the Netherlands), *Ph.D. thesis*, University of Amsterdam.

Nieuwenburg, C.F.K., 1969, New evidence on the determinants of the demand for money: an empirical study of Dutch households, *European Economic Review*, 1, no 4 (Winter), 257-274.

OECD, 1989, *Electronic Funds Transfer: Plastic Cards and the Consumer*, Organisation for Economic Co-operation and Development, Paris.

Paroush, J. and D. Ruthenberg, 1986, Automated teller machines and the share of demand deposits in the money supply: the Israeli experience, *European Economic Review* 30, 1207-1215.

Payne, L.C. and H.M. Morgan, 1981, UK currency needs in the 1980s, *The Banker*, (April), 45-53.

Perlman, M., 1970, International differences in liquid assets portfolios, in: D. Meiselman (ed.), *Varieties of Monetary Experience*, University of Chicago Press, Chicago, 299-337.

Persson, T., 1979, Alternative transactions variables and the empirical evidence of economies of scale in money holdings, *Economics Letters* 2, no 4, 349-355.

Porter, R.D. and A.S. Bayer, 1984, A monetary perspective on underground economic activity in the United States, *Federal Reserve Bulletin* 70, no 3 (March), 177-188.

Ravensloot, K.A., 1990, *Afrekenen Kost ook Geld!* (Checking Out is not for Free!), Facet-onderzoek detailhandel (March), Economisch Instituut voor het Midden- en Kleinbedrijf, Zoetermeer.

Resek, R.W., 1967, Uncertainty and the precautionary demand for money, *Journal of Finance* 22, no 4 (December), 657-664.

Santomero, A.M., 1971, Optimal transactions behavior and the demand for money, *Ph.D. thesis*, Brown University.

Santomero, A.M., 1974, A model of the demand for money by households, *Journal of Finance* 29, no 1 (March), 89-102.

Santomero, A.M., 1979, The role of transaction costs and rates of return on the demand deposit decision, *Journal of Monetary Economics* 5, no 3 (July), 343-364.

Schimmelmann, W. von, 1985, EFT developments in Germany, in: *Texts of the Presentations at the Seventh European Financial Management and Marketing Association Convention* (March 28), European Financial Management Association, Paris, 41-46.

Selden, R., 1956, Monetary velocity in the United States, in: M. Friedman (ed.), *Studies in the Quantity Theory of Money*, University of Chicago Press, Chicago, 179-257.

Snyder, C., 1934, On the statistical relation of trade, credit and prices, *Revue de l'Institut International de Statistique* 2, 278-291.

Sprenkle, C.M., 1967, Is the precautionary demand for money negative, *Journal of Finance* 22, no 1 (March), 77-82.

Sprenkle, C.M., 1969, The uselessness of transactions demand models, *Journal of Finance* 24, no 5 (December), 835-847.

Sprenkle, C.M. and M.H. Miller, 1980, The precautionary demand for narrow and broad money, *Economica* 47, (November), 407-421.

Tanzi, V., 1982, Underground economy and tax evasion in the United States: estimates and implications, in: V. Tanzi (ed.), *The Underground Economy in the United States and Abroad*, Lexington Books, Lexington Mass., 69-92.

Temmerman, G., 1990, Comparing denomination structures, *Working paper*, (July), National Bank of Belgium.

Tinbergen, J., 1939, *Business Cycles in the United States of America*, 1919-1932, League of Nations, Geneva.

Tobin, J., 1956, The interest-elasticity of transactions demand for cash, *Review of Economics and Statistics* 38, no 3 (August), 241-247.

Tobin, J., 1958, Liquidity preference as behavior towards risk, *Review of Economic Studies* 25, no 67 (February), 65-86.

Trundle J.M. and P.V. Temperton, 1982, Recent changes in the use of cash, *Bank of England Quarterly Bulletin* 22, no 3 (December), 519-529.

Uyttewaal, R.A.I.M., 1981, Maandelijkse indexcijfers van de betalingen met Nederlandse bankbiljetten van 1966 tot 1980 (Monthly index numbers of payments with Dutch banknotes from 1966 to 1980), *A&E Note* 1981/1, University of Amsterdam.

Verrijn Stuart, G.M., 1935, De maatstaf der geldvoorziening (The measure of the money supply), *De Economist* 83, 695-707.

Virén, M., 1989, Financial innovations and currency demand: some new evidence, *Working paper*, Bank of Finland.

Virén, M. and T. Kokkola, 1989, Rahalajien Kysyntäennuste vuosille 1989-1994 (Demand forecast for different types of money 1989-1994), *Working paper*, (February 20), Bank of Finland.

Vogel, R.C. and G.S. Madalla, 1967, Cross-section estimates of liquid asset demand by manufacturing corporations, *Journal of Finance* 22, no 4 (December), 557-575.

Voigtlaender, H., 1976, *Falschmünzer und Münzfälscher*, Numismatischer Verlag H. Dombrowski, Münster.

Wessels, R.E., 1982, Overdraft Facilities and the Demand for Money by Firms, *Ph.D. thesis*, University Leiden.

Whalen, E.L., 1965, A cross-section study of business demand for cash, *Journal of Finance* 20, no 3 (September), 423-443.

Whalen, E.L., 1966, A rationalization of the precautionary demand for cash, *Quarterly Journal of Economics* 80, no 2 (May), 314-324.

Whitehead, D.D., 1982, Explaining the cash explosion, *Economic Review*, Federal Reserve Bank of Atlanta, no 3 (March), 14-18.

Whitesell, W.C., 1989, The demand for currency versus debitable accounts, *Journal of Money, Credit and Banking* 21, no 2 (May), 246-251.

Wilbratte, B.J., 1975, Some essential differences in the demand for money by households and by firms, *Journal of Finance* 30, no 4 (September), 1091-1099.

Wolff, P. de, 1969, *Bedrijfsstatistiek* (Business Statistics), Samson, Alphen a/d Rijn.

Zillinger Molenaar, J.L.N., 1986, Waar, waarvoor en waarmee betaald wordt (Where, what for and how we pay), *Bank- en Effectenbedrijf* 35, no 12 (December), 372-374.

Zijlstra, J., 1948, *De omloopssnelheid van het geld en zijn betekenis voor geldwaarde en monetair evenwicht* (The Velocity of Circulation of Money and its Significance for the Value of Money and the Monetary Equilibrium), Stenfert Kroese, Leiden.

SUBJECT INDEX

FINANCIAL AND MONETARY POLICY STUDIES

* 1. J.S.G. Wilson and C.F. Scheffer (eds.): *Multinational Enterprises*. Financial and Monitary Aspects. 1974 ISBN 90-286-0124-4

* 2. H. Fournier and J.E. Wadsworth (eds.): *Floating Exchange Rates*. The Lessons of Recent Experience. 1976 ISBN 90-286-0565-7

* 3. J.E. Wadsworth, J.S.G. Wilson and H. Fournier (eds.): *The Development of Financial Institutions in Europe, 1956–1976*. 1977 ISBN 90-286-0337-9

* 4. J.E. Wadsworth and F.L. de Juvigny (eds.): *New Approaches in Monetary Policy*. 1979 ISBN 90-286-0848-6

* 5. J.R. Sargent (ed.), R. Bertrand, J.S.G. Wilson and T.M. Rybczynski (ass. eds.): *Europe and the Dollar in the World-Wide Disequilibrium*. 1981 ISBN 90-286-0700-5

* 6. D.E. Fair and F.L. de Juvigny (eds.): *Bank Management in a Changing Domestic and International Environment*. The Challenges of the Eighties. 1982 ISBN 90-247-2606-9

* 7. D.E. Fair (ed.) in cooperation with R. Bertrand: *International Lending in a Fragile World Economy*. 1983 ISBN 90-247-2809-6

8. P. Salin (ed.): *Currency Competition and Monetary Union*. 1984 ISBN 90-247-2817-7

* 9. D.E. Fair (ed.) in cooperation with F.L. de Juvigny: *Government Policies and the Working of Financial Systems in Industrialized Countries*. 1984 ISBN 90-247-3076-7

10. C. Goedhart, G.A. Kessler, J. Kymmell and F. de Roos (eds.): *Jelle Zijlstra, A Central Banker's View*. Selected Speeches and Articles. 1985 ISBN 90-247-3184-4

11. C. van Ewijk and J.J. Klant (eds.): *Monetary Conditions for Economic Recovery*. 1985 ISBN 90-247-3219-0

* 12. D.E. Fair (ed.): *Shifting Frontiers in Financial Markets*. 1986 ISBN 90-247-3225-5

13. E.F. Toma and M. Toma (eds.): *Central Bankers, Bureaucratic Incentives, and Monetary Policy*. 1986 ISBN 90-247-3366-9

* 14. D.E. Fair and C. de Boissieu (eds.): *International Monetary and Financial Integration*. The European Dimension. 1988 ISBN 90-247-3563-7

15. J. Cohen: *The Flow of Funds in Theory and Practice*. A Flow-Constrained Approach to Monetary Theory and Policy. 1987 ISBN 90-247-3601-3

16. W. Eizenga, E.F. Limburg and J.J. Polak (eds.): *The Quest for National and Global Economic Stability*. In Honor of Hendrikus Johannes Witteveen. 1988 ISBN 90-247-3653-6

* 17. D.E. Fair and C. de Boissieu (eds.): *The International Adjustment Process*. New Perspectives, Recent Experience and Future Challenges for the Financial System. 1989 ISBN 0-7923-0013-0

18. J.J. Sijben (ed.): *Financing the World Economy in the Nineties*. 1989 ISBN 0-7923-0090-4

FINANCIAL AND MONETARY POLICY STUDIES

19. I. Rizzo: *The 'Hidden' Debt.* With a Foreword by A.T. Peacock. 1990
ISBN 0-7923-0610-4
*20. D.E. Fair and C. de Boissieu (eds.): *Financial Institutions in Europe under New Competitive Conditions.* 1990 ISBN 0-7923-0673-2
21. R. Yazdipour (ed.): *Advances in Small Business Finance.* 1991 ISBN 0-7923-1135-3
*22. D.E. Fair and C. de Boissieu (eds.): *Fiscal Policy, Taxation and the Financial System in an Increasingly Integrated Europe.* 1992 ISBN 0-7923-1451-4
23. W.C. Boeschoten: *Currency Use and Payment Patterns.* 1992 ISBN 0-7923-1710-6

*Published on behalf of the *Société Universitaire Européenne de Recherches Financières* (SUERF), consisting the lectures given at Colloquia, organized and directed by SUERF.

Kluwer Academic Publishers – Dordrecht / Boston / London

MIX
Papier aus verantwortungsvollen Quellen
Paper from responsible sources
FSC® C105338

If you have any concerns about our products,
you can contact us on
ProductSafety@springernature.com

In case Publisher is established outside the EU,
the EU authorized representative is:
Springer Nature Customer Service Center GmbH
Europaplatz 3, 69115 Heidelberg, Germany

Printed by Libri Plureos GmbH
in Hamburg, Germany